NEVER DISCUSS A CHILD'S SHORTCOMINGS
IN HIS PRESENCE.

SHOW THE CHILD THAT YOU ARE FOND OF HIM.

Britta Holle

Motor Development in Children
Normal and Retarded

Preface by Annalise Dupont, M.D.
Lecturer at the University of Aarhus

A Practical Guide for Sensory-Motor Stimulation

BLACKWELL SCIENTIFIC PUBLICATIONS

OXFORD   LONDON   EDINBURGH
BOSTON   MELBOURNE

Motor Development in Children Normal and Retarded
First edition 1976
Reprinted 1981

Cover by Poul Breuning

Printed in Great Britain by
Butler & Tanner Ltd, Frome and London
ISBN 0-632-00065-1

Photographs: Anna Albeck

Drawings: Steen Jensen

Distributed in Great Britain, and the British Commonwealth by
Blackwell Scientific Publications Ltd
Osney Mead, Oxford, OX2 0EL
8 John Street, London, WC1N 2ES
9 Forrest Road, Edinburgh, EH1 2QH
52 Beacon Street, Boston,
  Massachusetts 02108, USA
99 Barry Street, Carlton,
  Victoria 3053, Australia
in the United States of America by
Blackwell Mosby Book Distributors,
  11830 Westline Industrial Drive,
  St Louis, Missouri 63141
and in Canada by
Blackwell Mosby Book Distributors,
  120 Melford Drive, Scarborough,
  Ontario, M1B 2X4

Preface

»Why does he walk so badly?« asks the mother of a young mentally retarded boy. »Why do so many of these children hold themselves so badly?« asks the new school doctor. »Can nothing be done to help my pupil guide his hand properly when he is writing?« asks the new teacher.

Can these conditions be improved, perhaps prevented, by stimulation which is based on precise knowledge of the circumstances?

This is the question which Britta Holle, the writer of this book, has asked herself and which she has gone a long way towards answering through her work with the mentally retarded. Based on a fundamental knowledge of the many aspects of the normal child's development it is possible to survey the handicaps of the retarded child in question. Specially adapted stimulation is then started from the stage of development which the child has reached and attempts are made to proceed along the lines which are known from the normal child's development.

When you have read this book – and know the subject – you will find it obvious that it is possible to work in this way. But although many of the ideas are simple and quite self-evident, careful study is needed to put them into practice. It is well known how easy it is to miss the optimal moment for teaching a new skill, and how important it is to begin training in the right way. However, there are special pathological conditions with which the book does not deal and advises against treating. In the book the writer points out some of these cases.

The book is written for, among others, professional workers in institutions, schools, hospitals etc. who are directly concerned with the mentally handicapped and their families. Therefore all the technical words and expressions are explained.

But others also, parents, siblings, etc., will benefit from this book. With regard to parents, however, it should be pointed out that it may be difficult to train your own child. Some are successful, and there are parents who can carry out training and exercises with their retarded child. For others, a program and a book like this seems too frustrating, and may possibly, in some instances, spoil the relationship between parent and child. These parents should ask for special help and get others to work with the child. However, in any case, their knowledge of the subject will be a support for their child.

There is no reason why parents of adolescent or adult retarded children should feel guilty on reading this book. Although many things in the book are evident and simple, they are the result of broad theoretical and practical experience and the way they are arranged in this book is new.

Work with the mentally retarded requires a teamwork of specialists, and the deployment of professional skills from a variety of disciplines. Many of these professional workers: teachers, psychologists, doctors, speech therapists, nurses, physical therapists, etc., will see their professions dealt with in this book in a somewhat unusual way and in a new connection. This approach is necessary to describe the new developments in physical education. For the retarded child there is a risk that the primary retardation, whatever the cause, easily leads to inactivity and further retardation, which then hinders further development. When retarded adults seem to function worse than they should do, it is because of this vicious circle.

The book does not just recommend letting the retarded have some physical exercise to improve their form. To see the problem in that light is too simple.

In the past, mentally retarded children often stayed on the waiting list for years before they received treatment or special training, but now every effort must be made to start special treatment, training, and stimulation very early. By following the directions in this book you can start suitably training the retarded child or the child at risk, right from infancy. Everyone who deals with children, normal or retarded, has the possibility of gaining new wisdom and inspiration from this book.

Annalise Dupont
Risskov, Denmark

ACKNOWLEDGMENT

The inspiration of this book I owe to hundreds of children, normal and retarded.

Without the help of experts in the areas dealt with, this book would not have been possible. I would like to thank all who have been helpful during its preparation. The manuscript, or parts thereof, has been read and usefully commented on by Annalise Dupont, M. D., Lecturer in Mental Retardation, University of Aarhus, Erik Hansen, M. D., Professor of Neurology, University of Odense, Lasse Rydberg, B. A., Headmaster, Educational Consultant, The Danish National Service for the Mentally Retarded, Birte Margrete Rydberg, B. A., Educator, Erik Forchhammer, B. A., Speech and Hearing Consultant, and Nancy Fluhr, B. A., Munksgaard.

In addition I owe thanks to Erik B. Poulsen, Headmaster, for support and encouragement during the many years I worked at the boarding school at Gamle Bakkehus.

Grants to carry out studies in the U.S.A., Canada, Australia, England, France, Holland, Norway and Sweden have been received from The Danish Physical Therapy Association, The Danish National Service for the Mentally Retarded and Tuborgfondet.

Finally I wish to thank Margaret Mølgaard, B. A., for undertaking the translation of the book into English.

Britta Holle

Contents

III Motor Skills Seen in Relation to Perception

IV Readiness for Reading and Writing

V An Example of a Sensory-Motor Evaluation Form

Introduction

The principles in stimulation

This book is the outcome of preparation for teaching and lecturing. My experience of this subject comes originally from work with normal children and, during the past fifteen years, with retarded children. I began with the educationally sub-normal (I. Q. 50–75), but, after studies in Europe and the USA it seemed natural to go on to children at a lower stage of development, the severely sub-normal (I. Q. 25–50).

Experience shows that the stages of a retarded child's development follow the same order as a normal child's, but the retarded do not progress so far in many important particulars, and they take longer to do it.

This book is intended for

all who deal with children. For example, primary school teachers, P. E. teachers and nursery and kindergarten teachers will find many of their problems discussed, especially in the last part of the book, where educational gymnastics and motor skills such as writing, ball play, etc., are analyzed.

In particular, this book is intended for people dealing with retarded children. A normal infant's movement pattern and perceptual development can be recognized in much older retarded children and, in many cases, in retarded adults.

Perceptual and motor development

The child's first stage of development is the sensory-motor, and before this stage has been completed, the child cannot develop further, e. g. he cannot be expected to learn to read and write. In school, this rule is often disregarded.

Perceptual and motor development lie on the borderline between education and medicine, so the physical therapist naturally enters into the picture when the retarded child needs help towards further development. The physical therapist's aim will be – in cooperation with others who deal with the child – to try to bring the child from a state of sensory-motor handicap to a better level of functioning.

I have described the normal child's sensory-motor development and in relation to this the retarded child's development in general terms, disregarding the intelligence quotient and the reason for retardation, since I regard the subject chiefly from my standpoint: motor development.

However, motor and perceptual development are so interrelated that I have been obliged to discuss perception in those areas where it is connected with motor development, if for no other reason than to point out how necessary it is to analyze each skill in order to judge whether the child is really able to carry it out.

Because of it, the book is very detailed. From my practical experience I have learned that we often fail to help a retarded child because we leave out the details, with the result that he gets nothing out of his education.

Whether it is called treatment, education, or stimulation, the help we can give to a retarded child must be given at the most suitable time for each stage of learning.

The specialists – and those who have daily contact with the child

Each speciality is now so demanding that few specialists are in a position to understand completely the »whole« child. Therefore it is necessary for the one to know what the other is doing and what the aim is at any particular time, so that those who are responsible for the daily care of the child can implement the instructions and treatment in the child's everyday life.

In one's entirety, i. e. the whole person, no area can be divided off as something separate, something independent. There is a continuous interchange between motor ability, perception, mind, speech and thought.

For example, it is not enough that the child is treated twice a week for half an hour by a speech therapist, a psychologist or a physical therapist, or that a welfare worker occasionally pays a visit, if the child is not helped by being trained all day by the same methods. It is the frequent daily repetitions which count. Guided by the aforementioned specialists, it is the parents, nurse, nursery school teacher and later the teacher, on whom the child's development really depends.

Mentally backward – late developers

The expressions »mentally backward« or »mentally retarded« are not used in this book, because a child cannot be only mentally retarded, but is more or less retarded in all respects; somatic (body), mental, perceptual and motor. Therefore I have chosen to call the child purely and simply »retarded«, thus stressing the slow development rather than the mental retardation. Thus the child may be tempo-

rarily backward in development, but otherwise normal, or he may be more or less severely mentally retarded. The procedure is the same for both: to help the child towards further development and experience at his own pace, beginning from his current level of development.

Cerebral palsied and psychotic children

are not dealt with in this book, since they are outside its scope. The same applies to more specific neurological or other defects. Nevertheless, many of this book's suggestions can be useful in the treatment of these children.

Causes of retardation

Knowledge of whether a child is brain-damaged or has suffered from a non-stimulating environment, whether his backwardness is due to congenital, metabolic or other reasons can help with prognosis (predicting the course of an illness) and can determine the medication or other medical treatment, and is of the greatest scientific interest, especially in preventive work.

Examination and developmental diagnosis

However, this knowledge helps the teacher, or others who deal with the child, to only a certain extent.

The help given to the child must be based on the psychological, the motor and the perceptual level of each individual child.

This is where the developmental diagnosis is most important. If the investigation and recommendations are not sufficiently detailed, the treatment and the stimulation will also be imperfect.

The special knowledge of the doctor (pediatrician, neurologist, psychiatrist, eye or ear specialist) must be made available in language which is easily understood by everyone.

Furthermore, if necessary, a team composed of educationalists, social workers, psychologists, speech therapists, occupational and physical therapists, dentists, etc., should examine the child, each with his own specialty in mind. Here too it is important that they express themselves in such a way that all can understand their recommendations.

The principles in stimulation and education

Adults as well as children usually find pleasure in learning something new, as long as it is not too difficult.

Retarded children also show the same pleasure everytime they feel that they have learnt something. It gives them more self-respect.

It is not enough to »have a good time« with the child. The adult must also establish a »working contact« with him, and stimulate him to constructive work, in all possible aspects, beginning from his actual level.

The principles governing stimulation can be sketched briefly as follows:
1) All who deal with children should first of all learn about the development of normal children and know all its aspects down to the smallest detail.
   This is a prerequisite for every kind of stimulation, treatment or education.
2) A child's development must be judged in all its aspects (see Folding Chart). For example, it is not enough to say that the child can walk, but how does he walk, and to what stage of development does his walk correspond?
   Therefore the adult must learn to »see« and learn what to look for. As soon as one grasps this idea, the whole thing appears logical and the stages of development become obvious.
3) The child is stimulated beginning from his present level of development, which is not always the same in all areas. There can be large gaps. So the area in which the child is most retarded should preferably be stimulated first. Try to improve on every step for as long as it takes the child to reach the next step. Thus one avoids encouraging

the child to perform a function which he cannot manage because of his stage of development.
   On the other hand, do not underestimate the child, for then he will lose interest. This requires fine judgment, which is not so hard to attain if one has learned to »see«.
4) It may be difficult for a retarded child to take part in other children's games, and so he misses the development and pleasure which contact with other children can give. Therefore the child must learn »to play«.
   He must, step by step, learn all the elements of each game, for example, handling a ball, playing ball with an adult and playing quickly and competently by himself, before he can be expected to play ball with other children.

A normal child can have many problems to solve during the developmental process, but although some of the problems may present great difficulties, the child can often solve them by himself.

A retarded child has more difficulty in solving his problems, and this often makes him give up completely.

The problems are there, even if we cannot discern them, and it is therefore essential that we try to obtain absolutely as much knowledge of normal development as possible, so that we can enter into the child's situation and thoughts, and so that nothing can escape our notice.

The earlier in life suitable stimulation is given, the better will be the result. From experience we know that a retarded child cannot afford to omit any step, without the next step being partly spoiled.

Evaluation

To judge a retarded child's development requires a detailed examination of the child. Page 183 gives an example of a suggested evaluation form.

Development Chart

(Folding Chart at the end of the book)

One of the difficulties in stimulating retarded children is their uneven development in different areas. For example, arm patterns, leg patterns, vision and speech development in the same child can be at very different levels in comparison with those of a normal child.

On the chart we see the problems of development horizontally – chronologically – in each area, and vertically, giving information on how far the child has progressed in each area at a given time.

As far as possible, development in all areas should be brought to the same stage.

Each section of the book corresponds in general to a horizontal line on the Development Chart, so that perception and motor development should keep pace with each other and with the development of the central nervous system.

A careful study of the chart in conjunction with the book will reveal many interesting details of the child's development, and, what is most important, will reveal the overall picture.

The Folding Chart gives the average age for normal children and should not be taken too precisely, for there are great variations within the norm.

Suggested exercises

As experience has shown that it may be difficult to vary daily work of the child, more examples of exercises are included in the book than are strictly necessary for understanding.

The exercises are arranged generally in order of difficulty.

»Training programs«

The intention is not to provide ready-made »training programs«, rather the contrary.

It is a question, as mentioned, of obtaining information about the child's general development and getting guidance from available specialists in each case in order to help the child to progress and to be able to take part in daily life according to his individual stage of development.

Materials

A wide choice of excellent materials and educational toys is available. However, the adult's understanding of the individual child, of his development, and of the method of teaching required, are more important than expensive teaching materials.

For example, the child should not be forced to learn about shapes only with the help of set materials, but should be stimulated to occupy himself with the world around him and be motivated to »want to see« and thus to experience and understand what he sees.

Almost everything in nature and in the environment can be used, and many home-made materials can provide quite satisfactory stimulation.

Bibliography

As the book may be used as a reference book by all groups of people dealing with children, I have mentioned earlier works on similar subjects only in the bibliography.

Educational-psychological literature is included only where it directly relates to motor development. Only a few works on drama, rhythmics and mime are named, as my starting-point has been otherwise.

Experience and research

The book describes observations which all parents will have made regarding their children, as well as conditions investigated by other authors. In addition I have wished to make available my own experiences with the kinds of stimulation described in the book, although these experiences are not yet all supported by controlled scientific research during longer or shorter observation times. In the future, long-term research comparing the development of normal and retarded children in many of the areas mentioned would be desirable.

May this book inspire all who deal with children to find the level of each child – normal or retarded – and thus to stimulate to further development, so that each child at his own pace can reach his individual potential.

February 1976   Britta Holle

I. Motor development

Motor development

The normal child

Reflex movements of the newborn

The nervous system is far from fully developed at birth. In the newborn infant, the cerebral cortex (where the nerve cells are) has no influence on the lower regions of the brain, because the myelin sheaths (a kind of insulation around the nerve fibers) are not yet formed. Myelination (insulation) is necessary, so that impulses from a nerve center can pass along the nerve fibers into the nervous system. There is therefore a strong connection between myelination and development of physiological activities, including the child's movements.

However, the spinal cord is already myelinated at birth, thus making possible all the newborn's movements. These movements are all reflex actions, that is, involuntary motor reactions which may be entirely spontaneous (e. g. the child lies and kicks) or are caused by stimuli in his surroundings (being handled, sounds, etc.). *A reflex movement is always performed in the same manner after the same external stimulus.*

The newborn's motor activities are usually lively, and the infant cannot help making them because of his lack of control. The newborn's movements are not yet inhibited by the cortex, and they are not voluntary. (Corresponding patterns of reflex movements can be studied in animal experiments in which the cerebrum (the brain proper) has been separated from the lower parts of the brain.)

Mass movements and associated movements

The newborn infant moves arms, legs and the whole body at the same time (mass movements) because he cannot yet differentiate separate movements.

Associated movements can occur throughout life in situations in which an unaccustomed, complicated movement is being made, e. g. an adult trying to spread out his stiff toes may unintentionally spread his fingers at the same time.

Neurological development

As the cortex and the myelin sheaths develop, connection with the spinal cord is established. Mass movements lessen and voluntary, directed movements become more and more accurate.

The nerve tissue must be sufficiently developed before a particular movement is possible. Practice in performing the movement is also needed because the interaction between the development of the nerve tissue and its practical use are mutually enhancing. A path must be established for impulses from the brain out to the muscles through the synapses (points of communication between the branches of two nerve cells).

Thus the child's motor development corresponds with the development of his central nervous system.

Roughly, there are four stages:

1) Reflex movements (uncontrolled by the brain).
2) Symmetrical movements (with brain-control just beginning), e. g. similar movements of both arms.
3) Voluntary, motivated, differentiated movements.
4) Automatic movements; habitual movements such as walking, for example, eventually become automatic.

The coordinated movement

A well-coordinated movement requires a close interplay between sensory and muscular functions; the movement is easy, unhampered and purposeful, because the muscle contractions are made with the intended amount of force at the right moment and for the right length of time.

Good coordination is not inborn but develops in conjunction with the maturation of the central nervous system and is aided by the kinesthetic sense, and the senses of touch and sight, as well as by experience.

Coordination is synonymous with automation of particular types of movement patterns. Repeating the correct movement improves coordination. Therefore every new movement must be learned and then repeated again and again until at last it becomes automatic.

The more movements that have already been learned, the easier it will be to learn new, similar movements.

Reflexes and primitive movement patterns

The normal child

In my opinion, certain reflexes and primitive types of movement are of particular interest only to doctors, nurses and physical therapists, but there are many reflexes which should be known by everyone who has daily contact with children. Without knowledge of these reflexes

it will be difficult and often impossible to help retarded children.

Therefore, in what follows I shall only deal with the reflexes and primitive types of movement patterns that may be of interest to the non-specialist.

Each reflex will first be described separately. The following section, which deals with movement patterns and describes how the child can be helped from one stage of motor development to the next, will make for a clearer understanding of the reflexes and of their importance in the development of children.

Some reflexes are present at birth, and some develop later. Some disappear at $3\frac{1}{2}$ - 4 months of age, some later, and some appear and remain throughout life.

The reflexes should be the same on both sides of the body, and the child should be calm and relaxed when the reflexes are tested.

Seeking, sucking, swallowing and biting reflexes
See page 48

Eye reflexes
See page 65

Prehensile reflex (handgrasp reflex)
See page 34

Plantar-grasp reflex

This reflex is present at birth and can be elicited by pressing the sole (under the toe joints) with the thumb, causing the foot to grip around it.

In small infants this reflex may also be caused if the ball of the foot touches the supporting surface. This reflex, therefore, must be inhibited (under control) before the child can stand. He must be able to stand with flat feet without curling his toes (see Fig. 1).

Babinski reflex

The Babinski reflex is usually present from a few days after birth until the child begins to walk. If one strokes the outer edge of the foot

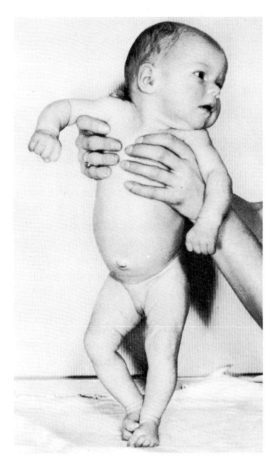

Fig. 1. Supporting reflex. Note the bent toes. (By permission of Henning Andersen, from his book »Barnets første år«).

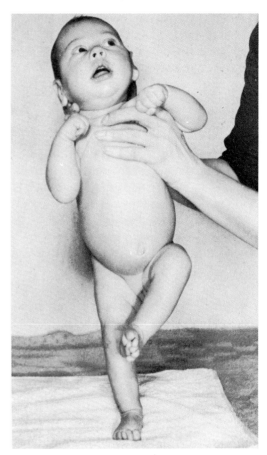

Fig. 2. Walking reflex. (By permission of Henning Andersen).

with a fingernail or a pointed object, the big toe will bend up (and perhaps the other toes spread out). On the newborn's small foot, stroke from the toes towards the heel, for if one tickles under the toes instead, the plantar-grasp reflex will result.

If the Babinski reflex lasts for too long, it will be found that the big toe does not assist in pushing off during the act of walking, as this movement requires that the toes bend downwards.

Supporting reflex

Up to 4–6 weeks, if an infant is held upright with the soles against the supporting surface, he will stretch his legs. He holds his feet close together, and does not bear his weight (Fig. 1).

Walking reflex

If the child is held in the above position, supporting his head and then leaning him forward a little, he will make a reflex walking movement. The legs have a tendency to cross, and there is no accompanying movement of trunk or arms as in the real walking movements that begin some months later. The legs are not yet sufficiently developed to bear the weight of the body.

This reflex is usually seen from birth to 4–6 weeks (Fig. 2), after which time touching the underlying surface will no longer cause the walking reflex. It is important that it has been present, however, because it serves as the foundation for the walking movement that occurs a little later. In many cases this walking reflex develops directly into a proper walking movement.

A retarded child may not have this reflex or he may continue with reflex walking for a long time. Do not confuse this with the beginning of a real walking movement.

Anal reflex

(Anus: posterior opening of alimentary canal). With the child lying relaxed on his back, lift both legs up till they are almost vertical. Touch the skin around the anus lightly, and the muscles around the opening will contract, as well as the muscles in the buttocks.

The anal reflex is present from the first day after birth.

Tonic labyrinthine reflexes

The labyrinth is an organ of balance which is situated in the inner ear and produces several reflexes, the effects of which are not yet fully understood. The following reactions are thought to originate in the labyrinth:

a) Changes in the position of the body will cause the head to move in such a way that it regains an upright position. E. g. if an infant of 2–3 months is turned on his stomach (prone position) and lifted up horizontally while being supported under his chest, he will lift his head. Even before this time many infants will be able to hold their heads horizontally for a mo-

ment and some will make short reflex attempts to lift the head. If the child is held in the same way on his back (supine position), he will lift his head from about the 5th month.

If the child is held up at an angle of about 45°, the head will be raised by a sideways bending of the neck (spinal column). Eventually, orientation by sight also influences the head movements.

Later the reflex is inhibited, but adults still show residual effects, e. g. if, from a standing position, they lean sideways, the head will not fall outwards. However, this is not a genuine reflex, for on command the subject can let his head fall, and as a rule a practiced gymnast will do so at once.

b) On the other hand, changes in head position will cause changes in body position – which is intentionally made use of in diving from a springboard or turning somersaults.

See page 123. Labyrinthine senses.

Amphibian reaction

This can be elicited when the child is lying prone on the floor. Gently lift up one side of the pelvis, causing the pelvis to rotate. The leg

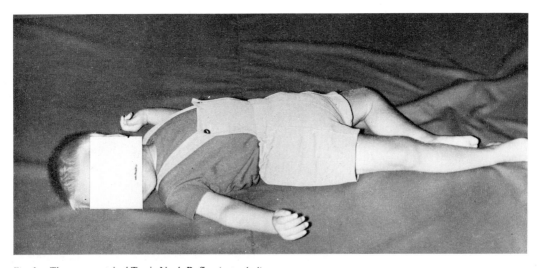

Fig. 3.   The asymmetrical Tonic Neck Reflex (retarded).

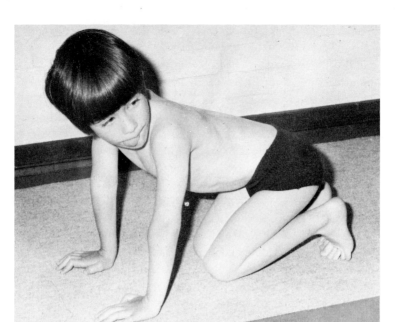

Fig. 4.   The symmetrical Tonic Neck Reflex, shown in an older retarded child. Head and arms are stretched, legs bent.

at that side will bend at all joints and be drawn up to the side, while the other leg will extend (see Fig. 13). This movement is a preparation for active crawling, where the child slides forward on his stomach with the aid of both arms and legs, and is a prelude to crawling on all fours.

The amphibian reaction appears at an age of 6–7 months, and lasts throughout life, but it can be consciously controlled later. This movement presupposes flexibility of the spinal column.

The Tonic Neck Reflexes (T. N. R.)

These are called neck reflexes because the position of the head and neck influences the muscle tone of the limbs through the sensory cells in the neck muscles.

They are called tonic reflexes because they alter the muscle tone of the limbs, and this tone lasts as long as the head position is maintained. The altered tone of the limbs causes quite characteristic types of movement patterns.

Here I shall deal with the asymmetrical and the symmetrical Tonic Neck Reflex.

The asymmetrical Tonic Neck Reflex

There is uncertainty as to whether this reflex is found in normal children (Fig. 3). Some authors think that the reflex is found from about 1–3 months in some normal children, while others think that this reflex is found only in children with defects of the central nervous system. In any case, any child who has this reflex should be watched, especially if the reflex continues after the 3rd or 4th month.

It may be difficult to elicit this reflex, and the child should be calm and completely relaxed. The reflex is seen when the child's head is turned to one side, either passively or actively, whereupon the arm on that side will be stretched out slowly and the other will be bent. If the head is turned to the opposite side, the arm pattern is the reverse. The legs will follow the movement but to a lesser degree, with the arm and leg on the same side bending (or stretching) simultaneously.

The symmetrical Tonic Neck Reflex

This reflex appears when the immature child's head is bent back, causing him to extend his arms and bend his legs. Conversely, if the head is bent forward, he will bend his arms and stretch his legs.

Thus, if the child is sitting back on his heels (Fig. 4) and supporting himself on his out-stretched arms, he is unable to rise on all fours (on hands and knees) without the arms bending and the head falling forward. At the same time the legs will stretch slightly as the child lifts his buttocks from his heels (Fig. 5). He ends up with his legs completely extended and lying on his stomach.

When the symmetrical T.N.R. has been inhibited, the child can stand on all fours and move his head in all directions, and also bend it forwards and backwards without the position of the limbs being affected. The child is now ready to begin to crawl (Fig. 11) and to play while crawling on the floor.

The reflex is shown in this way at 9-10 months of age, after the forward Parachute (falling) reflex has been developed (see below) and means that the child can now carry a great part of his weight on his outstretched arms.

Elements of the symmetrical Tonic Neck Reflex seem to remain in adults. When on hands and knees, the adult will unwittingly stiffen his elbows when he lifts his head, and when he bends his head he will bend his elbows a little and move his body weight more forward over his arms. An adult can consciously control the reflex, so there is nothing abnormal in this. In a practiced gymnast there will be no sign of the reflex.

Fig. 5. The symmetrical Tonic Neck Reflex, shown in an older retarded child. If the head bends down, the arms bend as well and the legs straighten.

Parachute reactions (falling reflexes)

Legs
If the infant is lifted up under his arms and then lowered rather quickly onto the floor, he will instinctively stretch both legs to reach out with ankles bent and feet flat. This reflex appears at the 6th month and lasts throughout life.

Arms
Reaching forwards: If the infant is sitting without support and, losing his balance, begins to fall forward, from 6 to 7 months of age he will save himself with his outstretched arms. His arm and fingers will stretch out to place his hands flat on the floor.

Reaching to the side: If a child of about 6 to 8 months sits on the floor without support, and, losing balance, tips sideways, he will reach out (save himself) with the hand on that side.

Reaching backwards: If the sitting child falls backwards, he will either move both arms behind him or he will turn around and save himself by extending one arm. This begins at about 11 months of age.

All these falling reflexes last throughout life. A person who trips or is about to fall will involuntarily stretch out hands and arms to try to save himself, partly in order to protect his head.

Only when these reflexes have developed will the child feel safe in a sitting position, and he will then be able to reach out for an object or turn to look at something without falling. He will feel secure.

The retarded child

All voluntary (willed) movements are brain functions

Motion as well as perception are functions of the brain, for voluntary movements can be performed only with the help of the brain. The normally gifted child goes through a stage of sensory and motor development before he can make further intellectual progress, and the retarded child must follow the same path, as well as he is able.

To stimulate the retarded child's motor development it is necessary that all who deal with him know in detail the types of reflex and primitive movement patterns of the normal child, so as not to stimulate the retarded child to perform movements which are too advanced or are unnatural at his stage of development. Abnormal movements should not be encouraged, as it is difficult, later on, to root out ingrown bad habits.

If, for example, a mother in ignorance thinks that it is time her retarded child began to walk, and forces him to attempt walking when neither head nor body balance are stabilized, and when he is afraid of falling, even from a sitting position, because he cannot yet save himself by stretching out his hands, he will be nervous and stiff when walking. If the child at his own speed had been helped to balance his head, to roll, to save himself from falling, and to crawl, he would have had a better chance of learning to move around freely and safely. This does not say that the child will be able to achieve this, however, for that depends on the nervous tissue being intact, and on the individual child.

It is to be regretted that this natural development in certain cases does not take place, and that a severely motor handicapped child must, for example, be held up in a frame, or can walk only by holding on to rails, but one cannot always attain perfection. If the doctor judges that the child will never be able to support his body, or use his legs, artificial aids must be provided, so that the child has better conditions for intellectual development than if he is bedridden. It also is important for the development of bones and joints that they gradually begin to support weight at the proper stages. Crawling, for example, is an early step in this progress.

The retarded child's first years of life

The retarded child must have the time he needs to develop and, above all, a chance to move about – not for five minutes once or twice a day but for most of his waking hours.

A child's development may suddenly stop at some stage and some time may pass before he can advance further. Perhaps the central nervous system is not sufficiently developed, or perhaps the child is busy developing other skills, such as speech, etc. In any case, do not try to hurry the child, but reinforce his present stage of development as much as possible so that he can easily and naturally go on to the next stage if and when that becomes possible.

Here I must strongly emphasize the importance of the adult's hands when working with a little child. To be able to handle a child well, to notice his tensions and guide his movements in a natural direction using one's hands, is a gift not always fully appreciated. Not all are born with this ability, and it must be perfected through experience and through knowledge of the motor development of the normal as well as the retarded child.

The older child

Natural movements must be developed through a natural progression

Experience with older retarded children has shown that if a formerly unused movement can come into use, there is a possibility that this movement may become part of the child's daily movements in a natural way – but it takes time.

Even if the central nervous system has matured, old ingrown habits will not be altered by simply allowing the child to move around freely in his usual way. Any faults must be eliminated and the corresponding natural movements practiced, starting at the first stage at which they appear in normal children and going through all the stages step by step.

This method requires body awareness and cooperation on the part of the child. The correct movements must be repeated again and again until he learns them, after which »refresher courses« should be given at longer but regular intervals to keep him from relapsing into his old bad habits.

How far the child can progress, and how long it will take, is another matter, and is often difficult to predict. The child cannot be made normal, not even in motor ability, but he can be helped to go through the stages of development in the right order and thereby to get as far as he, as an individual, possibly can. In the case of a retarded child, no stage can be omitted.

Stimulation and inhibition of reflexes

If certain reflexes last longer than usual, this may indicate abnormality of the central nervous system, and a doctor should be consulted.

The retarded child's reflexes may be late in appearing, or some which are present and should have been inhibited by development of the brain are not yet controlled; both situations hinder the child's motor development.

Abnormal reflexes are found frequently in cerebral palsied children. Whether the young retarded child should be diagnosed as slightly spastic or as merely a slow developer will, in some cases, be a matter of opinion. The diagnosis »cerebral palsy« is based on such criteria as the development of reflexes and the presence of primitive movement patterns. The spastic child shows other abnormal signs, as well as reactions which are never found in normal children. All the various symptoms are taken into account in making the diagnosis.

If, for example, the case report says that a child had some signs of spasticity (a form of cerebral palsy), but that these were absent during a later neurological examination, this may be because the central nervous system has developed in the meantime and thus now controls the reflexes which previously were symptomatic of a possible cerebral palsy.

Late-developed reflexes may be stimulated, and late-controlled reflexes inhibited, provided that the corresponding nerve tissue exists.

It is most important that the diagnosis can be made as soon as possible so that stimulation and any necessary treatment can be started

straight away; preferably right after birth. Unfortunately, however, the diagnosis often cannot be made that early.

A few examples of early stimulation:

Rooting (searching), sucking, swallowing and biting reflexes are dealt with on page 48.

Anal reflex

If toilet training of a retarded child is difficult, in some cases it helps to elicit the anal reflex a few times just before a visit to the toilet, so that the child is made aware of the contraction and relaxation of the muscle which closes the entrance to the bowel (the anus). Thus, using the sense of touch and the kinesthetic sense, one may succeed in producing awareness of this mechanism, and hence an understanding of how it works.

The asymmetrical Tonic Neck Reflex

Certain retarded children may have an asymmetrical Tonic Neck Reflex, and may retain it for many months or years. In some cases the reflex may be so strong that the head always turns towards the outstretched arm, making it difficult to see anything that is being held by the arm that is bent.

A long-lasting asymmetrical Tonic Neck Reflex will hinder a child from rolling from his back onto his side. When the child turns his head in the direction he wants to roll over to, the arm on the same side will stretch out and hinder him from rolling over.

In extreme cases this reflex delays self-feeding because the head will turn away from the arm that is bending to bring the spoon to the mouth.

Even a small remnant of this reflex will hinder motions requiring hand and eye-hand coordination. It may be present in merely a slight bending of the fingers of one hand, together with an almost unnoticeable increase in stretching the fingers of the other.

To inhibit this reflex, try to correct the aspect that seems easiest to deal with, whether it is the position of the head or of the arm (or even the leg).

The purpose of the following exercises is to stimulate the child to act against the reflex, that is, to turn the head towards the bent arm until finally, if possible, head and arm may be moved independently. E. g.:

Place large playthings in front of the child, so that he has to stretch and bend both arms to take them up. Later, when he can do that, place the toy in such a way that he must turn his head towards the bent arm. It may help to have an adult holding the other arm. Get the child to look at an object held by the bent arm and hand.

Get the child to suck his thumb, so that his face is turned towards the bent arm.

Get him to hold a small object in one hand and afterwards to put it in his mouth.

»Clap hands« with the child, symmetrically and across.

Have the child sit on the floor, with both legs bent to the same side supported by one outstretched arm (supported at the elbow by an adult), while he tries to pick up an attractive object with the other hand.

When the stage of amphibian reaction is reached – but only then – can crawling on the stomach be practiced. Eyes and head should continually follow the arm that is bent. These exercises may be a little difficult initially and at first should only be undertaken with the help of an adult and following the advice of a physical therapist. The exercise is exhausting when the child performs it actively, and therefore is excellent training for all the muscles as well as for respiration (breathing).

Amphibian reaction

When a child is lying prone one can elicit the amphibian reaction by lifting one hip slightly up from the mattress and so stimulate a crawling movement towards a toy in which the child is interested (Fig. 13).

This movement requires enough flexibility of the spinal column so that it can rotate on its own axis. Rolling movements must therefore have been mastered already.

Tonic labyrinthine reflexes

can be employed for the purpose of improving head balance when the child's body is held in various positions. This will stimulate vertical positioning of the head.

Parachute reactions (falling reflexes)

Many older retarded children are afraid of falling. This may be because the child has not yet developed the natural falling reflexes and therefore hurts himself when he falls because he does not put his hands out quickly enough. So the child becomes afraid of falling; he walks stiffly, often with legs apart and dragging feet, as if he is afraid to lift them off the ground.

This child's fear can be alleviated to some degree by playing »falling«.

Child and adult sit on a large mattress on the floor and take turns pushing each other forwards, sideways and finally backwards, in other words, in the same order as in the natural development of the falling reflexes. Afterwards practice falling from a kneeling and finally from an upright position.

At first it may be necessary to support the child's outstretched arm at the elbow, to keep it from bending. If the child hurts himself, there is no point going on with the »game« and the whole thing is spoiled for a long time.

In many cases these reflexes can be learned quite quickly. The child enjoys the »game« and gains confidence and self-reliance, even when in the upright position.

There can be many other causes of fear of falling and poor balance, such as mental factors, muscular weakness, ataxia (a form of cerebral palsy), etc., but in most cases, stimulation of the falling reflexes will be advantageous.

The symmetrical Tonic Neck Reflex

To see a normal 10-month-old child crawl is like watching a beautiful, agile animal in motion. The child's whole body moves rhythmically in rotating, bending, etc., and the head moves freely in all directions while he crawls.

Fig. 6.   All joints can be bent in the prone position, but are straightened when on the back (retarded).

All who deal with young children should know that this simply cannot take place freely and naturally before the symmetrical Tonic Neck Reflex is inhibited. Therefore they should attempt to stimulate the child in such a way that he can eventually hold up his head and straighten his arms, even when his body weight comes forward over his arms.

One exercise is to rock to and fro from the heel-sitting position, supported by outstretched arms (Fig. 7) in the hopes that this eventually will lead to crawling. The adult must always make sure that the child does not fall face down on the mattress; this can be done either by supporting the child's chin with a couple of fingers, causing him to extend his arms, or by supporting the straightened elbows.

Other reflexes

Cerebral palsied patients may have retained a reflex that causes them, when prone, to bend every joint in the trunk and limbs and, when on the back, to stretch the whole body. In extreme cases the spastic child becomes so stiff when on his back that he is supported only by his neck and his feet.

Retarded children without other signs of cerebral palsy may present the following symptoms:

Lying on his back, the child will slightly resist passive bending of arms and legs (movements carried out by another person) because the dominant movement in this position is stretching.

When prone, the child will gently resist another person's trying to stretch his arms upwards along the floor and straightening his legs because the dominant movement now is bending (Fig. 6).

These reflex patterns will also hinder head lifting in either of these positions because they prevent these movements.

Suggested exercises

On the back: Alternate bending and extending of elbows. First passive, then active.
On the back: Alternate bending and stretching of legs. First passive, then active.
A fairly slow tune which the child likes may

Fig. 7. Heel-sitting position. The child rocks to and fro until he gets into the crawling position. Support the child's chin if the head tends to fall. (The child in this picture is normal and is able to crawl.)

accompany the exercises at first. The movement thus becomes a conditioned reflex, that is, the tune activates the movement. Afterwards, change the tune, and finally the child should be able to perform the movements unaccompanied.

When on hands and knees lift legs backwards alternately. The hip should be fully stretched. (The child should know where his back and buttocks are, before this exercise can succeed (see page 97)).

Lying prone, lift each leg in turn with knees straight (Fig. 42).

Encourage the child to lift his head, whether lying on back or stomach.

Lively reflexes

Saying that a child has »lively reflexes« means that all his reflexes (including tendon and skin reflexes, see footnote) respond strongly to slight stimuli. Such a child often seems unusually ticklish and the least touch produces involuntary movements. Such a child should always be handled with a quiet, firm grasp, and he should also be told beforehand when and where he will be touched.

Tendon reflexes are elicited by a light tap on a tendon, e.g. below the knee-cap: the patella reflex. Skin reflexes are elicited by light stroking with a pointed object, whereby an involuntary contraction of the underlying muscles is caused, e. g. on the stomach: the abdominal reflex.

Movement patterns

The normal child

Head balance

Lying on the side

The newborn infant has no control over his head movements; for this reason he is usually laid on his side during the first few weeks so that the head is placed in what is, for him, a comfortable position.

Lying prone

When lying on his stomach the newborn child will instinctively try to turn his head to one side in order to breathe.

Control of the head begins when prone, so it is important to place the child in this position as soon as possible, and when handling him to accustom him to lying on his stomach. The prone position also helps to straighten the hips, which is essential for the later standing position.

Even though a child may not like lying on his stomach, head control and hip stretching are acquired most easily in this position, so why make it more difficult for the child? If the child does not lie on his stomach, he may also not crawl before he can walk (see page 21).

During the first weeks, when lying on his stomach, the child lifts his head for a moment but drops it again. This is a reflex movement.

At about 3 months the child can hold his head up with his face turned frontwards; when he is lying supported by his forearms, he can look around to all sides. This is a conscious and motivated movement (Fig. 8).

When the head is lifted all the posterior muscles are tensed – in other words, the muscles of the back as well as the hip extensors (buttock and thigh muscles).

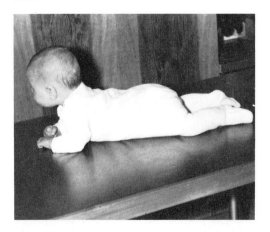

Fig. 8. The child supports himself on his bent arms. The hands are slightly clenched.

Lying on the back

It is more difficult to lift the head when lying on the back than on the front, and is a later development.

Up to 3 months the head will fall back if the child is made to sit up by pulling on his arms. Later the head will also rise, not as a reflex movement, but because the child wants to sit up.

When the child is about 5 months old he will help by lifting his head at the beginning of the movement.

Sitting position

The sitting position would certainly seem the easiest position for maintaining head balance, since the weight of the head is not a factor, as long as the head is held upright.

Even in the first week of life the infant sitting in his mother's arm can hold up his head for a moment, but, without support, it falls again at the slightest movement off the vertical.

At about 4 months, head balance is established and the child, in a sitting position, can move his head in all directions.
See also under Eye focus, page 65.

Arm patterns

During the first 2 months of life the bending pattern is predominant, and the arms make symmetrical, unrhythmic reflex movements. At first it is chiefly the shoulder that moves, with the elbow joining in later. All the arm joints – shoulder, elbow and wrist – are either stretched or bent without differentiation between the separate joints. The child's primitive »see-reach« movement develops from this arm pattern.

This symmetrical arm pattern (both arms moving in or out simultaneously) still seems to force its way into the arm pattern for several years, when the child becomes excited, e. g. if he expresses sudden joy or anticipation. These arm movements are then accompanied by jumping.

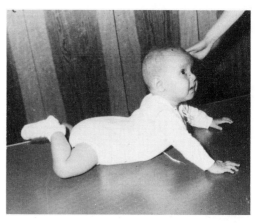

Fig. 9. Arms and fingers are stretched, thereby raising the chest.

Looking at and playing with his hands (body knowledge) is an important stage in development which usually appears at 3 months.

The symmetrical position of the limbs may also be observed in the 4-month-old child sleeping on his back with both arms above his head and his knees bent.

Lying prone

The newborn infant keeps all his arm joints bent. At about 3 months he can support himself on his forearms while raising his head. The elbows are bent and the hands partly clenched (Fig. 8). At 5 months the head can be lifted high and held up while the arms and hands are extended; the chest is thus lifted higher than before (Fig. 9) and the back is made flexible by bending backwards.

At about 9 months the child will support himself on his outstretched arms and hands while sitting back on his heels (Fig. 7), but if he tries to rise on all fours his head will fall forward and his arms will bend as in Fig. 5 (the symmetrical Tonic Neck Reflex).

Eventually the child in the heel-sitting position will rock forwards and backwards and crawl on his stomach with the help of both arms and legs. At about 10 months he can crawl on all fours in a cross-pattern, i. e. he brings one arm and the opposite leg forward at the same time, or rather, almost simultaneously, since the arm moves a fraction of a second before the leg, and perhaps thereby gives the impetus to follow (Fig. 11).

Leg patterns

As with the arms, the legs of the newborn infant are controlled by the bending pattern.

Lying on the back

The legs will perform unrhythmic kicking reflex movements. At first the feet do not touch the underlying surface, then the heels touch, and at about $3\frac{1}{2}$ months the bending pattern is less evident, and the whole sole of the foot touches.

Lying on the stomach

For the first few weeks the legs are drawn up right under the body and all three joints, hip, knee and ankle, are tightly bent. In this position, too, kicking movements can be seen, increasing in vigor.

The legs straighten little by little, so that the hips are extended partially at about 2 months but completely only at 4 months.

When the child can sit up on his heels, the ankles are usually kept bent at first (Fig. 4), i e. all three leg-joints follow the same pattern, that of bending. Only when the child begins to crawl does he usually extend his ankles (Fig. 11), such that the foot lies along the floor no matter how much the hips and knees move and bend.

The rolling movement

If the infant's head is turned to one side when he is lying on his back, the whole body will follow in a complete movement, without rotation of the spine itself.

The child may often spontaneously make the same movement, when he is lying and kicking, and suddenly he has worked up such speed that he rolls over. The child is barrel-chested during this stage, which facilitates rolling.

From about $3\frac{1}{2}$ months the rolling movement becomes more complex. If the child lies on his back and one turns his head to one side, first the shoulders, and then the hips and legs follow, through rotation of the spinal column itself. Rotation occurs in reverse order if one leg is lifted over the other. This is passive rolling, but it is a preparation for active rolling, which the child can carry out himself consciously at 5-6 months. The child sees something beside him, wants to get hold of it, turns his eyes and head, lifts his head, reaches over his body with the arm that is furthest away, which raises the shoulder, and the hips and legs follow. This is the natural rolling movement, where the spinal column rotates on its own axis, and this movement continues to be used throughout life (Fig. 12).

A motivated rolling movement, whether from lying on the back or on the stomach, is initiated by head-lifting. Rolling over from the prone position begins earlier than from the supine, because head balance is acquired earlier in the prone position. Moreover, the arms are of help in this position.

Rolling from the back almost onto the front is used – with accompanying leg bending – to get into a sitting position, later into a crawling position, and from squatting to standing, with greater or lesser hand support.

Up to about 4 years of age, the child will rise from his back in this way. Only then can he get up like an adult by lifting his head and body and rolling up into a sitting position, bending his legs and standing up by pushing with one hand.

The sitting position

When head balance is established, body balance also begins to develop, and at about 6-7 months, if the child is placed on the floor, he can sit there without support. At first the back is much rounded, so the position should not be held for long. Sitting with straight legs is particularly conducive to a round back, so usually

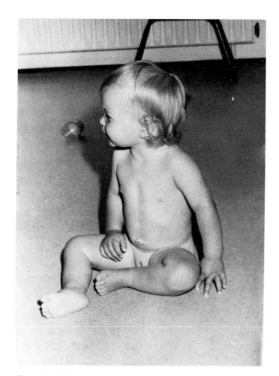

Fig. 10. Sitting position with good leg support.

or can find other ways of getting around the room, until they can crawl properly.

Crawling on the stomach

Letting a child play on the floor stimulates him to move, to roll over, to sit, to crawl on the stomach and on all fours, and thus to develop naturally his motor ability.

The most primitive form of moving from one place to another is to crawl on the stomach. This can be done in several ways.

With the help of the arms alone, the legs being passive. This is no preparation for crawling on all fours.

Crawling on the stomach using the arm and leg on the same side simultaneously, which is a very immature movement pattern.

The natural and the most advanced method, crawling in cross-pattern, that is, moving the opposite arm and leg simultaneously (Fig. 13).

Crawling on the stomach can be an excellent preparation for crawling on all fours. It promotes rhythmic movement and coordination of all four limbs. At the same time the spine becomes more flexible and its rotation improves as a continuation of earlier rolling and amphibian movements. Moving the bent leg forward along the floor requires hip rotation.

Crawling on all fours

When the symmetrical Tonic Neck Reflex is inhibited, movements of the arms and legs no longer depend on head and neck movements, and the child is usually ready to crawl on hands and knees at about 10 months (Fig. 11).

A small child needs plenty of clear floor space – not too slippery and not too cold – so that crawling can be encouraged.

The child uses several types of movement according to his stage of development:

He pushes himself forward on his bottom as described above.

the child will sit with bent legs, turned out at the hips, and with thighs and lower legs resting on the floor. This enlarges the supporting surface, and gives better balance for the trunk, as well as making it easier for the child to sit with a straight back (Fig. 10). Much lying on the stomach has already exercised the back muscles, so now the posture reflexes can be exercised as a preparation for standing.

Sitting on the floor, the child will support himself at first with both hands, either on the floor or on his own legs. The falling reflex is being developed, so if the child falls, he reaches out in front or to the sides, and, some months later, he will reach out behind him as well.

When the child is about 9 months, he can sit himself up from a supine position by rolling almost on to his front, bending his legs and pushing with his arms. Head and body balance are now extremely good, and the sitting position seems to be well established by the time the child can get himself into a sitting position.

In this position some children can now slide themselves forward on his bottom by pushing with one leg, perhaps with the help of one arm,

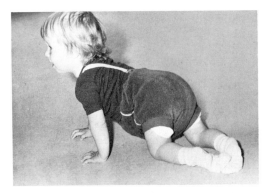

Fig. 11. Crawling position. Right arm and left leg move together in cross-pattern.

On all fours he moves forward using both arms and both legs alternately, like a rabbit jumping.

A well-developed crawl in cross-pattern. Many variations of the above.

Some children will not crawl or lie prone. They fight against it and cry. It is difficult to determine why this is so, but some hypothetical explanations are:

Unknown psychological causes: The child, becomes afraid because, for example, he lacks head control or he cannot see around him very well.

He has poorly developed head-control, so his head falls suddenly and he either hurts himself or is frightened. The adult should guard against this, supporting the head.

Dizziness may occur when the child is turned over, or he may get an upset stomach.

Retarded inhibition of the reflexes, the bending pattern still being dominant in the prone position, making it difficult to raise the head or stretch the arms.

Weak arm muscles, so that the arms cannot be extended to bear the weight of the body.

Walking upright has been introduced too early, so the child has not needed to crawl.

Many normal children seem to get on very well without having gone through a regular crawling period, or, more correctly, they have developed so quickly that the few times they have crawled on the floor have been sufficient to develop the skills relating to crawling, possibly even after they have begun to walk.

Advantages of crawling on all fours

Crawling has many developmental advantages:

The child practices holding his head up and moving it freely in all directions, since he follows up all auditive and visual stimuli that catch his attention.

Eye fixation develops. Head turning is not always sufficient for seeing something high up or far out to the side, so the eyes become accustomed to moving to extreme positions.

Arm muscles, especially those used for stretching, are trained.

The hand is bent back at the wrist, and the fingers are spread, bent slightly and pointed forwards, which is preparation for the natural positioning of the hand when holding objects, tools, etc.

The leg pattern becomes more advanced, because the hips and knees alternately bend more or less while crawling, but the ankle is generally stretched since the top part of the foot usually rests on the floor all the time. The central nervous system's development thus allows a finer differentiation of the movements of these three joints.

The cross-pattern movement – one arm and the opposite leg simultaneously – brings about small rotations and side-bendings in the spinal column, which lead up to a natural, supple, upright walk.

Rhythmic movements of the whole body are practiced while crawling.

Crawling is a good beginning exercise in balance, because the center of gravity is not as high as in the standing position, and there are four supports if the child stays still, three if he reaches for something, and two when he is actually crawling. From time to time the child kneels, and practices balancing when the center of gravity is slightly higher. Shifting one's weight from arm to leg and from side to side is practiced, making crawling a natural preparation for walking upright by teaching body-balance without support, which is something not attained to the same extent by the child pulling himself up in a playpen.

The playpen

Playpens can be useful, enabling the adult to turn his back on the child for a moment, but should be limited in their use.

For most of his waking time, when he reaches the crawling stage, the child should be allowed to explore the whole house to gain experience and thus develop perceptual and motor skills, to feel, lift, grasp, and push, and to experience distance and direction during constant changes of position.

The distance between the bars should be wide enough to let the child's feet poke through. If they are not, his legs will be turned outwards while he is standing.

Moreover, the playpen should be placed so that the child can follow what is happening in the room.

Infant seats and bouncing apparatus

A limited use of one of the infant seats made of plastic or canvas is permissible, but the child must not sit for too long, as he is strapped into the seat in a fixed position and has difficulty in moving his back and pelvis.

The seat should not be used for more than 10-15 minutes at a time before the child would naturally sit up for the same length of time. The seat should not be allowed to rob the child of the experience of lying on his stomach or of moving around on the floor according to his stage of development.

The same guidelines apply to the use of a bouncing apparatus. To be allowed to use the bouncing swing or chair, the child must be able to hold his back straight.

Movement patterns of the retarded child

The following pages should not be regarded as a training program. They simply put into practice ordinary good sense founded on knowledge of a normal child's motor development. If the child is severely retarded, it will always be useful to seek the advice of a physical therapist, and ask her to decide when the child is ready for the next step. Any adult who knows and understands children will be able to help the child develop in the following natural progression.

It depends on the individual child how early in his life it is desirable to begin stimulation, but this stimulation can seldom be started too early, and in any case it should be started as soon as retardation is diagnosed.

The primitive types of movement of the normal infant often are obvious in the older retarded child, and the succession of developmental stages is the same for both.

Follow the principle that if a child performs an action badly, it is not this action that should be dealt with. Rather, encourage the child to perform the action which *precedes* this in development. If the child walks badly, then crawling on hands and knees must be practiced, and if he crawls badly, he should practice crawling on his stomach. If this does not look natural, he should practice rolling over, etc.

In order to stimulate the retarded child's development, the stages of a normal child's development must be known and followed closely, but help and stimulation can only be given when the child himself is on the way to that actual stage, that is, when he has satisfactorily mastered the preceding stage.

Furthermore, the child must never be forced and should never be frightened, e. g. his head must not be allowed to drop. If necessary, the adult must support the head so that the child feels safe.

Motor development has such a close connection with perceptual development (see page 61) that if the former is delayed, the latter will have such poor prospects in most areas that the child will be retarded in all aspects. Body awareness, kinesthetic sense, touch, sight, and the interplay between these senses must therefore always be stimulated along with motor ability, in accordance with the child's actual stage of development.

The adult must observe the child closely. If the child is in an unsuitable position, or if his movements look too unnatural, the position and possibly also the movement should be altered, so that the child is led into a natural, possibly a more primitive, movement pattern.

Prone position

If the normally developed infant is laid on his stomach with his arms along his sides, he will immediately try to draw his arms up. The movement required for this can be stimulated by a light pressure on the opposite buttock.

When the child later begins to lift his head, this movement can be stimulated, partly by showing him interesting things, so that he raises his eyes and head to look at them, and partly by supporting his chin lightly with two fingers or tickling his neck. The child can also be laid on his stomach, so that he has a chance to follow what is happening around him.

If the arms have a tendency to slip out to the sides when the child tries to raise his head, using his bent arms as support, the adult should help by holding the child's arms in close to the body many times in the course of a day. Alternatively, a sandbag can be placed at the side of each arm for a short time each day, thereby stimulating the child to raise his head. This should be done only if the child can hold his head up but is prevented from doing so by the sliding out of the arms, and only if an adult can be close by (particularly useful for mongols).

Back position

When lying on his back, the child should be encouraged to hold his head in the mid-position as well as to turn it from side to side.

If the child is about ready to lift his head when being pulled from a lying to a sitting position by his arms, it is a good idea to do this »exercise« with the child every time he is »changed«. Support the head with one finger and give it a slight push, so that it is stimulated to rise with the body movement.

If the child is inclined to hold his head always turned to one side, place his bed so that he is forced to look the opposite way if he wants to see what is going on in the room. The child is also attracted by light from a window and this should also be taken into consideration in positioning the bed.

Fig. 12.   Good rolling movement with rotation of the back.

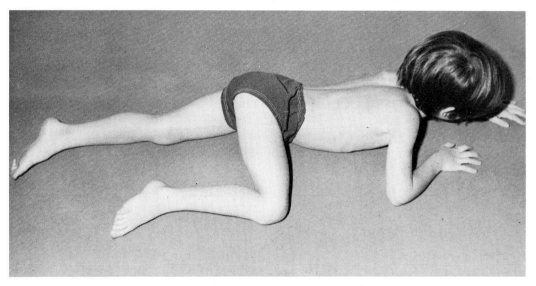

Fig. 13. Crawling on the stomach. The back is slightly rotated because the right hip is raised a little from the floor. Without the rotation the child cannot crawl.

Rolling movement

Lay the child on his side and get him to roll onto his back, then from his stomach onto his back, and later from his back to his stomach. Help the child, if he is almost ready to roll over by himself. If not, delay this exercise. Possibly encourage the child to roll over, by laying toys beside him at a suitable distance (Fig. 12).

Afterwards let the child practice rolling by lifting one of his legs over the other, until the whole body follows. Or turn and lift the child's head and at the same time pull one arm across his body, so that the shoulder follows, and finally the hips and the legs.

Little by little the child himself will help with these movements, and eventually he will be able to carry them out by himself. Only then will he be able to change naturally from lying to sitting and crawling, and the back will thus be exercised in all directions and become flexible.

Prone position

When the child has learned to hold his head up while supporting himself on his forearms, he may be stimulated to reach for objects with one hand, to lift his head even higher and finally to support himself on his extended arms. In this position, the fingers should be outspread. Give a little support under the chin if the head is not yet quite steady, so that it does not suddenly drop and cause the arms to bend.

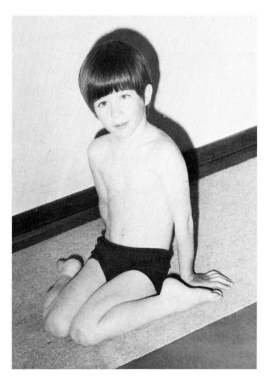

Fig. 14. This position should not become habitual over a longer period of time, as it may have a detrimental effect on leg position when walking.

When the child is lying prone, test the amphibian reaction in order to encourage the child to crawl forward on his stomach (Fig. 13).

Sitting position – Parachute (falling) reflexes

When head control has become established in both supine and prone positions, practice the sitting position, first with back support and later without. It helps to place the child in a position natural to his development, that is, with legs bent as in Fig. 10, to give better balance.

When the child is sitting, practice the falling reflexes by pushing him gently as soon as he shows a tendency to save himself, but never frighten him. Help him by placing one of his arms out at the side and steadying his elbow.

To strengthen and stimulate the child to hold himself up, he can be carried by holding him with his back to the adult who is carrying him. At first, support the child around the chest, to assist head-raising, then at the pelvis to stimulate the activity of all the back muscles, and finally right under the hips, so that the extensors of the hip may also be activated. From any of these positions the falling reflexes may be practiced by gently pushing the child forward over a table. The arms will stretch forward and the hands will be supported on the table.

It is important to notice whether eye fixation, head balance and arm pattern progress together naturally. For example, if the arm pattern remains too long at the symmetric stage, the child should be encouraged to use one hand at a time. To enable him to use his arms alternately, get him to reach for toys with one hand, and to creep and crawl in cross-pattern, etc.

From the prone position through heel-sitting to crawling

When prone, supported on outstretched arms, the child is helped to sit on his heels, still supported by outstretched arms and hands (Fig. 7). Here let him rock to and fro, until one fine day he will find himself on hands and knees,

perhaps with slight chin-support. The symmetrical Tonic Neck Reflex is now under control, and the child can move his head freely in all directions, and even bend it to look down without his arms giving way.

The child is now ready to crawl, perhaps at first like a rabbit, moving both arms and both legs alternately, and a little later in the natural cross-pattern.

When the child can move around the house, he develops quickly, partly because of all the new impressions and experiences he gains.

Immature types of crawling

The older retarded child

To encourage an older retarded child to crawl, whether in play or as a definite exercise, does not mean encouraging regression to infancy. When the child has finished crawling for that day, make him take a good run, because rhythmic crawling in cross-pattern, followed by running at an ordinary speed, helps him to walk better and more rhythmically as soon as the running is over.

The older retarded child's way of crawling can give a clear indication of his stage of development, so I shall mention a few types of retarded crawling:

One often sees the head bent when crawling (Fig. 15), which results in the arms also being more or less bent.

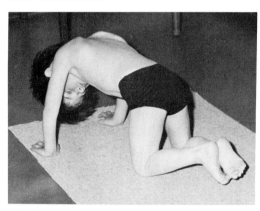

Fig. 15. Some retarded children show this crawling pattern with bowed head and lifted feet.

Examples of exercises

   In the prone position, head-lifting and arm-stretching.

   Crawling on the stomach.

   Heel-sitting supported by the outstretched arms and hands.

The back may be rounded when crawling. Poor head balance when lying prone may have caused poor development of the back muscles, or perhaps the child was unwilling to lie on his stomach. Or perhaps the primitive fetal, flexed position is still dominant in the prone position, and this causes the rounded back as well as the bowed head.

Examples of exercises

   Let the child lie prone on the floor with lifted head, supported by the forearms and later by the outstretched arms.

   Let him crawl on his stomach.

   Stimulate the falling reflexes, and also

   Stimulate the child to look up when he is lying on his stomach.

The hands may be clenched when crawling, which is a sign of underdeveloped grasp, or rather, that the child has difficulty in letting go of an object.

Examples of exercises

   Practice grasping by »give and take« play with various objects.

   Teach the child to stretch his fingers when he is lying prone, leaning on his extended arms.

   Do the same when heel-sitting (Fig. 7).

His arms and legs may be spread too far apart, usually because of poor balance.

Arms and legs may advance unevenly and this may mean that one side of the body is better developed than the other. Train the weaker side after consulting a physical therapist.

Examples of exercises

   Exercise the muscles of the weaker side.

   Crawl on the stomach, moving each side' equally.

   Crawl, walk and run with steps of equal length.

Leg movements may still be influenced by the fetal flexed position, so that the knees are bent too much for the feet to reach the ground. The ankle joints also are bent too much (Fig. 15).

Examples of exercises

   Crawling on the stomach.

   Heel-sitting and rocking so that the buttocks finally come to rest on the outstretched feet.

   Crawling on all fours, starting from heel-sitting.

Some children crawl and walk homolaterally, that is, the arm and the leg on one side move forward simultaneously. This could be due to a very early stage of development, and if it occurs in older children, it is usually connected with a stiff back, as this type of gait frees the child from the necessity of rotating the spinal column.

Examples of exercises

   Supple the back by exercises belonging to an earlier stage, e. g. :

   Rolling with rotation of the spinal column.

   Lying on the back with knees bent and feet on the floor and then swinging the knees from side to side (Fig. 55). Crawl on the stomach in cross-pattern as soon as possible (begin with the amphibian reaction).

The wrists may be stiff, and the hands bent toward the little finger (ulnar flexion) (see Fig. 30 a).

   It is important to notice and treat this defect early, because it can hinder an effective grip. Training is usually successful. The child with this defect will crawl with his hands far apart and fingers together, and pointing outward, with the whole arm turned outward. »Cheating« in this way avoids maximum bending of the wrist. When the fingers point forward and the hand is in mid-position while crawling, the wrist should bend backwards to the fullest extent.

Examples of exercises

   Practice grasping in »hold-release« play, getting the thumb and index finger to play a major role. Strengthen the wrist muscles by bending the hand backwards and the finger muscles by spreading them. Bend the hand deliberately towards the thumb-side. Crawling exercises with fingers pointing straight forward, spread and slightly bent.

Standing – walking – running

The normal child

A child may be able to walk, but how he walks, and to what stage his walking has developed, is another matter. For the normal child the whole process takes about 3 years from the day he takes his first step until he can walk, properly balanced, with rotation of the spinal column, good articulation of the foot, a natural arm swing and no regression to tiptoeing. Good foot articulation involves putting the heel on the ground first, carrying the body weight over onto the leg, and »rolling« forward over the foot so that the toes are the last to leave the ground (Fig. 20).

From birth, the supporting reflex and the walking reflex are present, but without weight-bearing and with curled-up toes (the plantar grasp reflex).

These reflexes disappear gradually, and at about 5 months, if the child is held upright, with the feet touching the mattress, he will stretch and bend both legs simultaneously as if he were jumping. There is some weight-bearing, but the hips and knees are not fully extended, and he is often inclined to point his toes. When the child is 7-8 months he will, with support, be able to stand on flat feet and jump or make walking movements supporting almost all his weight. This is no longer a reflex, but the first stage in learning to walk.

Later the child can walk sideways, holding the bars of the playpen with both hands.

A few months later the child can stand for a moment without support. The standing posture is bow-legged with legs apart to preserve balance. Hips and knees are slightly bent, the stomach sags and the lower back consequently is curved.

Not long after this, the child can roll over from his back onto his stomach and from a squatting position he can raise himself up to stand without support, and thence to walk. This occurs usually at about 1 year (between 11 and 18 months). There are great individual differences in the acquisition of this and other skills.

At first the child leans slightly forward, and, to prevent falling, moves instinctively one leg forward. He goes so fast that it almost becomes a kind of »run« that cannot stop, ending with the child running into the furniture or a wall, or falling down. Thus the child seems to »run« before he can walk, because slower motion requires better balance.

At first the child walks just to practice walking, but his walking soon becomes motivated and directed.

Early walking goes straight forward, with legs apart, no rotation of the back or hips, and no articulation of the feet, which are flat on the floor (the older retarded child's walk may be recognized here). The arms are lifted, but, as balance improves, they are lowered and held at the sides, so that they can swing slightly, along with the rotating movements of the trunk.

From being bow-legged, he progresses to straightening his knees, which then go to the opposite extreme and tend to become knock-kneed. Finally the knees reach equilibrium, at the same time as they start being fully extended when walking.

The ankles also become more stable and straight, and, as balance improves, they just pass each other when swinging.

The hip muscles help to correct foot and knee positions, because the force exerted on these joints changes as the hip muscles become stronger.

The hip extensors become stronger so that the hips can be fully extended when walking.

The hip muscles are now strong enough to balance the pelvis, and the child can stand and hop on one leg. This helps his balance in that stage of walking in which he stands on one leg while swinging the other leg forward.

With better balance there is time to completely extend the hip with each step, a move-

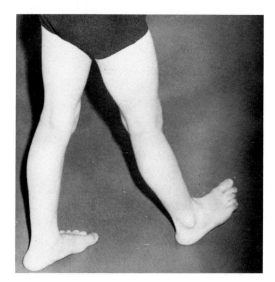

Fig. 16. Right leg: bent hip, straight knee, ankle bent and toes stretched.

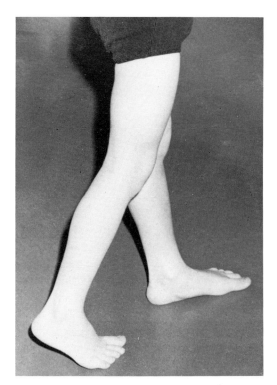

Fig. 17. Right leg: hip and knee straight, ankle and toe joints bent. Immediately afterwards, the knee will be bent and the leg will swing forward.

ment which also helps towards development of a natural run.

Fig. 16 (front leg) shows that ankle and hip joints are bent while the knee is straight. Fig. 17 shows another stage in the movement of the same leg, where hip and knee joints are straight while ankle and toes are bent.

The child turns his face forward to orient himself visually. With the rotation of the spinal column, the natural movement is for one shoulder and arm to swing forward at the same time as the opposite leg and hip also swing forward. This rotation of the body occurs along its own central axis and requires flexibility of the spinal column, a flexibility which has been acquired by rolling and crawling.

Maturation of the central nervous system is so clearly mirrored in the leg patterns of crawling and walking that these patterns can be used as indications of a child's level of motor development.

It is tiring for a little child to walk for a long time. He lacks the motivation to go on walking, and furthermore walking must first become automatic before it can be light, gliding, rhythmic and easy.

With regard to running, see page 129.

Foot movements when walking

The ankle must be bent and stretched alternately when walking – foot articulation, as it is called (Figs. 16, 17) – and this needs good coordination and an advanced development of the central nervous system.

At about 2 years of age, foot movements begin to be a part of the walking movement. It seems as if the calf muscles must first be trained in the correct coordination to keep the ankle joint in a suitable position. The child will have a tendency for a year or two to walk occasionally on tiptoe.

The toes spread a little when pushing off, because that is the part of the foot that leaves the ground last. This can only be done when the joints at the base of the toes can bend freely.

The muscle that draws the big toe outwards (abductor hallucis) also helps to hold up the

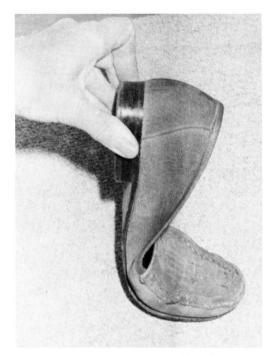

Fig. 18. The sole of the shoe should be flexible and able to bend at the toe joints.

arch of the foot. If this muscle is weak, it will cause faulty articulation of the foot and toes when walking; the big toe will be pressed against the other toes, and there will be a tendency towards flat-footedness.

A little child appears to be flatfooted, but this is only because there is a »cushion« of fat under the foot; this disappears after the foot has begun to be used.

Footwear

Unsuitable footwear can hinder the natural movement of the foot when walking. It is important that the sole is flexible enough to bend up at a right angle at the toe joints, even in winter footwear (Fig. 18). Otherwise the gait is likely to be flat-footed, with turned-out legs.

Pointed shoes can squeeze the big toe in towards the other toes and thus hinder its spread when pushing off; this contributes to flat-footedness.

The toes should be able to stretch out completely in the shoe, but on the other hand, the foot should not be able to slip back and forth,

which can happen if the instep does not fit the foot properly.

The heel of the foot must be well supported by the heel of the shoe, especially in the case of valgus positioning (fallen arches) and flatfoot. In these cases especially, good arch support is required as well.

Finally, the shoes must not be too heavy, especially for children who walk badly or have weak muscles.

Slippers should be soft, with ample room for the toes to spread. Remember that a child who has been ordered arch supports in his shoes should also use them in his slippers, or should not wear slippers, because the foot will fall back into the wrong position again each day and the support will have been useless.

All flatfooted children, and especially those who have arch supports, should exercise barefoot each day and likewise should walk barefoot in sand and soft earth whenever possible.

It is important to work towards developing strong feet, so that the arches are stabilized, but it is also important that the feet be flexible, so arch supports should not be used longer than is absolutely necessary (for foot exercises, see page 128).

Immature walking patterns

The young child

Put off encouraging the retarded child to walk until his motor development has advanced sufficiently, in other words, until he has passed through the development that finally ends in walking, as described in the section on the normal child's development.

As in all attempts to help the retarded child develop, it is important to begin one stage lower than the child's present level of motor ability, and patiently, with much repetition, to establish the child's abilities so well at this stage that he himself tries to go further.

The older child

It is not proven, but it is probable, that the spinal stiffness and uncoordinated gait seen in retarded children is partly due to premature attempts to walk. If the child feels unsure, he becomes nervous and stiffens his whole body, which prevents free walking movements. It is easier to balance on four points of contact than on two, and therefore it is advisable to postpone walking until the child has developed sufficient balance. One should also consider the presence or inhibition of the various reflexes.

In the case of older retarded children who can walk, but whose walking pattern is immature and poorly coordinated, in many cases this can be improved by energetic, purposeful training, given that the child is not too old. The methods of directing and training these older children are in principle the same as those described for normal children.

If the child lacks eye control, this should be trained. If the back is stiff, it must be made more flexible. If the falling reflexes are absent, they must be developed.

When the child has mastered all these and other »preliminaries«, training for a natural walk should follow in natural progression.

Never try to correct a child's gait, as it is a part of his personality. Correcting the gait usually has no effect on the gait but only makes the child feel uncertain and miserable. Instead make an effort to improve all the primitive movement patterns (rolling, crawling, etc.) and then the gait will improve by itself, partly because the child then will be able to walk naturally, and partly because the child feels more sure of himself and has gained more self-respect, as he realizes that he was able to learn.

I will mention a few examples of the most usual faults in the way retarded children walk, and suggest a few exercises:

Frontal gait:
When a child has a frontal gait there is no spinal rotation, and this must therefore be exercised:
  Rolling movements.
  Amphibian reaction.

Crawling on the stomach.
Crawling on all fours.
Let the child run until he is out of breath, so he forgets to think about how he should walk, and so discards his old habits. Then tell the child to walk until he has gotten his breath back. As a rule, his gait will be more natural and free than before the run. The natural, rhythmic movements of the primitive patterns of crawling and running have transferred to the walking movements.

Walking with feet apart:
A straddling walk may be caused by poor balance and fear of falling, or because of weak hip muscles. Examples of exercises:
  Falling reflexes.
  Crawling while playing on the floor.
  Exercising hip muscles.
  Walking on a line 8 cm wide.
  Standing on one leg, first with support, later without (right and left).

Shuffling gait:
A shuffling gait may be a sign of poor balance, as the child thus avoids standing on one leg while walking. It can also be a sign of general late development, poor sight, or, in particular, weak leg muscles. In the last case all the muscles should be exercised, and in the first case the same exercises as for walking with feet apart should be used, or, for instance:
  Walk between the rungs of a ladder laid on the floor. When the child has walked for some minutes, he will continue to raise his legs after the ladder is removed, at least for a little while.

Knock-knees
Pronounced knock-knees unfortunately cannot be improved or corrected by exercises. This condition can possibly be kept from worsening by training feet, leg and hip muscles, so that the weight on the knees is better distributed. This is work for the physical therapist.

Slightly bent legs
Many retarded children still walk with slightly bent hip and knee joints and on flat feet

Fig. 19. The normal child at 3½ years jumps with feet flat and hip, knee and ankle joints bent.

without articulation. When walking, the hip is not fully extended. This, again, is a residue of the normal child's primitive walking pattern. This bending of all three joints prevents the child from jumping and running well enough to take part in the games of his age group.

The child jumps like the normal 3-year-old, that is, with feet completely flat (Fig. 19).

There may be psychological reasons for this, or poor sight may mean that the child does not dare to lose touch with the ground, but most of it stems from retarded movement patterns. In most cases the procedure is the same:

Draw the child's attention to his back, and to the fact that it can be trained to produce the hip stretching.

Proceed to hip-stretching.

In the same way, through body awareness and kinesthetic sense, the child can learn to know his feet and their movement possibilities, and so improve their functioning (see page 128).

It is interesting to see how this method, in some cases almost immediately after only a few exercises, will facilitate a springy jump. Yet the child may practice for months before he can use this acquired foot movement normally in daily life, though often he does succeed.

Flatfoot and turned-out legs
If the legs turn outwards, the feet will turn too and more weight will fall on the inner edge, resulting in flat feet. The foot does not articulate when walking, and the walk becomes heavy and flatfooted.
Sample exercises:
Long-sitting with inward rotation of both thighs.

All foot exercises may be used (see page 128).

Walking on a broad line.

Go to the wall while I stand behind you. I want to see the whole sole of your foot, while you push against the floor with your toes (older children) (Fig. 20).

Round back
There can be many reasons for a round back, such as:

The child may have been allowed to sit for

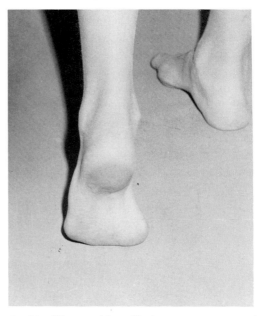

Fig. 20. When pushing off, the toes are supported along their whole length, while the sole of the foot is visible from the back.

too long at a time, before he was really ready to sit up.

The spine is stiff.

The child is shy and always looks down.

The back muscles are weak.

The child does not know the back of his body.

Poor balance, which makes the child look down to see where he is treading.

Sample exercises:

Practice awareness of the back and the buttocks (see page 97).

Training of back muscles (see page 157).

In many cases the abdominal muscles and the hip extensors must be trained.

Suitable posture when sitting and when lying (sleeping).

Arm movements when walking

In rare cases the arm and leg on the same side are brought forward simultaneously in an ambling gait. This primitive pattern should have been superseded when the child was crawling on his stomach. If it has persisted, this may be due to a very stiff spine and hence an inability to rotate.

Sample exercises:

Roll with rotation.

Crawl in cross-pattern.

Exercises to supple the back (ball play).

Skipping.

With some children the arms may be turned in and held slightly out from the body, which is also a primitive pattern. Here practice turning out at the arms and shoulders and exercise the shoulder muscles.

Other children with no rotation of the spine swing both arms forward simultaneously when walking. Treatment here is as described for the ambling gait, because rotation of the spine determines the natural arm swing.

The child who falls often:

Many retarded children fall down often, and this may be due to many different causes, such as:

a) The legs are turned in, so the child falls over his own feet. This may be a muscular fault, and the leg position will be rectified when the thighs are trained to rotate outwards, but it can also be caused by an unusual position of the upper part of the thigh bone, in which rare case nothing can be done.

b) Weak hip muscles, especially those moving the leg backwards and outwards, are those which must be exercised.

c) Poor balance may be due to brain defects, e. g. a slight ataxia (a form of cerebral palsy that causes balance difficulties). Here may be recommended:
Muscular training.
Training »to fall« from the kneeling or standing position. Balance exercises helped by sight (the ataxic child cannot keep his balance when his eyes are shut).
Horseback riding.

d) Poor balance is usually due to late development. Even older retarded children may lack falling reflexes, and these must then be taught. This can usually be done quickly, and will give the child a more assured gait, because he will be less nervous of falling when he knows that he can save himself by putting out his hands.

With regard to developing balance, and for various balance exercises, see page 123.

Handgrasp

The normal child

Grasp reflex

The newborn child generally hold his hands clenched. If you insert your finger in each of the child's hands his grasp will be so strong that you can lift him up this way. This is a reflexed movement elicited by the sense of touch. By about 2 months the grasp gradually becomes more relaxed, and it is easy to straighten the child's fingers.

The first way of holding is with one hand, with the three ulnar fingers (little, fourth and middle fingers) flexed against the palm (Fig. 21a). The child grasps an object only if it touches his hand.

When the child grasps with one hand, the other will be clenched at the same time, that is, there is a corresponding movement of the other hand. The task is still so difficult, and coordination so unsure, that too many nerve centers are activated and too many muscles involved.

The grasp reflex is inhibited gradually, so that, by the 5th month, the child can consciously, though still with difficulty, let go of an object. Thumb and first finger now take part in a radial-palmar grasp and both hands can be used at once.

In the next phase of development the child will be able to pick up small objects using all his fingertips, since it is no longer necessary to press the object in against the palm. Finger coordination has improved, and the child can

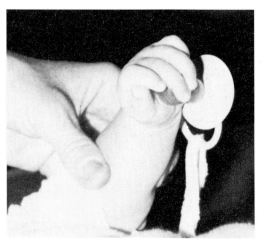

Fig. 21a. Thumb and index finger are not used in the child's first grasp.

Fig. 21b. Retarded grasp. The grasp begins with simultaneous finger and elbow stretching. (Mongol, 2 years).

now use one hand without a corresponding movement of the other, as long as the movement is one he is used to. A month later, the child will begin to use a pincer grasp with thumb and index finger, when for example, he wants to pick up a crumb from the table.

Coordination

Side by side with motor ability comes development of all areas of perception (sight, body awareness, touch, kinesthetic sense) which are prerequisites for the child's understanding of what he is holding.

At first the grasping movement is uncoordinated. The child often misses his aim because eye-hand coordination are still uncertain.

Likewise, at first a child will hold things too firmly, but he soon learns by experience to fit the strength of the grasp to the weight of the object. This is continued throughout life. For example, a guest in a strange house may lift a lamp from a table and, misjudging the weight, may almost throw it up to the ceiling.

One function at a time:

When grasping begins to develop, the child will be able to perform only one function at a time. Later he will be able to do several. E.g.:
Lying on the back and grasping.
Lying on the front, lifting the head, without grasping.
Lying on the front, lifting the head and grasping.
Sitting.
Sitting and grasping only one object.
Sitting and grasping an object, which he then drops as he picks up another.
Finally, a child can hold an object with one hand, while the other hand reaches for something else.

Stretching movements in hand and fingers:

When the child wants to grasp an object, the development also follows a definite pattern.

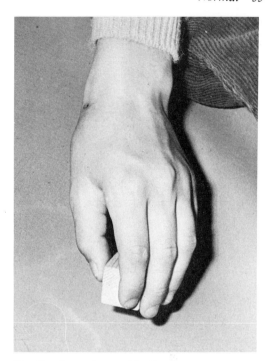

Fig. 21c. Normal grasp. The fingers are stretched just enough to grasp the object, and the elbow need not be stretched at the same time.

Arm, hand and fingers are stretched to the maximum before the object is grasped (Fig. 21b).

The stretching occurs at the last moment, and the hand opens just enough to grasp the object (Fig. 21c).

To let go of an object:

It is harder for a child to let go than to grasp. The reflex bending-grasping movement is present at birth, but finger-stretching is learned subsequently, as the central nervous system develops.

When the child amuses himself by throwing everything within reach on to the ground, this is a necessary stage in development. The child is practicing holding, letting go, observing the speed of the fall, getting an idea of the distance to the floor, and hearing the noise when the object hits the floor. Thus the child gains experience.

Playing »give and take« is a useful exercise.

Coordination within the bending-stretching pattern is difficult. At about 8 months the child

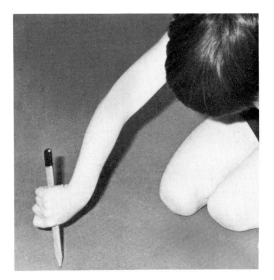

Fig. 22.   The turned-in primitive, cross-palmar grasp.

Holding writing tools

The child's first grasp on a writing tool is a cross-palmar grasp (Fig. 22). The whole hand clutches the chalk or pencil, and usually the arm is turned inwards. The arm is not supported on the table, so the child draws with gross motor movements. The hand is only a tool for holding and does not take part in the movements.

A little later, almost the same grasp is used, but the child notices that he can guide the pencil better, if he extends his index finger (Fig. 23).

Around 3-4 years of age the child often uses a »brush grasp«. The writing tool is no longer held within the hand, but instead only the fingers are used. In most cases the hand is still turned in, but there is some movement of the wrist, even if the fingers do not move (Fig. 24).

Some children, particularly older children with poor finger coordination, often use a cross-thumb grasp (Fig. 25) where the pencil is held between the clenched hand and the thumb. The child's hold is high on the pencil

can let go of an object when it is resting on a table or on the other hand, for example, but only at one year can the object be released in the air. The grasp-release function is now under control.

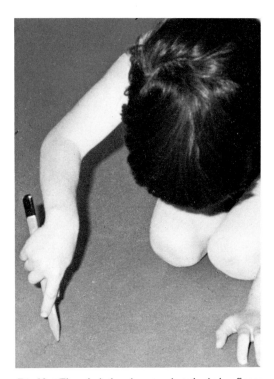

Fig. 23.   The whole hand grasps, but the index finger guides.

Fig. 24.   »Brush grasp« A finger grasp, rotated inwards.

and the forearm is still unsupported. This also involves gross motor movements without using the fingers.

The child notices eventually that adults support their arms on the table, and that this helps them guide the pencil. In some cases a child uses a low cross-thumb grasp before he goes over to a grown-up grasp with the arm supinated (turned outwards).

The »adult grasp« requires well-developed finger coordination (see under Writing, page 170) and corresponds to a late stage in neuro-muscular development.

If the child's finger dexterity is developed early by the use of suitable educational toys, it is possible that one or more of the above mentioned stages will be omitted.

Holding spoon and fork

The grasp of eating implements follows the same development pattern. For example, the 2- to 2½-year-old child who can feed himself with a spoon or fork will quite naturally use a turned-in cross-grasp (pronated cross-palmer grasp). Later, he will stretch out his index finger in order to guide the fork better. Making him hold the spoon with a supinated, more adult grasp will make the business of eating far too complicated and in some cases will spoil mealtimes for him for years.

It is therefore advisable to let him use a simpler, less advanced, grasp, so that the child does not have too many difficulties to overcome at once.

Using scissors

Cutting is difficult and needs much motor ability, eye-hand coordination and finger strength. To require the child to cut accurately is of no benefit. Most children can only cut out well at about 6 years of age.

It may be mentioned that using of the thumb and middle finger, supported by the index finger, often gives the best grasp for cutting.

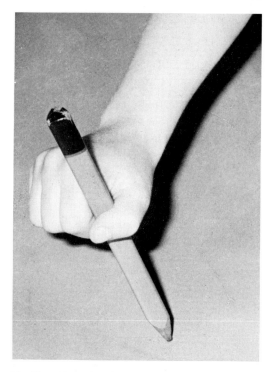

Fig. 25. »Cross-thumb« grasp.

A ROUGH OUTLINE OF THE HAND'S MOTOR DEVELOPMENT

From; turned-in (prone) grasp
to: turned-out (supine) grasp.

From: palmar (within the hand) grasp
to: finger grasp.

From: maximum stretching of fingers and arm
to: stretching adapted to the object's size.

From: difficulty in releasing
to: easily letting go.

From: ulnar-palmar grasp *without* using thumb or index finger,
to: a) radial-palmar grasp (hand in mid-position using all fingers and against the palm),
b) finger grasp (no longer completely within the hand),
c) pincer grasp with the tips of the thumb and index finger.

Grasp of writing and eating implements follow the same progression:

High grasp:
The forearm does not rest on the table.

From: The child grabs the top end of the implement or uses a pronated cross-palmar grasp. The implement is held within the clenched hand,

to: a) pronated cross-palmar grasp with straight index finger (gives better control of the implement),
b) cross-thumb grasp (rather rare in normal children),
c) pronated finger grasp, as if holding a brush or a fork,
d) supinated finger grasp, as holding a pencil with »adult grasp«.

Low grasp:
The forearm rests on the table when writing or drawing.

e) cross-thumb grasp (rather rare in normal children). Gross motor movements.
In this case the writer has difficulty in seeing what he has written,
f) »adult« ordinary grasp, which uses fine motor movements. Supine hand.

(See: Ball play page 135).

The immature hand

Relation between motor development and perception

If a child cannot use his hands properly, he is deprived of a whole world of experiences, and this will greatly affect his life.

Possibly it will prevent him from being able to take care of himself; he may not be able to dress or feed himself, or handle things around him. Furthermore, later in life all manual work will be difficult, if not impossible, and the social and psychological consequences are obvious.

Motor development accompanies perceptual development, and it is essential to know the sequence and all forms of normal development if we wish to help the retarded child. First of all, we must know what a natural movement looks like at a certain stage. We must learn to observe in detail the motor patterns of the hand. If the hand does not look natural when handling a certain object, the object is unsuitable for the child at that time.

Perception of direction and space, as well as eye-hand coordination, will improve if the hands can be used naturally.

The child must be trained gradually to grasp things handed to him from different directions, e.g. when he is sitting on the floor surrounded by his playthings.

Sensibility (touch) and stereognostic sense (see page 87) must be trained and practiced. The child must learn to be aware of his hands and fingers, and of their movements. He must have an opportunity to manipulate numerous different objects – not just the same six or seven all the time – in order to experience form, structure, consistency and weight.

If a child does not perceive the different characteristics of an object, the object will not be of any interest to him, and consequently he will not be motivated to tell the name of the object or describe it. Thus, handling an object and perceiving it through all senses also helps speech development.

Motor development

With regard to the motor development of the hand, as with general motor development, it must be remembered that every new skill must be learned, and the more diverse skills the child already has acquired, the easier it will be to learn new ones.

Before there can be a question of learning the more complicated grasping movements, the grasp reflex must be completely inhibited, that is, the child must be able to let go of any object quickly and easily.

Sample exercises for small children
Correct, natural movements can best be

learned through play, with as few formal exercises as possible.

Practice holding and releasing.

Play »give and take« with objects that require the use of the thumb in grasping, so that the hand is weaned from the ulnar position (bending toward the little finger) and is held in the mid-position.

Crawl and play on the floor.

Take a natural hold of various objects, regardless of their position.

Build towers of blocks and of 2.5 cm cubes. The difficulty here is to release the blocks precisely.

Pincer grasp is practiced by putting beads in a box.

Handle all kinds of objects, light and heavy, big and small.

Grasp of eating or writing implements

A normal child may take up to four years to pass from the pronated cross-grasp to the supinated »adult« grasp. Remember this, when a retarded child is learning to feed himself or to write.

Often the child eats better with a primitive grasp, so there is no need to force a development which seldom produces any improvement.

The child can often be helped by using a slightly thicker implement, because it will be easier to hold. However, there are limits to the size a small child can manipulate.

If the child continues to develop, the primitive grasp will become stable and the child will himself attempt to use a more advanced grasp.

Sample exercises for older children

In the case of older children, who have not developed a natural hand grasp after an adequate amount of time, more formal and purposeful exercises should be initiated.

It is necessary to begin with body awareness, because knowledge of the hands, and of their movements and the names of the fingers, can promote their use. For example:

Body-awareness (see page 97).

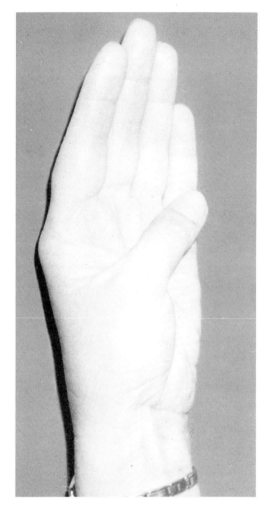

Fig. 26a. The thumb should rotate on its own axis. The nail outside.

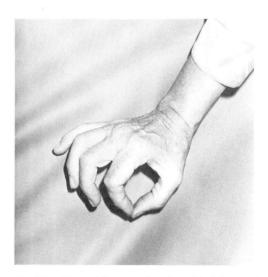

Fig. 26b. Normal finger prehension with full opposition of the thumb.

Dip the hand in paint and make a clear print with outstretched fingers on a piece of paper. Point to the fingers and name them.

The child lays one hand on a piece of paper and traces around it with the other, naming the fingers.

Draw in the nails.

Movements of the thumb

To improve finger movement the thumb must be flexible, as shown in Fig. 26a. The nail faces out. This movement is called »opposition« and consists partly in bringing the thumb opposite to the other fingers and partly in rotating it on its own axis. Flexibility of the thumb means that it can easily meet the tips of the other fingers in all fine movements (Fig. 26b).

»Opposition« seems to come quite late in a child's development and should be practiced carefully by retarded children (Fig. 27a).

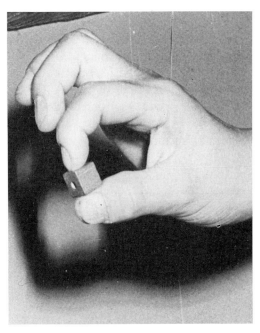

Fig. 27b. Insufficient opposition of the thumb. The finger grasp is performed by taking the object between the tip of the index finger and the side of the thumb. The sensitivity of the fingertip is not fully utilized.

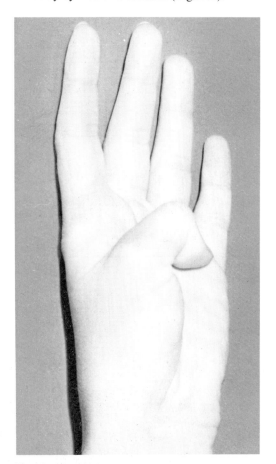

Fig. 27a. Incomplete rotation of thumb.

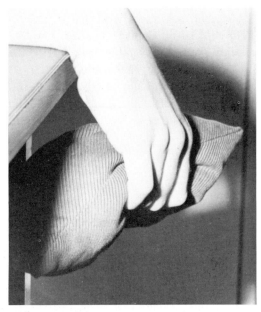

Fig. 28. Begin with the wrist bent.

If the thumb does not rotate on its own axis, the pincer grasp will be performed as in Fig. 27b. The object is held between the point of the index finger and the side of the thumbnail. This makes for an uncertain grasp and does not make use of the feeling in the fingertip.

All finger movements which include the thumb must be exercised:

Put the tips of the thumb and first finger together, so that they are slightly bent and form a ring. Repeat with the other fingers and the tip of the thumb (Fig. 26b).

It promotes the development of opposition if the adult takes the child's hand in his, and with his other hand gently bends the child's thumb so that it turns in over the hand, with the nail uppermost (Fig. 26a).

Bending back the wrist

The wrist must be bent well back to get a natural, strong grasp, e.g.:

Crawl on the floor with the fingers spread a little and pointing straight forward.

Lay the forearm and hand flat on a table and clap the table several times without lifting the arm.

Lay the forearm over a corner of a table, so that the hand hangs over the edge. Move the hand up and down, with the wrist bent well back (the adult may help a little). When the movement is good, take something heavy in the hand and repeat the exercise (Figs. 28-29).

Sideways movements of the wrist

If the hand is much bent towards the little finger (instead of in a middle position), which often occurs in retarded children (Fig. 30a), this means that the child has not yet quite discarded the ulnar grasp using the third, fourth and fifth fingers, and that the motor ability of the thumb and index finger is not yet fully developed (Fig. 30b).

This sideways movement of the wrist will mean that the wrist cannot be bent back fully and that the fingers cannot be properly spread.

Bending the wrist towards the thumb (radial flexion) must be persistently practiced before the grasp can be improved, e.g.:

Lay the forearm on the table and hold it so that it lies still and does not move when an attempt is made to bend the hand towards the thumb. An adult may help by applying a light pressure in the opposite direction, so that it is harder for the muscles to carry out the movement.

Place the hand in mid-position on the table and then spread the fingers out and bring them together again.

Much play with a large ball, which requires spreading the fingers to catch or to aim a throw.

Practicing coordination and speed

After this, coordination, reaction time and speed of movement must be trained. Every ex-

Fig. 27c. Is this child right- or left-handed? Which hand is most developed?

Fig. 29. Lift the sandbag, bending the wrist back as much as possible.

ercise should be repeated daily ten times, first with the dominant hand, then with the other hand and finally, for some of the exercises, with both hands together. The exercises should

become quicker and quicker, but avoid sloppiness. Encourage the child by timing him to see how often he can perform each exercise in, for example, 30 seconds, or how long it takes to do a certain number of exercises 10 times each:

Press the tips of the two index fingers lightly together. Repeat with the other fingers.

Lay the forearms and hands on the table. Alternate closing the fist and opening it, with fingers spread apart, or

Close the fist and stretch out one finger at a time. This is easy with the index and the little finger. The ring finger may be stretched together with the little finger, because otherwise it is too difficult for children.

Lay the hand on the table in the piano playing position so that only the tips touch the table, and lift one finger at a time without raising the others.

Put bigger, and later smaller, beads in a small bottle. For example, three beads with

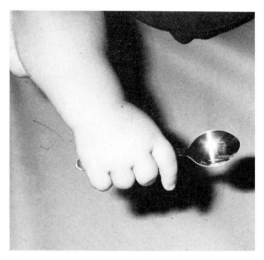

Fig. 30b. Ulnar-palmer grasp. Two-year-old retarded infant. Index finger and thumb are not used sufficiently.

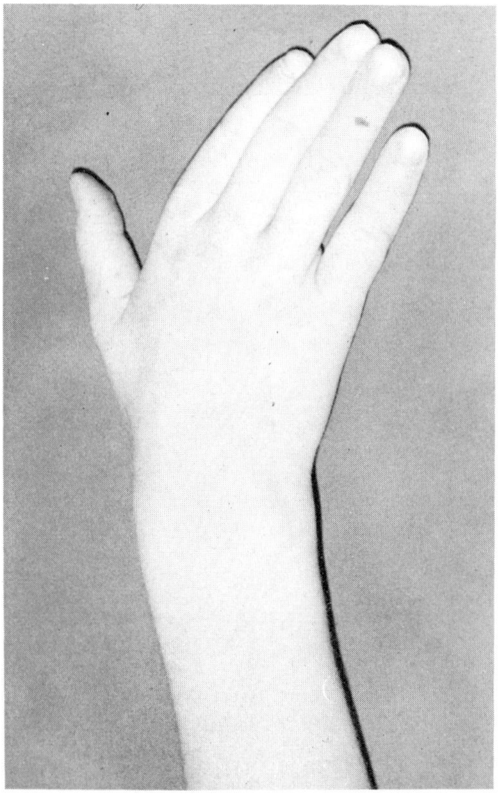

Fig. 30a. Wrist always bent towards the little finger causing poor grasp.

the thumb and index finger and three with the thumb and each of the other fingers.

Build a tower with 0.5 cm wooden blocks.

Play pegboard games, using all fingers in turn.

Play with a small ball (see page 135).

Gradual training in strength

Muscle strength should usually not be trained separately before motor ability, the movement patterns, looks natural. If the hand can be used naturally, the muscles will gradually gain strength. It is possible to increase muscular strength even in severely retarded children, but, if the motor pattern is not sufficiently developed, this is of no benefit.

Exercises

Hook both index fingers together and pull. Repeat with the other fingers two by two.

On hands and knees. Place the fingertips on the floor in the piano-playing position, in other words, with slightly bent fingers. Bring as much bodyweight as possible forward over the fingers.

Hold the corners of a loosely-filled sandbag weighing from 3-10 kg and hold firmly. By bending the elbows, raise and lower the bag slowly 10-20 times in succession without dropping the bag (Fig. 31).

Lift various heavy objects, according to the hands' ability, so that the grasp becomes stronger.

The child holds a smooth stick firmly with both hands and another child tries to take it from him.

Hang on the wall bar for one minute or less. It is easiest to hang with the face towards the wall, especially if the child has stiff shoulders or back.

If the exercise makes the child nervous, let him put both feet on the lowest bar and take hold with his hands as high as possible. Slip the feet out and hang down. The child feels that he can almost reach the floor. Overweight children cannot bear their own weight when hanging by the fingers (hands).

Investigation of thumb opposition

In an investigation of 104 educable subnormal children of school age, 20 could not rotate their thumbs at the beginning of the school year. At the end of the school year only six of the oldest children could not rotate the thumb (perhaps they started learning too late). The other 14 had learned very quickly.

Fig. 31. Training strength and endurance of grasp (normal child).

Function of the bladder and bowel

The normal child

The child is born with an »emptying« reflex that is activated when the bladder or bowel reaches a certain degree of fullness; at first the level of activation is very low.

Emptying the bowels

During the first weeks, bowel movements are frequent and sporadic, but at 4 weeks there will only be three or four movements daily, usually when the child wakes, or in association with a mealtime. When the child is about 2 months old, the number of movements often decreases to two.

When the child is about 18 months old, this central nervous system is so far developed that he understands simple associations. Only then he can be expected to understand the use of the pot.

Conscious control of the tension of the sphincter muscles (the ring of muscles that opens or closes the orifices of the bowels and the bladder) must precede a conscious sphincter relaxation. This is why, when a child of about 18 months is put on the pot, he often does not move his bowels until he is taken off again. He can hold in, and tighten, but he cannot yet completely relax. A few weeks later, when a child is put on the pot at the time that he usually has a bowel movement, suddenly the motion comes at once, and often explosively. This means that the child responds to being put on the pot by contracting the sphincter

muscles strongly and then relaxing them too suddenly, since muscle control is not yet coordinated. The motions may still be irregular, and »accidents« happen up to $3\frac{1}{2}$ years of age, but less frequently.

A new complication can occur when the child is about $2\frac{1}{2}$; he feels that he has good control over the sphincter muscles, so he holds in for several days, with consequent constipation. Actually, the child is practicing tensing his muscles.

All this intricate process can be complicated by various psychological factors, change of diet, change of environment, etc.

Bladder emptying

The stages here are similar to those for the bowels. At about a year the child does not like a wet diaper, but conscious control first begins about 18 months. The child can make a sign in several ways, but often too late. At 30-36 months the child is usually »dry« during the day, with only a few accidents.

At about 20-21 months, urinating is often more frequent, either because the child thinks he should not have his bladder so full, or because he cannot judge how full it is. Later there can come a time when the child is so absorbed in play and other activities that he forgets to notice the feeling in his bladder.

At $2\frac{1}{2}$ years the child can often go for long periods without urinating, and has contracted so strongly that he may have difficulty relaxing. At 3 years the child can put off urinating until he is just on the point of wetting himself, and so occasionally lets go too soon.

After this age, sphincter control should be complete during the day.

It is difficult for a child to keep dry at nights, for he does not notice the warning signs when he is asleep.

By 2 years, 50% of children are usually dry at night, at 3 years, 75%, and at 5 years, 90%.

Complete control of the bladder is acquired later than control of the bowels.

Involuntary wetting (enuresis)

Enuresis has several causes. There may be delayed neuromuscular control over the sphincter muscles, or there can be psychological reasons. Perhaps toilet training has been too energetic and the child has been punished for »accidents«.

Sphincter control may be delayed if the child cannot be taken to the toilet as soon as he wants to go, for example in large institutions with many children and few staff.

Enuresis is more common among boys, who at this stage develop more slowly than girls do.

When can toilet training begin?

As said before, the time to begin toilet training depends entirely on the child's neurological and psychological development.

Spontaneous movements give natural satisfaction, and toilet training does not fulfil a child's need at this period, but is something which is imposed on child by adult. Children's natural reflexes must be curbed for the sake of society, and conscious control established. However, even wild animals establish a certain sphincter control for practical reasons.

The child must have reached a stage of development where he understands what is required and has the neuromuscular ability to fulfil this requirement. A warm and loving mother-child relationship is the most important preparation for easy and natural toilet training.

A child must never be punished for an »accident«. He must not be made to feel inferior because he has made a mistake.

Before a child can walk there is seldom any question of beginning conscious training. That there is some connection between the upright position – which is partly influenced by muscles on the inner side of the thigh – and toilet training has not been fully proved. Tension in these muscles will cause reflex tension at the base of the pelvis, which again has a certain connection with tension of the sphincter muscles. The characteristic position for sitting on the toilet helps to relax these muscles (Fig. 32).

This process is further complicated because the muscles of the abdomen must be tightened for defecation, but the base of the pelvis and the sphincter muscles must relax, which is so complicated that it corresponds to a fairly late stage in neuromuscular development.

The child informs an adult about urinating first, often by pointing at the wet diaper, later by saying that he is urinating and finally by telling just before. Only then has the right time come for toilet training.

As soon as the child indicates that he is wet and does not like it, his diaper should be changed, but that has nothing to do with training except that it accustoms the child to the comfort of a dry diaper.

Later the child can go to the toilet by himself, but needs help afterwards in wiping. The child's rhythm should be noted and followed closely, the same time schedule should be kept each day, especially after meals, which give a certain impulse toward defecation.

As soon as the child himself begins to be able to indicate a movement, it must be carefully noticed at what times he does so, and he should be put on the toilet or pot at once. It naturally helps the child if his parents take him with them when they go to the toilet themselves.

If the child himself says nothing, ask him after every meal or at the times when he usually has a movement.

Toilet training thus is highly individual, but should be complete when the child is about 6 and can manage all by himself.

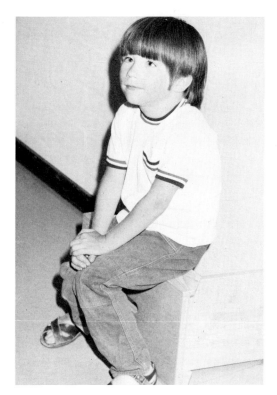

Fig. 32. Toilet position.

Until the child has reached this stage, he should:

not sit too long, for prolapse of the bowel may result,

learn to tear off the paper properly, without pulling the whole roll, and

take his time doing up his clothes, washing his hands, etc.

Finally it should be said that it is important to sit in a relaxed position during defecation, with hips, knees and ankles well bent (Fig. 32). The position is most relaxed if there is foot support, so, in institutions, toilets should be of different heights or, lacking that, suitable foot stools should be put in front of the toilets (or possibly a potty with a foot rest).

In institutions, toilet training is harder for the child because it is not always associated with one person. If a child is looked after by another person during the day, the parents and this other person should work together.

Good toilet habits help good digestion and therewith the child's growth and well-being.

The retarded child

All that has been said regarding the normal child's toilet training applies equally to the retarded child. More patience is needed, and the child must have developed sufficiently before he is required to be continent.

In cases where it does not seem possible for the child to reach the required neuromuscular and psychological development which conscious continence requires, the necessary reflexes must be exercised. For example, touching the pot may activate urination or, if the child is put on the pot regularly after each meal, there may be a reflex: eat – sit on the pot – defecate. To keep the child continent is thus a different thing from a child being continent.

To elicit the anal reflex a few times (see page 14), with subsequent tension in buttocks and lower pelvic muscles, can in some cases help retarded children to understand about tensing and relaxing their sphincter muscles (kinesthetic and tactile senses).

If the right time for toilet training has been missed, if the child has been allowed to be a baby for too long in relation to his general development, sometimes it can help to let the child run around for a few days without his pants so that he sees as well as feels when defecation takes place,

Defecation requires concentration and relaxation. The overactive child may have special difficulties. Perhaps he unwinds all the toilet paper or cannot sit still for a minute at a time. So training in concentration must be undertaken before toilet training is possible (see page 114).

Development in feeding and speech

The normal child

Feeding

It is important for speech development that feeding is normal from birth, because the same organs are used for both functions. The better the feeding habits are, upon which speech is built, the better are the motor possibilities of speech.

The baby's food intake is entirely controlled by reflex movements. There is a reflex chain-reaction: – seek, suck and swallow – where the one regularly activates the next.

Rooting reflex (seeking reflex)

The child seeks the nipple or the bottle, and the mother helps by touching the cheek, lip or corner of the mouth, whereupon the child turns his head towards the side that is touched.

Sucking reflex

The child's mouth takes hold of the nipple, and this contact elicits the sucking reflex.

Swallowing reflex

When the milk touches the back of the tongue and oral cavity, it elicits the swallowing reflex.

At this stage the tongue is already involved in both sucking and swallowing movements.

Breast-feeding versus bottle-feeding

Since breast-milk is the most suitable food one can give an infant, it cannot be too much emphasized that the mother should make every attempt to breast-feed her child. This also makes the child immune against many infections.

Breast-feeding gives so much contact, security and pleasure to both mother and child that this more than compensates for the inconvenience.

Spoon-feeding

When the child begins to eat with a spoon, the tongue becomes more active than before, for it throws the food, purée or the like, down into the throat. When the child is sitting up, the tongue has to work harder than when he is lying down.

The seeking and sucking reflexes gradually diminish as the child is weaned onto spoon-feeding.

Sucking through a straw requires a sucking movement, but in this case it is no longer a reflex, but a voluntary movement. The tongue has more work to do than in breast-feeding, because the head is bent forward while sucking.

Biting and chewing movements

The biting reflex develops later. At this stage the child puts everything in his mouth and bites on it. The jaws open and shut with an up-and-down movement that is activated by feeling something in the mouth. This movement appears a little before the first chewing movements at about 6 months, when the child begins to get more solid food.

The child gradually learns to consciously control the biting reflex. At about 3 years, he can, for example, quickly learn not to bite on the dentist's mirror when it touches the teeth or other parts of the mouth.

When all the teeth have erupted at about 2½ years of age, the chewing movement will no longer only go up and down, but will include a sideways movement. which results in a fully developed grinding, chewing movement.

The tongue is exercised because it moves the food from side to side in the mouth.

A few other reflexes deserve mention in connection with feeding.

Vomiting reflex

The vomiting reflex is a strong, sudden contraction of the diaphragm and stomach muscles involved in exhaling and can be activated by several things; for example, if the food is pushed too quickly into the throat, if the stomach is too full, or if the child gets solid food before he can chew, so that lumps of food stick in his throat. In addition, vomiting can be nervous, or it may be connected with stomach troubles.

Burping

Burping in a baby occurs when the air the child has swallowed comes up again, often bringing the food along with it.

Coughing reflex

Coughing is usually caused by irritation of the mucous membrane or inflammation of the lower respiratory passages or, when food, for example, by accident slips down into the windpipe, and a sudden, strong exhalation with open mouth is done to clear the windpipe.

Sensibility (feeling, touch)

Sensibility in the oral cavity plays a large part in eating and digestion, since seeking, sucking, swallowing, biting, and chewing reflexes are all activated by the sense of touch, just as an increased secretion of saliva during meals is partly induced by the sense of touch, and partly by smell, taste and thought.

Good eating habits

The child should take the time to chew his food and to move it around in the mouth, because the food should be mixed with saliva to promote digestion. Learning good eating and chewing habits thus has a wider implication. It is the basis for good digestion, for good nourishment and for the development of the organs of speech.

The making of sounds

From the neurophysiological viewpoint, speech is one of the most complicated processes the child must learn. But before the child has reached the stage of talking, he has been prepared for it in several ways, of which I shall explain the motor aspect, in particular.

Crying

The newborn child's cry becomes gradually more differentiated, according to whether it expresses hunger, wet diapers, pain or desire for company. Crying is thus the child's first mode of expression, the first »language«, which the mother soon learns to understand and which helps her to satisfy the child's various needs.

Respiration (breathing)

Respiration develops in several ways:
By crying. The child exerts himself and draws deep breaths.

By all the sounds a child can produce.
By movements of all kinds as well as
By yawning and
Sneezing.

Yawning

A yawn begins with a slow deep inspiration through the mouth and raising of the soft palate followed by a vigorous widening of the whole throat. Then follows a long, deep expiration (breathing out).

To yawn is a reflex movement, activated by lack of oxygen together with fatigue, sleepiness or sitting still for a long time.

For speech, the soft palate must also be movable.

Sneezing

Sneezing is a reflex, elicited by irritation of the mucous membrane in the nose, and consists of a sudden deep inspiration through the mouth followed by a vigorous expiration through the nose.

Sound and speech

(See also Hearing, page 81).

Along with the development of the organs of speech through eating, the sounds the baby makes develop as well, depending primarily on anatomic and neuromuscular changes, but also on the infant's environment. Every mother talks to her baby and repeats the sound made by the child, whereby the child is encouraged to make more sounds. Both show their pleasure, and this encourages further development of speech.

The child first produces single sounds without using his tongue very much, for example »aaahh«, but later the lips and tongue are used more and more for producing sounds and the child begins to babble with two-syllable sounds, for example »ba-ba«.

The child can produce many different sounds at an early age, sounds that may not be found in his native language. In spite of this, he may later not be able to produce the same sounds, because the sound combinations – e. g. double consonants – or the sequence of sounds may be hard to reproduce.

The strength of the voice increases as respiration becomes more differentiated, and the child babbles cheerfully at about the time that he begins to sit up.

The child practices sounds solely because he enjoys making them. The sounds can now be produced with differing strength, pitch and length, because the child has observed how breath can be varied.

The movements producing sounds are repeated again and again, and coordination is established between hearing and movement.

One of the chief functions of the child's babble is thus an intensive auditory and kinesthetic learning by experience, a combination between the sounds heard and the corresponding movements.

In the first months of life it is believed that children of every nation produce the same sounds, but later the sounds are influenced by the language environment.

Control over the pitch, strength and rhythm of sounds improves towards the end of the first year, and the child has reached the stage where he imitates not only his own sounds but also the more differentiated speech sounds that he has heard. He begins to repeat over and over a word he has heard, even though he does not always understand that the sound is a word with a definite meaning.

Which sounds are the most difficult for a child to produce and therefore come last in development depends on what movements the sounds require. For example, the labials »m« and »b« and later »p« develop partly from the sucking movement and partly from practice with the lips closing on the spoon, whereas »f« needs a separate movement of the lower lip and requires the presence of at least a few upper front teeth. It, therefore, occurs some months later.

At about 12 months the child makes long strings of babbled words resembling the mother's speech in rhythm and tone because he wishes to communicate with his mother.

This is a preparation for being able to say

the first meaningful words, for example, »ma-ma« at about 11-12 months. This often occurs just about the time the child can stand up and begin to walk.

During the following months the child uses single words but usually says only the accented syllables and omits the less clear, unstressed syllables.

Sometimes a new difficult word is repeated for days on end, until the child has quite mastered it, in other words, until the movements have become automatic.

Later, babbling disappears, and at around 2 years of age the vocubulary increases noticeably to about two or three hundred words. However, the child understands many more words than he can say – because the motor aspect of the affair is still difficult. Furthermore, to use a word in speech the child needs to know and remember the word far better than just to recognize and understand it. The so-called assertive age is certainly to some degree caused by the child's irritation at not being able to make himself understood.

At about 4 years the child talks in long sentences, and vocabulary increases rapidly if the child's environment is stimulating.

A child asks questions not only to get information, but also to establish contact and to practice talking; this corresponds to how adults learn foreign languages.

When the child is about 5 or 6 years old he usually talks correctly from the standpoint of pronunciation and intonation as well as grammar. He knows grammatical structure and can decline all words. Only exceptions to the rules present difficulties. For example: »I goed« for »I went« or »two sheeps« for »two sheep«.

Along with the correct syntax, the child develops a feeling for the pitch, melody, strength and rhythm of the language. It requires fine coordination between auditory perception, respiration and the movements of the organs of speech before well-modulated, differentiated speech can be mastered.

Speech defects

To facilitate further reading on the subject, it may be of use to explain the following:

Dysphasia

Dysphasia (dys = bad, phasis = speech) is a congenital or very early defect in the brain itself and hinders the development of speech.

Dysphasia can be either impressive or expressive but is most often a combination of the two.

Impressive dysphasia is a defect of aural perception, in other words, difficulty in understanding the spoken word.

Expressive dysphasia means difficulty in expressing oneself in speech.

Aphasia

Aphasia usually describes a defect in the brain which occurs later in life, after speech has been fully developed, and thus is not dealt with in this book. The term aphasia is nevertheless sometimes used to denote dysphasia.

Dysarthria

By dysarthria is meant poor articulation due to motor difficulties or to defects in the organs of speech.

It is difficult to draw a line between dysphasia and dysarthria, because many retarded children have to contend with both, and the conditions for good speech depend greatly on the interaction between perception and motor ability, as already mentioned.

Dysphasia as well as dysarthria can in many cases be influenced by suitable stimulation, but it is difficult to predict how far the child's speech will progress, since this also depends on the child's level of development in other areas. The child must be able to listen, to understand words and then to use them in the right way, so that they say what they mean and can be understood by everyone. Here motor ability comes into the picture.

Retarded eating and speech development

Seen from the motor standpoint

The retarded child should be stimulated to develop all the skills and functions that affect speech, in the same order of development as the normal child and carefully following the same sequence. Everything needs thorough practice, and each step must be mastered before the next is introduced. It may be necessary to begin by improving the child's method of eating.

Feeding problems

Try to improve the feeding situation in all ways, emotional as well as perceptual and motor. The child must feel secure, he must have love and attention. Take the small child on your lap, but not lying horizontally, for this hinders swallowing. An inclination of 45° or more is best. In case of difficulty hold the older child's hand or in some way let him feel contact with the adult. He ought to sit as nearly upright as possible, partly to facilitate swallowing and partly to be able to see what is going on, what food is offered, and when the next spoonful is coming.

If the child is a very late developer, and the chain-reaction »seek – suck – swallow« is imperfect, it may first be necessary to elicit seeking reflex or to teach the child to suck.

The hole in the feeding bottle should not be too small, nor so large that the lips and the tongue do not need to work very much.

If the child cannot swallow properly, it will make things worse to hurry him at meals. In some cases swallowing can be stimulated by lightly stroking the front of the neck with two fingers.

In other cases the adult may put a finger under the child's chin, to help him to close his mouth on the food.

Head balance and, later, body balance must be attained, so that it becomes possible for the child to eat sitting up without head support and later without back support.

When the time comes to take solid food, make the purée thicker and thicker, and then use crackers or bananas, which are easily softened by saliva, and later bread, small pieces of carrot, peeled apple, etc.

It may be necessary to resort to such details in feeding as to place the food on the less active side of the mouth, so that the tongue has to be exerted to move the food.

It may also be necessary to try to inhibit a biting reflex that should have been under control long before. This must be done consciously, and the child's attention should be drawn to it.

When spoon feeding, do not shovel the food into an already open mouth or scrape the food off with the front teeth, but get the child to take an active part. Hold the spoon a little away from the mouth, so that the child has to move forward to meet the spoon, hold it with his lips, as far as he is able, and so stimulate the chewing and swallowing reflexes. This also keeps the spoon from going in so far that it touches the soft palate, which could be unpleasant for the child and in extreme cases cause vomiting at this somewhat inconvenient moment. Before feeding begins it is necessary to look first into the child's mouth to judge the depth of the mouth cavity, according to how much space the spoon will take up.

The time spent in teaching a retarded child to eat in a natural manner will earn a rich reward later. It will be easier to feed the child, his possible refusal to eat will disappear, and meals will take place in a happier atmosphere for the child and his companions.

If there are feeding difficulties, see that the child gets enough liquid. Dehydration can have serious effects. Ask a doctor how much liquid the child should take.

Retarded speech

It is important to talk constantly to a child, even if he has not yet reached the stage of talking himself, and even before he can understand words. One fine day he may reach the stage of development where he begins to understand, and after he has heard a word many times in a certain context, he may be able to grasp its meaning.

At the same time as the organs of speech are developed through eating, all baby-talk should be stimulated. The child must be motivated, he must wish to gain contact through speech with those surrounding him, and adults should therefore in many cases talk to the retarded child, even an older child, in the same loving manner in which a mother chats to her normal baby.

There is a close relationship between the development of speech and general perceptual and motor development. Speech is learned through its use in meaningful situations. If the child, for example, is to learn the word »chair«, it is not enough that he sees a chair, but he must have a chance to examine it and use it, so that it becomes more meaningful. The child will not use the word »chair« until the sound – the word – is associated with the object which he now knows. Therefore it is a great help to the child if the chair can be experienced through vision, touch, the kinesthetic sense and hearing.

The word »chair« is a noun, and a chair is a concrete object, so this word is not as hard to learn as other, more abstract, words. If the word »chair« is learned first, this helps in learning adjectives describing chairs, such as big, heavy, smooth, hard, because these words become real through and in conjunction with the chair.

It is important that each movement and action should be accompanied by speech. For example, if the child is taken out for a walk, it is natural for the adult to talk continually to the child and to get him to express himself not only in monosyllables, but to progress in speech development. It is necessary to speak clearly, in short, plain sentences without many un-necessary words, but yet to seek to increase the child's vocabulary day by day.

It is inadvisable to put pressure on a child about any sounds he cannot pronounce. Instead, the words a child cannot say should be used often, so that the word becomes a part of his impressive vocabulary.

As a rule, the older retarded child does not want to reveal that he has not understood what was said, because he already has had to admit failure too often. If he fails to understand even one word in a sentence, the meaning of the whole sentence is lost, and while he is wondering what was said, he does not listen to the next sentence, which is thus also lost.

The retarded child's frequent, dominant use of stereotyped, common expressions is a sign not only of retarded speech development but of poverty of thought as well.

A special form of imitative speech is »parrot-talk«, in which a child pretends to talk, but only repeats all, or the last words, of the other person's remarks. This shows a more or less conscious wish for verbal contact, combined with an attempt to hide poor understanding and a poor memory.

Finally it should be mentioned that pauses in speech development may occur – for example when a child is busy practicing a new motor skill, and such pauses indicate that speech should not be encouraged excessively, before the motor ability, if possible, is on a level with the child's general development.

Carefully planned cooperation among all who deal with the child is necessary, so that they all teach the same new words and skills. If not, the child may become quite confused, and, at the worst, speech development will cease.

Cooperation with a speech therapist is most important. If the child never learns to speak, this is an insuperable obstacle to further intellectual development.

Exercising the organs of speech

The organs of speech are: lips, teeth, tongue,

throat, hard and soft palate and the breathing passages.

The upper breathing passages are: the throat, oral cavity, larynx, nasal cavity and the sinus.

The lower breathing passages are: lungs and the bronchi.

The facial muscles which directly or indirectly affect speech should be included here as well.

If the organs of speech have not developed normally, neuromuscular exercises must be begun. Even with dysphasia these can be useful, because even the limited speech capability that is present should not be further impeded by limited movements, slight paralysis or slow and poory coordinated movements.

Training the speech organs is unfortunately not the same as improving speech; all it does, actually, is to make the »apparatus« better suited to being used in speech development.

For example, exercising tongue movements alone will not necessarily result in the child using these movements in speech. Exercising the muscles of the speech organs should therefore be followed immediately by a speech sound which uses the same movements. Such exercises can be a great help to the speech therapist, with whom there should always be close cooperation.

If eating develops normally, the child will learn to talk without being conscious of moving the organs of speech, but if the development is not normal, that is a different matter. Exercises will not always produce results before the child has enough body knowledge and kinesthetic awareness to distinguish which parts of the mouth are being moved in the various exercises. A perception of direction must be developed too, so that the child understands whether the tongue should be moved up or down, forwards or backwards.

Facial expression

Inability to imitate sounds may be due to poor brain development, or to a purely neurological defect. In certain cases, however, it is due to too little contact with adults during the first years of life and hence to too little opportunity to imitate sounds and too little time spent babbling and chatting.

It may be thought that the facial muscles can best be trained through drama, by playing »let's pretend«. This is not always the case, however, because a retarded child with a small vocabulary usually does not have many ideas either, so dramatic play may well be too difficult for him.

Often a child can more quickly learn to use his facial muscles if »paths« are made through the synapses. The physical therapist may do this by gently massaging the child's face, so that the child, through feeling and kinesthetic sense, becomes aware that he has a face, and that it can move. Massage is reinforced by exercises.

The child should be able to activate his facial muscles without contorting his whole face. If a movement is difficult for the child, the nerve impulses are so strong that it affects all the facial muscles. Similarly, the child should be able to talk without tensing the rest of the body more than is needed for the accompanying gestures.

To remedy this it is necessary to begin by training kinesthetic sense in the *whole* body; the child must be able to feel tension and relaxation in the larger muscle groups before he can be expected to perceive the small facial muscles.

The sequence of the exercises can be as follows:
1) *For facial expressivity.* (At this level of development, these movements are involuntary).
   Tactile: touch the face to produce movements. They may be movements to avoid the touch, smiles, etc.
   Auditory: talk, or make sounds or noises which will elicit different facial expressions.
   Visual: all forms of visual stimuli to which the child responds with facial expressions.

2) *Voluntary, conscious movements.* Tensing-relaxing.
   a) The whole body (see also page 95).
   Lying on the back:

Roll the feet (and both legs) towards each other.

Hold the head straight and let it roll to one side.

Lift both arms about 20 cm above the floor and drop them again.

Sitting on a chair:

Lift the arms sideways and let them fall.

Shoulder rotating in both directions.

Drop the head on the chest.

Neck and shoulder muscles must be relaxed enough that the jaw can move freely when speaking.

b) The facial muscles.

Lying on the back, comfortably, with a cushion under the head and neck.

Shut the eyes firmly. Open them and close them in the ordinary way.

Open the mouth wide and let it shut again.

Wrinkle the nose, then relax it.

Clench the teeth. Without opening the mouth, relax the jaw muscles.

Breathe in, so that the nostrils widen.

3) Natural facial expression

Try to improve facial expressivity through play and contact with other children, and through rather primitive creative drama, song or rhythm.

Respiration (breathing)

Training the respiration is most important in children with retarded speech development. The passage of air is what produces sounds, and retarded children often breathe rather weakly. The passage of air may be too weak or too uncontrolled.

Respiration must be natural and strong enough to produce clear sounds and speech. The frequency of respiration (the number of inspirations and expirations per minute) must be relatively low before speech can be fluent and a whole sentence can be spoken in one breath. Shouting and singing require good breathing.

Strong abdominal muscles are very important in breathing, and therefore these muscles must be included in breathing exercises.

It may be necessary for the physical therapist or speech therapist to help breathing by placing her hands on the child's chest and stomach.

A deep breath, where the lower part of the chest expands all around when breathing in, also aids speech, and may be practiced under the instructions of a therapist.

Remember to make sure that the child's nostrils are dry and unblocked before the breathing exercises begin.

Suggested exercises

It is fine to begin with blowing and sucking exercises, but they are not sufficiently trying to really improve respiration.

Blow on cotton, blow on tea or coffee to cool it, blow on something furry – a stuffed animal – or blow on soap bubbles (short, long, gentle or strong puffs).

Blow bubbles through a straw in a glass of water.

Blow out a candle or a match.

Suck through a long straw, possibly a rubber tube.

See how long the child can sing the same note in one breath.

More energetic breathing exercises (see page 166).

Sensibility (feeling, sense of touch)

Sensibility of the organs of speech and oral cavity can often be quickly improved by exercising, and for the child who has difficulty in making certain sounds, this has the advantage that he learns to feel where the tongue should be placed and how the lips should be used.

Sample exercises

With a spatula touch all the parts of the mouth, the tongue, the inside of the cheeks and the palate, if possible with the child's cooperation, so he tells where he can feel the spatula.

Something cold (not as cold as ice cubes) alternating with food or a liquid of a higher temperature can also improve sensibility.

The best thing to use is the adult's fingers. After massaging the face, they can also massage the inside of the mouth, so that the child becomes conscious of it (use rubber or plastic gloves to avoid infection).

Slobbering

Saliva is normally secreted constantly in the mouth, and spit is swallowed instinctively twice every minute stimulated by the tactile sense (sense of touch) of the presence of spit in the mouth.

A normal child usually stops slobbering before he is 15 months old, but the older retarded child often continues to slobber. This may be because his mouth is always open, or there are gaps between his teeth, or last, but not least, because his swallowing reflex is weak.

The saliva not only bothers the child but it also alters the resonance of the oral cavity, making speech less clear.

Treatment should be according to cause. Relaxation and/or training the lips, head balance, swallowing reflex and tongue movements (possibly straightening the teeth) as well as training the sensibility of the mouth. Slobbering usually can be cured.

The palate

The roof of the mouth consists of the hard palate in front and the soft palate at the back. The soft palate terminates in the uvula, which is a little finger-like appendage at the opening to the throat.

The soft palate moves during swallowing and yawning to close the passage to the nasal cavity.

The soft palate also helps to change the resonance in the oral cavity. If the palate is weak or does not completely close the nasal cavity, speech is snuffling. This is an open snuffle, whereas adenoids cause a closed snuffle.

Certain retarded children have a stiff palate, and this must be loosened by exercising its muscles so that it can be used in speech.

To succeed in producing the movement, try to produce the vomiting reflex with the aid of the spatula, but only a few times (do not make it a habit) and only after you have explained to the child beforehand what is going to happen. Then get the child to practice saying »ah« because then the soft palate is lifted and lowered consciously. This exercise may benefit from being performed in front of a mirror.

With advice from a speech therapist, a longer program can be worked out.

Teeth

The front teeth should meet when the child bites food. If the teeth protrude, this makes biting difficult. If any wrong tensions in the muscles of the lips or tongue are corrected first, a dentist may then straighten the teeth. A tense tongue which always presses on the front teeth from behind will bring about the wrong position of the teeth again very soon after the brace is removed.

Much thumb-sucking may cause protruding teeth if the thumb presses on the back of the front teeth.

The molars should meet when the child chews; otherwise the child swallows his food whole or almost sucks it in.

The position of the teeth has also a certain importance for speech, as protruding front teeth cause lisping.

Brushing the teeth should be practiced with each child in consultation with a dentist.

Pacifiers

Too long use of a pacifier can cause deformity of the teeth. A normal child should not use a pacifier after his 2nd year, but take care not to frustrate the child, in case the pacifier is removed.

A pacifier for children more than 1 year old should not be so thick that it hinders the closing of the jaw (proper ones can be obtained at a pharmacy).

Lips

The mouth should be kept closed but not too tight. Some of the causes of a constantly open mouth may be:

protruding front teeth,

nasal congestion,

a tight, short upper lip,

an enlarged tongue with poor muscle tone, possibly in connection with a small oral cavity.

The first two causes must be treated by a dentist or a doctor. The tight upper lip can in some cases be relaxed by massage and exercises, and the tongue may be trained.

The lip muscles may also be so weak that it is hard for the child to lick food from the spoon and to produce some of the labial sounds, and in this case the lip muscles must be trained.

Suggested exercises

Sucking exercises.

Eating practice. Close the lips on the spoon and do not smack the lips.

Say »b«, »p« or words that begin with these sounds.

Hold a piece of paper between the lips – firmly but without drawing the lips in (the adult pulls gently on the paper).

A button is fastened to a thin elastic, the button is held between the closed lips and teeth, and the elastic is pulled. Try it later with a smaller button.

Show the teeth and then close the mouth, alternately.

Smile widely, pout – and than relax.

Suck through a straw, first a thick and then a thin one.

Blowing exercises. Cotton, paper balls, feathers.

Blow the cheeks out (press the cheeks with two fingers).

Whistle.

Draw the upper lip down over the teeth with an active movement.

Jaws

The jaws must be able to open and shut, so that food can be taken into the mouth, and so that the child can chew and talk with good articulation. The chewing muscles must therefore be strong.

If the child has difficulty in opening his mouth widely, this can be practiced in several ways by encouraging the infant to play with things that are just big enough that he can, with a little effort, stretch his mouth over them when he wants to bite them. At mealtimes, heap the tip of the spoon rather high with food, but never give him such a big mouthful that he becomes nervous, or cannot rotate the food in his mouth.

The lower jaw should be able to move from side to side during the later »grinding« chewing. If the child, in spite of biting normally, chews with only an up-and-down movement, the grinding chew can be promoted in some cases by teaching the child to control the chewing muscles. They should not be so tense that the teeth are always clenched together.

Suggested exercises

Keep the mouth shut and press the teeth together. Relax afterwards so that the teeth are no longer touching, although the lips are closed.

Open the mouth wide, while the chin is drawn towards the chest, and then raise the chin so that the lips just touch, but the teeth do not.

If the chewing muscles are very weak it may be necessary for the adult to press the jaw up with two fingers around the child's chin, so that the mouth closes on the food. Then slacken the pressure for a moment and start again in order to induce a chewing movement.

With the mouth slightly open, move the lower jaw from side to side. Even though this exercise can be done, it does not follow that a grinding movement will immediately form part of the chewing movement, so the child should be given something nice to chew on, e. g. chewing gum, immediately after the exercise, so that the tongue will also take part in the movement.

The tongue

To use the tongue in speech it must be freely movable and flexible, and all movements must be able to be performed quickly.

In some cases it will be useful to poke the tongue with a spatula to provoke it into making an avoiding movement away from the spatula. In other cases the tongue will oppose the spatula's pressure, and a resistance exercise is done, which is a good method of strengthening.

A very big tongue usually has diminished muscle tone (hypotonia). If anything can be accomplished by intensive training from the first month of life, it would be of interest to investigate further. I have not found any literature on this subject, but my own experience shows that it can be done with good result.

With the tongue thrust forward it is difficult to hold food in the mouth, and the child should therefore be told to take small mouthfuls, to shut his mouth when chewing and then to swallow.

Samples of exercises
Especially for older children with speech defects, purposeful tongue exercises are very valuable, because they help the child to put the tongue in the right place for a particular sound.

The principle of the exercises is:
1) Involuntary movements.
   Licking jam from around the mouth or from the chin.
   Place some food between the teeth and the cheeks, and the tongue cleans the food remnants from the teeth.
   Wipe the lips with a paper serviette, so that a bit of the serviette stays behind and the child may lick it off.
   Place peanut butter several places in the mouth to cause the tongue to work at removing it.
   Lick ice creams cones and lollipops.

2) The same movements are now performed intentionally.
   The tongue reaches down on the chin and out to the sides.
   The point of the tongue licks the lips all the way around.
   The point of the tongue presses against the palate.
   The tongue is placed behind the upper front teeth and glides back along the palate.
   Keep the mouth shut and move the tongue from side to side.
   Try to touch the nose with the tongue.
   Open the mouth and place the tongue from a position behind the lower teeth and up towards the palate, alternately.
   With the mouth closed, clean the teeth on the inner and outer sides.
   Lift the back (root) of the tongue up towards the palate.
   Make the tongue alternately wide and narrow.
   Make the tongue alternately flat and high (thick).
   (The last three exercises are difficult).

3) Repeat the same exercises several times quickly.

4) Progress is tested by timing how often a movement can be made in, for example, 10 seconds. The exercises should be done more and more quickly, and change quickly from one exercise to another.

5) The practiced exercises should finally lead to sounds and words.
A mirror can be helpful to the child, but, when there are sideways movements, it may be confusing.

Short frenulum of the tongue

If the tongue-tie (the frenum) is too short it can affect the speech to a greater or lesser degree. The tongue-tie may be a thin thread under the middle of the tip of the tongue or a broader band that binds the whole width of the tongue. A short tongue-tie can bind to such a degree that the tongue becomes almost cup-shaped, with a perceptible hollow in the middle, corresponding to the tongue-tie's attachment to the underside.

A short tongue-tie can prevent the tip of the tongue from reaching the palate, and so disturb the child's speech, because sounds like »l« cannot be pronounced clearly. An extremely tight tongue-tie can be an obstacle to all speech.

A short tongue-tie can make swallowing difficult, because the tongue is prevented from throwing the food back towards the throat, and in extreme cases it causes tooth decay, because the tongue cannot clean the teeth after meals. It may also hinder grinding chewing, if the tongue cannot move the food around in the mouth.

The tongue-tie can be so short that the child cannot put his tongue out, and therefore cannot lick a lollipop or an ice cream.

If the doctor decides to cut the tongue-tie, it will always be advisable, before cutting (or before the operation in the case of a wide tongue-tie), to train the tongue intensively, so that it is certain that the innervation is intact and the muscles can be exercised. Moreover, the tongue should be moved soon after the operation, and should be stretched far out and upwards; in other words, it should practice performing the formerly obstructed and thus unaccustomed movements.

A speech therapist is absolutely essential here.

II. Perceptual development and its relation to motor ability

To sense and to perceive

The normal child

To sense

means that stimuli are received by the sensory organs; the eye, ear, skin, etc., and that these organs function.

To perceive

comprises much more than the mere functioning of the senses. The brain must be able to receive the stimulus and adapt it. The adapted sensory impression must be usable, first as an immediate response to the stimulus, e. g. by movement or speech – and, second, the received stimulus must be remembered and later utilized as material for further experiences. To perceive is therefore a widely embracing process which requires a corresponding development of the central nervous system.

The French educationalist Séguin wrote as early as 1846: »One cannot teach a child to read and write before his sensory organs function,« i. e. before his perceptual development has reached a certain stage.

It is customary to list five senses:
Sight and visual perception,
Hearing and aural perception,
Touch and tactile perception,
Taste, and
Smell.

In addition to these five senses there are several others, some of which are senses in their own right with special sense cells, as, for example, the kinesthetic sense (see page 93) and the labyrinthine senses (see page 123) and some are sensory areas which are more or less related to one or more of the five main senses, e. g.:
body knowledge and body awareness,
perception of laterality and dominance (preference for the right or the left side),
perception of direction,
perception of space (judging distance and comparing size) and
concept of time.

If the sensory and perceptual foundation is deficient, the child will have many difficulties and will certainly not be able to live a normal life.

If, for example, his temperature sense is undeveloped, he will not understand the request »Go get some lukewarm water« or be able to prepare his bathwater. Understanding of words relating to the senses depends to some extent on understanding and registering sensory impressions.

Likewise, a child often moves awkwardly and clumsily either because he lacks awareness of his body and its capabilities, or because his perception of direction and space is deficient.

There is a close connection between knowledge of the fingers' appearance, their names and their movement possibilities and the ability to use them.

The groundwork in all school subjects requires that the child can perceive through all senses. This applies particularly to reading, writing, arithmetic, and geography, where the perception of shape, direction and space are necessary prerequisites.

The very first lessons in both nursery and preschool should therefore be exercises in perception by all the senses.

It is important that all teaching should take place at the proper time, i. e. at the most suitable stage in a child's life (the sensitive periods) and that this point in time should not be missed.

It does not help the child much only to engage in occupations that develop his best areas of perception. This is easiest for all concerned and the child is more willing, but it is important to make the less developed areas so interesting to the child that he is motivated to exercise them.

If a child is deficient, completely or partially, in one sense, this can be compensated to a certain extent by planned, systematic training to develop what he has of this sense and also by training all the other senses. All senses can be educated to finer and more precise perception, and the more areas of perception the child has in readiness at any given time, and the better developed they are, the easier will be the next stage in his progress.

The relation between motor and perceptual development will be discussed further under each sense modality.

The retarded child

The natural perceptual development of the normal child should also be followed as far as possible in the case of the retarded child, but each step in development must be prepared for and then reinforced much more carefully.

The normal child persists in exercising each new skill, over and over, until he feels that »now it is easy«. The retarded child must also be given the opportunity to repeat over and over. It takes longer, and the retarded child does not progress as far ås the normal child. Furthermore, the result may not be so perfect, but, all the same, there will be some success if

the adult is patient and can inspire the child sufficiently.

The child must not be forced, by the use of certain materials, to realize certain properties or qualities, but he should be taught to use all impressions from his surroundings, to learn »to see«, »to listen«, »to feel«, »to taste«, etc., and the child should be motivated to wish to »see«, »listen«, etc.

If there is something the child cannot understand, the adult must first ask himself: »What have I omitted in teaching the child?« or »What preparation does the child need to enable him to solve this problem, which sense modality is insufficiently developed?«

Perceptual learning should not be drilled into the child, but should be part of his daily life, in step with his motor development. E. g.:

When the child is being washed, name the parts of his body as you touch them.

While dressing him, name the garments and their colors.

Talk all the time to the child, according to his ability, e. g.:

Bring the little chair here, – no, not the big one.

Lay the spoon beside the plate.

Milk is cold, tea is hot.

The biscuit is round.

Go and get the red socks from the bottom drawer.

Perceptual stimulation is a preparation for school and for the child's later education, and even if the child never manages to learn to read and write, the perceptual stimulation will always benefit the child in his social education and development.

We must meet the child at his own level. Often this is lower than we think, but on the other hand, we must never underestimate the child's capacity for learning or boredom will result.

Sight

The normal child

Visus: sight, visual: concerning sight.

Sight is normally the most important sense, since most sensory impressions are visual.

The eye receives light waves which are broken up by the lens of the eye in such a way that a picture of the object is formed on the retina. For an object to be seen clearly the picture must be formed on the yellow spot (fovea). This is, however, a most complicated neuromuscular function.

The fixational reflex

To fix upon an object means to look at the object in such a way that the picture falls on the retina. The eyes do not focus on every object in the surroundings, but attention and interest determine which details the glance is directed towards. The eye muscles move the eyes and thus they are part of the fixational reflex.

The accommodation reflex

(To accommodate: to adjust).

The accommodation muscle is within the eye, in a circle around the lens, and it can alter the thickness and the curvature of the lens and so adapt the eye to sight for different distances. Accommodation is not directly subject to the will, it is a reflex action controlled by the cortex. The accomodation reflex works only after the object is in focus.

Binocular vision

By binocular vision we mean a fusion of the two sight impressions – one from each eye – into a single picture. This takes place in the cortex, and fixation and accommodation both enter into this function.

The eye muscles

There are six muscles in each eye, and they serve to direct the glance towards any object of interest so that its picture can fall on the retina and thus can activate the reflexes which make a clear view possible. The accommodation reflex is also concerned in this.

Voluntary eye movements without definite fixation usually play a subordinate role, but can be performed. For example, it is possible, with the eyes closed, to move the eyes consciously in all directions. This is a well-known form of relaxation therapy, if it is difficult to relax a neurotic patient's eyes. Through conscious eye movements with the eyes shut, the patient can be brought to control and relax these as an important part of total relaxation.

Likewise the eyes can be ordered to look up or down or to the side in willed movements without focusing on anything special.

The eye muscles and the fixational reflex

The eye muscles contribute to eye movements in all directions. The muscles must work equally well in both eyes to give binocular vision, and the central nerve cells in both halves of the brain must be intact.

Among other things the eyes should be able:
to be directed towards a certain object,
to be kept still, as long as focusing is required,

to follow a moving object,

to move quickly and exactly from one fixation to another,

to perform these functions, regardless of whether the child's own body is still or in motion,

to assist in taking in the complete view both by focusing on one spot and also by moving around to take in details,

to study the contours of a larger object (e. g. a house) and so contribute to a more precise perception of this object,

to move, even without turning the head, e. g. in certain traffic situations, where to turn the head would take too long,

to assist in all functions that require eye-hand coordination, e.g. ball play, writing, dressing.

Furthermore, body balance depends considerably on eye movements.

Squint

There are several kinds of squint (strabismus, Fig. 33), but it is common to them all that the axes of the two eyes do not meet at the same point on the object observed, and therefore there is no binocular sight, and the child must be referred to an oculist. All children should be examined at a very young age, because many types of squint can be treated from the age of 1 year, and because the angle of squint may be so small that only an oculist can make the diagnosis.

In order to avoid double image, when squinting there is an inclination – through unconscious brain impulses – to suppress the

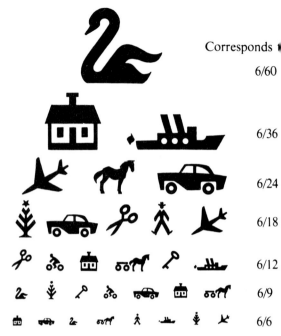

	Corresponds
	6/60
	6/36
	6/24
	6/18
	6/12
	6/9
	6/6

Fig. 34. Østerberg's chart. (By permission of Dr. G. Østerberg, M.D.)

sight of one eye, and this eye therefore becomes weaker, and in some cases blind.

When squinting starts in an older child, he may be seen to bump into objects, and also to have difficulty judging distances (threading a needle, pouring water, etc.). The child seems quite quickly to get used to judging distances with one eye.

Visual acuity

Acuity for distance

It is useful for adults who deal with children every day to understand what oculists do; so here a few words about eye testing.

To test older children a chart with letters of graduated size is used. For children who cannot read, a pictorial chart is used instead (for example Fig. 34, but larger).

The child is placed 6 meters away from the chart.

Acuity for distance is measured as follows: The eyes are tested singly (monocular vision)

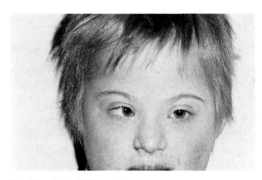

Fig. 33.   This child squints.

and together (binocular vision) (See footnote*).

Each line of the chart corresponds to the distance in meters at which it is possible for a normal eye to read the line in question, so that the top line should be readable at 60 meters, the next at 36 meters and so on.

Visual acuity is measured in fractions, e. g. 6/24 gives 6 as the child's distance from the chart and the number 24 means that the child at this distance can read the line in question (the third), which a person with normal sight can read at 24 meters.

Normal sight is expressed by the fraction 6/6 which means that at 6 meters distance the bottom line can be read.

Weak sight is indicated by fractions from 6/18 or 6/24 down to 6/60 which indicates that the child at best can read the top four lines of the chart.

Sight weaker than 6/60 classifies the child as blind, even if he is not necessarily completely blind.

If the sight is weak in only one eye, the child gets on all right by using the other.

To laymen, a strength of say 6/12 may sound shocking, but 6/12 is not too bad. Driving a car may in some cases be permitted with 6/12 in one eye and 6/24 in the other.

Acuity for near
The normal eye, which works satisfactorily at 6-meter distances, will be able to accommodate to shorter distances, so the acuity for near is not always tested.

If there are abnormalities in the eye, it is important also to test acuity for near, which is of such importance in a child's education and for his later possibilities of employment. A detailed diagnosis is most important for all who deal with the child, not least his teacher and workshop teacher.

Acuity for near can be tested in several ways. If there are definite abnormalities, the child must be sent to an oculist as soon as possible.

Form for testing small children

To test whether the child sees equally well with both eyes, test by covering one eye with a piece of paper (do not press in on the eye with the fingers) and let the child look at for example Dr. Østerberg's visual acuity chart (size as Fig. 34), from a distance of 1 meter exactly.

If there is a noticeable difference between the two eyes, a doctor should test the acuity as soon as possible.

Some remarks on the development of sight

The newborn
The eye muscles are well developed, and the eyes can be moved in all directions but are uncoordinated and often not together.

There is no coordination of eye and head movements. If the child's head is turned by someone else the eyes follow after a little while, but not immediately. This is called the Doll's eye reaction and disappears at about the 2nd week.

The accommodation muscle and some sensory cells in the retina and on the fovea (the yellow spot) are not fully developed, and myelinization of the central sight pathways is not yet complete (see page 7). However, the eye can react to certain stimuli, e. g. :

The reflex of the pupil is present, so that the pupil contracts if the eye is exposed to strong light.

The blink reflex is also present and can be elicited as a response to light. In many cases the child will close his eyes.

The newborn can see, but only to a certain degree.

Before the cortex develops further there can be no question of visual perception.

1 week
The child reacts to diffused light, for the head turns towards a window, no matter how he is placed in his bed.

---

*) As it often can be difficult for a child to concentrate on a particular picture on the chart, it can be useful to point to one picture at a time, or better still to cut out all the pictures and put them one by one on a flannel board.

4 weeks
The fixational reflex begins to develop. The child can focus on the mother's eyes for a moment. Eyes are bright and lively and therefore catch the child's attention.

Later the child stares at large surfaces for a long time.

4-6 weeks
The child can fix upon something for a short time and at 2 months the eyes can follow a person from a position in front to 90° at the side.

3 months
The eyes can now cross the midline and follow a person for 180°. The fixational reflex has developed so much that the child can be clearly seen to look at near objects for a short time, e. g. lie on his back and look at his own fingers.

Head balance is so good that when sitting up, with body support, the eyes can also follow an object in an up-and-down movement.

6-7 months
The falling reflex has developed, so the child, when sitting up without support and without falling over, can move his eyes together with his head or separately, in all directions horizontally.

The retina and fovea are now fully developed, and there can be binocular vision, but this is still not well established. Accommodation is being developed, but this emerges somewhat later.

The glance now moves quickly from object to object.

8-10 months
Body balance when sitting is now so well developed that extreme vertical head and eye movements can take place without the child falling.

12 months
The eyes are now anatomically well developed, although the accommodation is not always quite assured. The child can see to take a small

bead up from the table with two fingers, and his eyes can follow a quickly rolling ball.

2 years
Accommodation is not yet quite assured and binocular vision occasionally fails.

3 years
Fixational reflex and accommodation reflex are developed, but can still regress if the eye is not used for some time.

Focusing becomes quicker, as the child becomes able to perceive visual stimuli faster and more surely.

4 years
Binocular vision is so well developed by 4 years of age that it may be diminished, but not ruined, even if for some reason it is not used for some time.

5 years
Fixational reflex and binocular vision are fully developed.

The retarded child

Defects in the eye itself are the oculist's affair and his advice should be followed carefully. Glasses must sit level on the nose, should not slip down the nose and should be polished daily, etc. – all obvious, but things which are easily forgotten if the child himself has not yet learned to look after them properly.

It is important that the adults who are responsible for the child's care understand the doctor's diagnosis, so that they know what is wrong with the child's sight and thus can better understand his reactions to visual stimuli and can help him by choosing suitable toys, etc.

Treatment of a blind child lies outside the scope of this book, but the degree of sight which is present at any given time must in all circumstances be stimulated; the child should have as many visual stimuli as possible in the course of the day.

It seems as if much visual stimulation when nursing the child and when taking him up during the first year of life stimulates the use of the eyes and therewith the further development of visual perception.

It is advisable to stimulate the retarded child to as great an extent as possible, and to use his eyes, as described for the normal child. For example, as soon as he can be laid on his stomach, give him a chance to learn head control and at the same time to follow what is taking place around him.

The child's bed and playpen should be placed so that he can see the whole room.

Later the child should have plenty of opportunity to move around in the house by crawling and walking, so that he can receive many visual stimuli and have a chance to turn his head and eyes towards all that is happening around him. This means that the adults must arrange for things to happen that will interest the child.

The infant

The retarded infant can be stimulated in different ways, e. g.:

A flickering light, or a moving light.

A voice or a noise from the other end of the room may perhaps cause the child to look to »see what it is«.

Hang up brightly colored objects, so that they dangle in front of the child.

Take a tour around the house with the child in your arms, and stop before the most noticeable things.

Older children

Older retarded children can be stimulated in accordance with their handicap. Some children find it hard to fix because of lack of head balance, and here the first step is to practice head control. Others cannot separate eye movements from head movements, so to see around the room they must turn the head with jerks, as if they were wearing blinkers.

Just as the normal newborn child's eye movements are uncoordinated, so the older retarded child can have large jerky, uncoordinated eye movements. In extreme cases the eyes wander here and there without being controlled. Restless eye movements usually go together with restless movements of the whole body. This may have psychic causes, but may also be caused by other conditions.

It could be difficult to determine whether the primary cause is deficient fixational reflex and uncoordinated eye movements (possibly caused by slight ataxia – a form of cerebral palsy) or whether the cause may be found in slight asymmetrical paralysis. In any case, experience shows that purposeful training can give quieter eye and body movements and more lasting and more quickly established focusing.

The head will normally follow the eyes' movements to a certain extent when focusing, but in many cases the wholeness is perceived by letting the eyes roam around the room without moving the head. On other occasions the child »raises his eyes« or »peeps out of the corners of his eyes«. This requires free eye movement, and many retarded children just cannot do this.

All joints of the body ought to be more flexible than necessary for ordinary, daily movements. This is one of the factors that enables daily movements to be performed freely and easily.

Similarly, eye control in many cases can be improved by consciously excercising the eyes, and increasing the restricted eye movements in all directions.

Exercises

Fixating

For young children. Follow a moving object.

A toy car runs past the child and back again. The car runs all around the edge of a table, across the table, around in a ring, in a figure-of-eight.

A large ball is rolled to the child, who rolls it back again.

The head will automatically accompany eye movements.

The older child

An object is held in front of the child's eyes, at a distance of about 80 cm.

   The object is drawn slowly and quietly right out to the left, as far as the eye can follow it – quietly back to the middle – and then to the right.

   From the middle position the object is moved up or down and back.

   The object is moved diagonally and finally around in a circle at about the periphery of the field of vision.

The head will follow at first, but afterwards tell the child to hold his head still and move only his eyes.

   Note: Use only one or two exercises the first time, as this type of child is not used to moving his eyes, and the movements may be a little unpleasant or perhaps cause a moment's dizziness (notice here the influence on body balance if the eyes are not freely movable).

   Movements in the directions in which it is hard for the child to move his eyes should be given special practice.

   If one eye has special difficulty in following, the child can play »pirate« but *only for a few minutes daily.* With a patch over one eye the other moves in the directions described above, alternately the right and left eye (regardless of which eye performs the movements best) and afterwards both eyes at once.

Shifting fixation. Slow – fast

The child sits on a chair opposite the adult.

   Look at my eyes. How many have I? (this involves looking at the person he is talking to).
   Look at the window, at the wall, up at the ceiling, down at the floor, up at the right/left corner of the ceiling.
   Repeat without moving the head.

The child sits opposite the adult at a table, with his chin in his hands to hold the head still.

   Small objects are shown at different places in the field of vision, and the child says what they are, and describes them in detail.
   Show simple pictures in the same way. The picture should be held still in the same place while the child describes it, and then another picture in another part of the field of vision.

As above, but now do it quickly, change the pictures quickly.

   The child sits about 1 meter from a notice board with many small pictures on it. Without turning the head, in quick succession say what pictures the adult is pointing to.
   Practice all kinds of ball play.

Focusing while moving the body

The infant. Natural activities:

   Play crawling on the floor and looking at the surroundings.
   The child looks at a doll lying at the other end of the room, rises from lying on his back and runs to fetch the doll.

The older child:

   Swinging, see-sawing, trampolining (an old foam-rubber mattress or an upholstered armchair can be used).
   Play ball while running.
   Roller-skating (with good instructions and with the skates fastened to the boots) is within the range of possibility for many subnormal children.
   Pictures are shown in quick succession, while the child jumps, or moves in some other way.
   The child goes quickly around the room without stopping and tells what he sees.

An investigation of educable subnormal children's eye fixation

In 1967, I investigated the ability of 140 subnormal schoolchildren to follow a moving object with their eyes. The children were 9-18 years old, and those with nystagmus were excluded (see footnote).

Large, jerky, uncoordinated movements .. 20
Complete movement in all directions, but unaccustomed movements to the extreme positions, difficult or slightly painful 10

Unconcentrated (unaccustomed and/or influenced by psychic causes) 15
Quite unable to perform the required movement (they understood the task, but became
dizzy) 11
Limited movement 5

Total 61

Of the 140 children, 61 were treated for 5
minutes 4 times a week for 1-3 months, after
which, of the 61 children, there remained:

1 child with limited movements, and

1 child with large, uncoordinated movements.

Exercises (pages 69-70) were combined with
balancing exercises because of the relation
between vision and balance (see page 124).

What influence the training had on vision
itself I do not know, but in many cases it
improved the child's appearance, he looked
less disturbed than before and he could look at
the person he was talking to.

Since I was dealing with older children, the 3
month's training was certainly not enough to
stabilize eye fixation, and relapses may have
taken place. Follow-up examination was not
feasible, as the children were scattered over
the whole country shortly after the investigation.

The restless eye movements here described must not be
confused with nystagmus. Nystagmus can be
recognized by small, involuntary, rhythmic, jerky
movements, for which, as far as is known, nothing can
be done.

Visual perception

The normal child

Development of visual perception is a complicated process and has many aspects. In
reality the child must learn »to see«. He must
learn to use sight and its related brain functions
as they develop.

It is important for the child, right from the
first weeks of life, to have visual stimulation so

that the different aspects of visual perception
can all be developed. These are:

Body awareness with respect to the eyes and
their surroundings.

Perception of direction and space.

Perception of shape.

Color vision.

Figure-ground discrimination.

The peripheral visual field.

Eye-hand coordination.

Capacity for observation.

Visual memory.

Quick visual perception.

These subjects will be dealt with briefly in
terms of how they affect the daily care and
education of the child.

Relation to motor ability and to other senses

Motor ability: to be able to go up to an object,
in order to study it more closely, gives greater
experience.

Manual dexterity furthers eye-hand coordination in all manual tasks.

We have already dealt with the importance
of the eye muscles in fixation, accommodation
and binocular vision.

The sense of touch is of great value in visual
perception. The mouth as well as the fingers
take part: e. g. rough and smooth surfaces may
be differentiated by touch as well as by sight.

Sense of taste and of smell: e. g. the apple
looks good, it also tastes and smells good.

Hearing: a sound is heard and the head and
eyes turn in that direction: e. g. water boils in
the kettle, steam is seen and the whistle is
heard.

Kinesthetic sense: when throwing a ball, it is
better to look at the target than at your arm,
using the kinesthetic sense to tell you what
your arm is doing.

When writing, the kinesthetic sense is a
great help in learning shapes (see page 176).

Direction and space: (See pages 104 and 106).

Perfection

A few examples of highly differentiated visual perception:

Recognition of shape: An ornithologist recognizes birds in flight.

Recognition of color: Greenlanders discern many different shades of white in snow.

Observation: A detective notices the smallest details.

The retarded child

Awareness of the eyes and their surroundings

As the retarded child is often without awareness and knowledge of his eyes and their surroundings, body awareness should be trained in as natural a way as possible.

The young child

When the child is being washed, speak of »shutting the eyes« and »washing the eyes«, etc. (kinesthetic sense, sense of touch).

Point to your eyes.

Can you see that Linda is asleep?

What is Sally looking at? (direction of glance).

The older child

Each child cuts out a paper mask, and the children look at each other through the holes, so that they understand that it is the eyes they see with.

The eyebrows and eyelids are looked at in a mirror, touched, and the names learned.

Vocabulary

In order to perform the exercises described below, all unknown words connected with the exercises must first be learned, including all words for direction, shape, etc. E. g. straight, slanted, crooked, round, shut, open, stand still, stop, follow, balance, pointed, angular, same, different, high, low, wide, thin.

Visual perception of form

The normal child

When exactly the child begins to understand form is not quite clear, but recent investigations suggest that it is very early, at about the 2nd month or perhaps sooner.

At about 9 months of age, fingers and eyes replace the mouth as the most important sensory organ. The child examines everything carefully and shows his perception of form by being able to recognize simple objects.

The child is about a year old before he can understand that an object is the same when seen from different angles at different distances and against different backgrounds.

During the next 6 months the child learns to recognize pictures of cars, dogs, etc., and begins to be able to visualize objects which are not in sight and to turn a picture correctly.

At about 2 years the child can place simple geometric figures in matching holes, and at about 2½ years he can sort blocks in pairs.

Perception does not yet seem to include wholeness; instead, the child notices one quality at a time, e. g. only height or width. An object should be comprehended as a whole and not by separate elements, e.g. a chair is not only legs, but comprises also a seat and back, and a square is not four separate lines, but a whole.

At about 4 years the child draws primitive houses and people, and from the small child's observation of single details, development proceeds towards perception of the whole.

The retarded child

If the child has no form concept and therefore no form constancy there will not be much visual constancy in his surroundings. It is therefore necessary to teach the child to »see« the thing he is looking at. The procedure will be:

Show large, living, concrete things, before

small, abstract objects.

Three-dimensional objects, before two-dimensional pictures.

Perception of form is practiced first without the distraction of different colors and sizes. Finally, recognizing forms having different colors and sizes.

If the retarded child has great difficulties in recognizing form visually, the following progression can be followed:

A living dog, a large stuffed dog, a little toy dog, a picture of a dog and finally a line drawing of a dog.

Afterwards practice more abstract shapes, e.g. circle:

A large ball of a neutral color.

Smaller balls of neutral colors.

A large drawing of a circle, colored all over with a neutral color.

Smaller circles of the same kind.

Many round objects, later of different sizes and colors, and lastly

a line drawing of a circle.

For teaching geometric shapes, see Eye-hand coordination, page 78.

Sample exercises

Form constancy

A toy car. It is the same car, whether it is on the carpet, on the table, or in the hand, whether it is stationary or moving, and even if it is upside-down.

Differentiation

Point to several playthings.

Look at and handle blocks of different shapes.

Sort blocks according to shape.

Sort buttons, stones, beads, counters and the leaves of trees.

Distinguish between square and rectangular.

Picture lottery, where shape is the most important.

Mosaic and matching games.

Name all the things here in the room which are rectangular (have four sides).

Cut out pictures and figures (eye-hand coordination)

Patterns

Distinguishing patterns can be practiced with the help of all kinds of samples of cloth, e.g. dotted, checked, striped, flowered, multicolored. At first use samples that have only one pattern, but later the pattern may be mixed; it may be flowered as well as striped.

The child names the patterns on his own clothes and those of his friends.

Copying and eye-hand coordination

Mosaic, where the pattern is copied from a picture.

Legoblocks are combined according to a picture.

Copy matchstick figures.

Two blocks are placed in a certain position on a table and the child copies the arrangement with two other blocks. Afterwards use more, different-shaped blocks in more difficult arrangements.

Kinesthetic sense

Stand in one corner of the room and then go all the way around it along the walls.

Draw the shape you walked.

Walk around in a circle, in a triangle, etc.

Draw the same shapes.

Concept of wholeness

Show the remains of a broken toy. What did they come from?

Part of a shape is drawn and the child completes it.

Color vision

The normal child

In a newborn child, neither the retina nor the cortex is developed enough to recognize colors. During the first year the child prefers red and yellow to other colors, and when the child begins to speak, he usually recognizes and names these colors first. Later he distinguishes green and blue. So it would seem that the eye can recognize the red end of the spectrum first, and the blue, violet end last.

At about 3-4 years the child knows all the main colors, but green and blue are often mistaken, especially by boys. Girls seem to be more sensitive to color than boys are, and perhaps in this respect too develop earlier than boys.

Whether perception of color or of form develops first in children has been much discussed.

My opinion is that it probably depends on which area the individual child has developed first, either

1) the sensory cells for color sensitivity in the retina, or

2) perception of direction and space along with eye fixation.

As regards the retarded child, it is most uncertain which of the two areas develops first.

The retarded child

Color vision may develop so late that the child is considered partly colorblind, without being so. That many retarded children make mistakes in naming colors may not be because they lack ability to discriminate but because they cannot remember the colors or their names.

Exercises

Let the child's clothes be several different, bright colors corresponding to those he is learning. Have clear colors and patterns on walls, bed-clothes, etc.

Teach red, yellow, green, blue, white and black, one color at a time, and afterwards: brown, gold, silver, etc.

Pair small pieces of colored wood or cardboard (two of each color).

The colors should not be confined to only certain objects or shapes:

The child should later be able to distinguish all the colors in the room and in his clothes.

What is this color called?

Can you remember something else that is this color?

(Experience and recollection of what was seen previously.)

Shades of color

Picture lottery, mosaic or jigsaw puzzles, where color is dominant.

Cut out two pieces of material or paper in each shade (4-6 shades of each color), and match the pieces.

Investigation of color perception

In an investigation in 1965 at Gamle Bakkehus, which included 104 educable subnormal children aged 9-18, all the girls (32) knew and named the colors red, yellow, green, blue, white and black, while 1/3 of the boys (24 out of 72) confused green and blue. All the children learned to distinguish these colors clearly in the course of one school year. Experience seems to show that blue is the last to be recognized, so teach green first.

The school had a garden with a large lawn, so it was convenient to teach the color green before blue. When the child is sure of green, show him green and blue together.

Figure – ground perception

The normal child

Many different factors influence the ability to distinguish a figure from its background, and each of these must have reached a certain stage of development before a sharp distinction can be expected. Some of the requirements are:

A certain development of visual perception in general, including form concept, direction, space, and visual memory.

The child sees the mother's face, and first recognizes the bright, lively eyes. At about 2 months the child's eyes follow a person who moves about the room – movement makes it easier to separate a person from the background – and one fine day the child notices a block or a rattle, without, however, entirely differentiating it yet from its surroundings.

At 6 months the child sees and grabs everything lying near him, but half a year passes before the same object is recognized from different angles and in spite of different backgrounds (form constancy).

Three-dimensional objects are the first to be distinguished from their surroundings, e.g. the rattle from the carpet, the cupboard from the wall.

Later, two-dimensional figures and pictures are distinguished, e.g. a picture of a horse in front of a farm.

The retarded child

In addition to the other factors which influence the normal child's ability to distinguish figure from background, in the case of retarded children the ability to concentrate plays a large part as well. Often the child's eyes wander from one thing to another, so that they do not take in what is most important in a given situation; the child often cannot single out or concentrate long enough on the things that are important.

Exercises

Three-dimensional
  Lay several known objects on a patterned carpet. Where is the car? Where is the ball? Scatter blocks in various places. Find them. Tell me all the things you see in the room.

Two-dimensional
  Point to certain figures in a picture book.
  Lay many geometric shapes on a patterned carpet. Find all the triangles.
  What is this? A cup is drawn on a hatched background.
  Find the hidden figures in the lines of a drawing (different degrees of difficulty).
  Several geometric figures are drawn (circle, square, triangle, rectangle) so that they partly cover each other, and the child is asked to draw the outline of one with a colored pencil.

The visual field

The normal child

Visual field means that area which can be seen when the eye fixes on a certain point.

The central visual field is that part which is seen clearly, i. e. the point focused on, for this picture falls on the yellow spot in the retina.

The peripheral visual field is the rest of the area which is seen more vaguely. The visual field is limited by the nose, cheeks and forehead and reaches about 90° to each side, 60° towards the nose, 50° upwards and 70° downwards.

The peripheral visual field is used in taking in the whole room at a glance and is useful for orientation in traffic when it is impossible to look in all directions at once.

Thick frames on eye glasses, deep-set eyes, prominent forehead or cheek bones, or a high bridge in the nose can limit the visual field.

Judging the visual field

A rough estimation of whether the visual field is limited can be done in the following way:

The child sits about 1 meter from the wall and looks hard at a cross on the wall. The child tells when a hand, with moving fingers, comes into his view from one of the sides. A small flashlight can also be used.

It can be difficult to find out when the child can perceive the first stimuli from the peripheral visual field. As mentioned earlier, this depends largely on a clear form and figure-ground perception.

The child learns naturally to use his peripheral vision, e.g. when something moves at the periphery of his vision while he is crawling on the ground. Later in development he also notices motionless objects in the periphery, although he does not see their colors. The fixation must move to the colored object, or near it, to recognize the color.

The retarded child

The retarded child often is unable to use peripheral vision, even when it is not limited. It is as if the child has not realized its usefulness, or perhaps perception is not so sharp that the child has any use for this part of the visual field. Workshop supervisors are often puzzled because a young retarded workman cannot guide both hands at once when they are a certain distance apart. Kinesthetic sense and sense of touch play a part in this, but it is also attributed to poor visual perception of the hand movements when the hands are in the peripheral visual field.

Exercises

The following exercises develop awareness of the peripheral visual field (direction and form) and also the kinesthetic sense by two-sided, rhythmic, gross motor arm movements.

The child stands with feet apart facing a large blackboard, with a cross drawn opposite his nose (a vertical line down through the cross

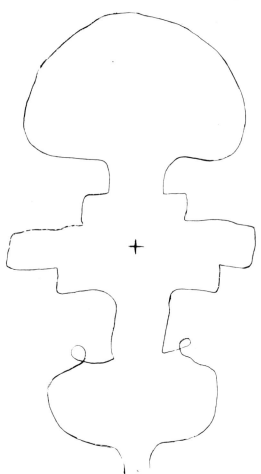

Fig. 36. Look at the cross and draw with both hands simultaneously. The drawing fills the whole blackboard.

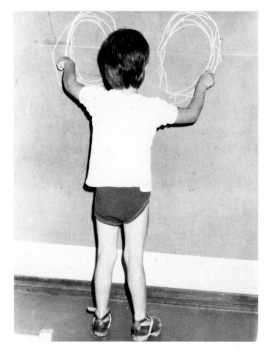

Fig. 35. Training the peripheral field of vision and hand movements.

may divide the board into two halves, one for each hand).

The child gets a thick piece of chalk in each hand, both pieces the same length, so that the movements and drawing of the two sides can be as similar as possible.

The exercise is to draw with both hands at once while the child looks steadily at the cross. The two-sided motion helps the child not to look at either chalk, but to focus on the cross, so that the peripheral vision may be understood and used.

1) Draw figures resembling circles (Fig. 35). The circles should be 20-50 cm in diameter, drawn rhythmically and more or less on top of each other, the one clockwise and the other counterclockwise.

When the figures are almost alike with both hands, try the other way around and finally both circles clockwise or both counterclockwise.

2) Vertical lines. (Vertical arm movements develop before the horizontal ones). Draw the lines up and down almost on top of each other, but without stressing this. The height should be about the same as the circle's diameter.

3) Horizontal lines may be drawn at different heights, first at eye level and afterwards so high and so low that most of the peripheral visual field is covered.

4) This exercise can be varied in several ways, with lines in various directions or with free drawing of identical shapes with both hands (Fig. 36).

Other exercises

Different known objects are brought into the visual field from outside.

Ball play with a large ball in each hand, e.g. bounce the two balls (see Ball exercises, page 135).

Eye-hand coordination

The normal child

(See also Handgrasp, page 34).

When the child of about 2 months holds an object, this shows the beginning of the connection between sight and the neuromuscular mechanisms, but the movement is still at the reflex stage. The child takes the object only if it is put near enough to touch his hand.

In the 4th month the child begins to reach for everything – »see – reach«, but the child often misses his aim, perhaps because of poor coordination of eyes as well as of hand.

At 6-7 months, balance while sitting is so good that the child can reach for things on all sides without tipping over. He now investigates everything within reach and so improves his eye-hand coordination through experience.

Towards 9 months of age the child looks at things for a little longer before he decides to

reach or perhaps not to reach; in other words, control of the »see-reach« reflex is complete.

The neuromuscular coordination is now so good that small articles can be picked up with the finger tips. The mouth is no longer the main sensory organ, but eyes and fingers contribute more and more.

The child no longer misses his aim, but reaches confidently, and everything is investigated and manipulated (handled).

At 1 year the child can build a tower with two blocks (2.5 cm cubes) but there is still difficulty in adding a third, because the child cannot let go quickly enough or confidently enough.

Later the child can judge the distance to an object with a quick glance, as well as judging its size and deciding if he wants it. It is no longer necessary to look at the object, but the child can look away and reach and grasp without the help of sight.

At 18 months there is no problem with reaching or grasping, and many movements are becoming automatic. He can now build a tower with three blocks.

When aged 2½, and making his first scribbles with a pencil, it is still hard for the child to get his scribbles to go in the direction he wants.

Around 3 years of age the child often uses his hands without looking at them.

To sum up, the eye is in advance of the hand in the beginning, for a child sees an object before he can pick it up. As development proceeds, the role of sight becomes less important, e. g. when handwriting becomes routine, sight acts only as a check.

The retarded child

The retarded child should be stimulated, as he develops, to do the same as a normal child, e. g.:

Eye fixation and head balance must be established first.

Offer the child different large and small objects, so that he is encouraged to grasp with both hands as well as with one hand.

When the falling reflex has been established

and the child can sit safely, toys and other objects should be handed to him from all sides.

Later use quite small objects so that the finger grip is stimulated.

The child crawls around and investigates everything.

Play »give and take«.

Build with blocks.

Exercises

Placing forms in the right holes.

Mosaic play.

Easy ball play with a large ball.

Threading large beads on a string.

Later in development follows:

Help in the kitchen and with laying the table at an early stage in the child's life. This is a natural way to get eye-hand coordination.

Modeling with clay, wax and wire.

Doing up large buttons.

Closing snap fasteners and zippers. Doing up smaller buttons.

Threading needles of different sizes.

Throwing bean-bags from a fixed distance into a wastepaper basket or a circle drawn on the ground.

Quoits: Throwing quoits over upright pegs.

Ball play, especially against a wall, so the ball comes back quickly and requires much eye-hand coordination. Boys should also practice this.

Train confidence, e. g. catch 10-15 times in a row.

Train speed, e. g. 20 times in how many seconds?

Drawing geometric shapes

Use large templates of thick cardboard, with circles, ovals, squares, etc. The figures should be large, e. g. a circle 10-15 cm in diameter, and well to one side of the cardboard so that there is room for a steadying hand.

Draw with chalk inside the circle. Trace the contours slowly and rhythmically several times until the shape is mastered. The child should be able to perceive with his arm movements

Fig. 37. The children are drawing on a large black-board, which should cover a whole wall. Good positions facing the board.

that, for example, two sides of a rectangle are longer than the other two, and that a triangle has three sides (Fig. 37).

1) Draw inside the cut-out templates.
2) Draw around cut-out figures (harder).
3) Freehand drawing, copying the same figure.
4) Freehand drawing following spoken direction with no model.

Other examples of exercises

Make about ten dots on the blackboard. Mark them with numbers, colors or pictures (Fig. 38) and the child draws lines from dot to dot.

Cut along lines, first a thick line and afterwards a thin one (Fig. 39). A normal child cannot cut along lines with a normal handgrasp until he is about six.

Cut out pictures, drawings and paper dolls.

Color over straight lines, curved lines, geometric figures, drawings and pictures.

Color figures and pictures. The child must learn first to follow the contours of the drawing and then fill in the drawing. It is not so hard to keep inside the lines when the

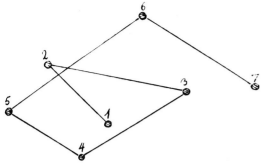

Fig. 38. Join the dots by lines in all directions.

Fig. 39. Cut out along the lines. Increasing difficulty.

technique is understood; this normally happens at about 5 years.

Cut out shapes drawn with a double line, keeping the scissors between the two lines.

Cut out one of two identical shapes and paste it over the other.

Draw a big circle on the blackboard, and draw concentric circles within it, about 4 cm apart.

Visual memory

The normal child

What is seen should be remembered and used as the foundation for further experience. As the child develops, his visual memory becomes longer. For example, the child first recognizes his mother; later he learns to expect to be fed after he sees certain visual stimuli, e. g. when he sees the bottle being taken out.

Eventually the child recognizes the whole family. At a year he can remember for a longer time what he has seen, and at 1½ years he recognizes pictures of a car, a dog, etc., points to his nose, hair and eyes when he is told to, and begins to be able to picture in his mind things known, but not present.

After this, progress is rapid. At about 3 years the child remembers many shapes and colors, and at 5 years he remembers the number symbols.

The foundation has been laid for further intellectual development.

The retarded child

The basis for visual memory is a clear perception of what is seen. This requires that all the areas mentioned under Sight and Visual Perception must be mastered. A great problem for the retarded child is whether the brain is able to retain for an extended period of time what he has perceived. This depends partly on how far the child has progressed in general development, and partly on repeating and being taught again and again at all levels.

Samples of exercises

Kim's game: 3-4 familiar objects are hidden by a cloth. The objects are uncovered for perhaps five seconds and the cloth is replaced. What did you see?

Later increase the number of objects to 5 and shorten the time.

Shut your eyes and say what is in this room.

Take a good look at Susan, shut your eyes and tell what she has on.

Different memory games (turning up cards) beginning with a few clear pictures and ending with a deck of cards, using a picture card game.

Show the child a picture of, e. g. a farm and tell the child to look at it carefully and, when the picture is removed, to describe it.

Tell what you saw on the way to school today.

Capacity for observation

The normal child

To observe an object is to look at it closely and notice the details. All the faculties constituting visual perception are used to teach the child to »see« what he looks at. Capacity for observation depends on motivation, on the child's interest in his surroundings, and is developed in conjunction with his visual memory, because he needs to compare what he sees with what he has seen previously. The central nervous system and perception must therefore have reached a fairly advanced stage of development.

The retarded child

The areas of perception basic to observation should all be developed to about the same level before observation can be practiced. This comprises all the areas named under Sight.

Examples of exercises
Picture lottery.
Mosaics.
What is the difference between these two books? (height, width, thickness, color, printing, pictures, letters).
Tell me everything you see in this picture.
Tell me how Peter's room was furnished.

Quick visual perception

The normal child

In all circumstances, it is important that visual perception be as quick as possible. For example, the child should be:

Quick to comprehend the traffic situation before crossing a road.

Quick to follow the ball on the field and to act accordingly.

Quickly perceptive when reading, watching movies, etc.

The retarded child

A prerequisite for quick perception is that the child has sufficiently developed all the perception areas mentioned in this chapter.

Training in this field, too, begins with three-dimensional figures, then two-dimensional ones, and finally more abstract forms, e.g.:

A familiar object is shown for a few seconds and then removed. What was it? When the child understands the method, show many different objects, one at a time in the quickest succession possible.

Single, clear drawings or pictures are shown in the same way.

Geometric shapes.

More complicated pictures.

Throw a dice and the child says as quickly as possible what the dice shows. It may be a color, a picture or dots.

A kind of film projector, a tachistoscope, which can show pictures in given fractions of seconds, is a great help and serves as a control in this kind of training.

The same procedure with numbers, letters, words, sentences.

Hearing

Auditory perception

Frequency and intensity of sounds

A source of sound causes sound waves which spread in all directions. These are collected by the outer ear and passed on to the inner ear.

Frequency

The pitch of a sound depends on its frequency, or the number of times per second that a sound wave vibrates. Notes in the treble range have a high frequency, and bass notes are low frequency notes. The human ear is capable of perceiving sounds which range in frequency from 100 to 20,000 cycles per second. The unit, cycles per second, is generally referred to as a hertz.

The ability to perceive high-pitched sounds decreases greatly with age. Many older people cannot hear grasshoppers (ca. 16,000 Hz). The frequency of ordinary speech lies between 500 and 2500 hertz.

Intensity

The intensity of a sound is measured in units of sound pressure, the pressure which the sound wave exerts on the ear. The ear is such a versatile instrument that the highest pressure it can bear is 1,000,000 times as large as the pressure of the faintest sound it can hear. For this reason, it is not convenient to measure sound directly as pressure. Instead, it is usually expressed as a ratio, based on the faintest sound which an average human ear can hear. This sound is called zero decibel, and the louder the

sound above this level, the more decibels it has. Some average sound levels are: broadcasting studio 20, suburban living room 45, conversation 70, subway train 95, threshold of pain 134. A hearing deficit of 15-20 decibels therefore lies within normal limits.

Audiometry

Auditory: connected with hearing, received by the ear,
metro: a measure,
audiometry: Measurement of hearing,
gramma: drawing, noting, registration,
audiogram: curve of hearing, measured by an audiometer.

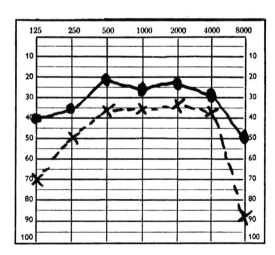

Fig. 40. Example of audiogram.
O - O, right ear.
X - X, left ear.
Hearing is a little weak for both high and low tones, and worst in the left ear. The area from 500–2000, corresponding to ordinary speech, is rather good.

Audiometry is done with the help of an audiometer, an instrument that produces sounds of known frequency (low-high notes) and intensity (soft-strong).

The audiometer tells which frequencies and intensities it may be difficult for the child to hear, and whether the hearing is the same in both ears. This can be read from an audiogram, which has two curves, one for each ear (Fig. 40).

The horizontal numbers give the frequency (hertz) of the sounds, and the vertical numbers give the intensity (decibel) needed in order for the child to hear the sound.

Audiometry requires that the child be able to cooperate and to indicate when he hears a sound in the earphones. Therefore it may be difficult or impossible to undertake the test with children whose I. Q. is much under 50, and so audiometry of retarded children should be undertaken by a person who already knows each child well.

It is now possible, however, with the latest equipment, to measure hearing even on infants. A computer/audiometer measures the child's brain impulses and gives an analysis of his hearing.

The normal child

The sense organs in the ear of a newborn child can receive strong stimuli, but the subsequent reaction is a sort of a reflex, and there can, in the nature of things, be no question of perception before the central nervous system is more developed.

When the child is about 2 months old, he usually reacts to a soft sound nearby. At 3 months he turns his head towards each sound that attracts his attention. In many cases however, these reactions do not occur until later, without there being any abnormality.

After 3½ months the cortex has developed so much that the child can listen, turn his head and look for the source of the sound. Now it is a completely conscious and motivated action.

The child begins to be able to recognize certain often repeated sounds and to remember what they mean. He understands, for example, that shaking the bottle means food.

The child becomes more and more interested in listening; he listens to voices, clocks, bells, etc. Listening is of great importance for the child's later development (see Speech, page 53 and Concentration, page 114).

To locate the sound, the child, until he is about 12 months old, will first turn his head to the side and then correct upwards or downwards.

The child later reacts to certain signal words, e. g. »no« »da-da« and to his own name, and can remember sounds and what they mean for quite a long time.

Now sounds can be localized surely and quickly with a single intentional movement of the head.

Between 18 and 24 months the child begins to be able to imagine sounds which he has heard before, and he enjoys moving to music.

Towards the end of his 2nd year the child understands simple instructions and likes to listen to short stories. He can locate sounds in an adjacent room, and tries to find out where the sound comes from and what causes it.

After this, development is rapid; the child understands words and acquires language. At 5 years of age a spoken instruction can be quickly carried out, with little delay between hearing the order and carrying it out.

Relation to motor ability and to other senses

A sound is heard better if one can turn the head in its direction, and by being able to move towards the sound, the cause of the sound can be investigated and experience gained. Through experience a child gradually learns to move away from sounds that warn of danger. Hearing is supplemented by other senses, especially by sight, but to a certain degree also by feeling and kinesthetic sense. These sensory impressions coordinate with, and thereby strengthen, auditory perception, e. g.:

A bell moves (sight), and it rings (hearing).

It is easier for a small child to imitate simple rhythmic patterns (clapping, drumming) if he can be watching at the same time.

The waves of the sea go high (sight and hearing) and wash over the body when bathing (feeling).

A well-developed visual perception of direction and space will supplement the auditory judgment of direction and distance. E. g. to have lived in and examined a house visually, kinesthetically, and by touch (feeling) will reinforce localization of sounds that come from different places in that house. Kinesthetic knowledge of the house here means that the child, by moving around the house, up the stairs and along the corridors, realizes the size of the house and the position of the rooms.

Perfection:

A few examples of finely developed auditory perception:

A musician distinguishes notes and remembers them.

An ornithologist recognizes birds by their song even without seeing them.

A linguist distinguishes slight variations in intonation and dialect.

The retarded child

To help the retarded child in his development of auditory perception, it is important to expose the child to different sounds and encourage him to listen, in order to widen his range of experience in sound recognition and discrimination.

It is a matter of finding the child's level of development; for example, when a child turns towards a sound, be sure whether it is only a reflex action or whether the brain is sufficiently involved that the child is interested in the sound and turns his head intentionally to find out where the sound comes from, and what causes it. At the first stage, when the sound can not yet be perceived, it would be most useful to expose the child to near sounds and to repeat them often, until the child's brain is so developed that it can realize what makes a certain sound. This is the method every mother uses with her normal child. In the case of a

retarded child at the same stage of auditory development, more time, more patience, and many more repetitions are needed.

First and foremost get the child to notice the sound. Unless he can concentrate on listening, he may not even hear the sound.

Why does the child not listen?

If the child does not listen, it may be for several reasons:

1) Defects of the sensory organs.
2) Defects in the brain.
3) Psychological reasons.
4) Environmental reasons.
5) Other reasons.

1) Defects of the sensory organs:

Deafness or partial deafness
If the sense organs in the ear do not function properly, a doctor should make a diagnosis and prescribe suitable treatment. It is never too early to take the child to the doctor. Hearing aids in some cases can be given from the age of 1 year, in order to further the child's whole development.

A speech and hearing therapist can help the child to use even a remnant of hearing. Special teaching for such children is outside the scope of this book. I shall only remark that to learn finger language requires a fine kinesthetic perception. Deaf children are not provided at birth with better sensory organs than other children, and a finer perception comes only through practice and experience.

Hearing aid
If a hearing aid is prescribed, the parents and others who deal with the child must learn to notice whether the child places the hearing aid correctly and, if the child cannot manage this, to put it right for the child, to clean the earpiece and see if the wires are in order and the current turned on. Also, the child's ears must be kept free of wax.

A hearing aid that does not work is worse than none. The adult must also remember that it enlarges all sounds, so being in a room with many noisy children can be most unpleasant. Moreover, it is the adult's duty to observe to what extent the child is dependent on the hearing aid.

Less serious hearing defects:
It helps a child with hearing defects if he is placed in the class in such a way that he can see the faces of his classmates and of the teacher. Hearing must be trained without the help of sight as much as possible, but with proper placement one may ensure that the child enters into everything the class does.

2) Defects in the brain

Low intelligence
The level of intelligence must be taken into consideration if there is to be any hope that the child can improve.

Impressive dysphasia
Impressive dysphasia means a defect of auditory perception. It concerns a poorly developed auditory understanding of speech (spoken words) as regards discrimination as well as memory span.

It often is difficult to diagnose dysphasia if it occurs together with defective hearing and low intelligence.

3) Psychological reasons
Besides various neurotic and psychotic conditions, which are outside the scope of this book, shyness and lack of concentration can be factors causing the child not to listen (see Concentration, page 114).

4) Environmental reasons
E. g. too little attention from adults. The child is not talked to enough, and the language used is incomprehensible to the child because it possibly is better suited to the child's chronological age than to his mental age.

In the case of older children, lack of social contacts means that they do not have a chance to listen to speech. For example, when the adult takes the child for a walk, he should talk to him all the time. It does not help the child's development if two adults converse over his head. The child should be included in an adult's activities, such as in the kitchen, and he should preferably help with the washing, ironing, cooking, shopping, etc., and continually be conversed with.

5) Other reasons
Colds and wax in the ears can cause temporarily defective hearing.

Vocabulary
The child must know the name of the source of the sound, and later say the word himself, so speaking and listening exercises go hand in hand.

Many words are necessary for the understanding of sounds, e. g. ring, rustle, cut, whistle, clap, tramp, hit, fall, sing, high, soft, strong, weak, etc.

Training listening and discrimination of sounds
Since a great deal of the child's intellectual development takes place through hearing, early training of hearing is important with due attention to the child's neurologic development and, if possible, in cooperation with a speech therapist.

The following pages give some examples of how the retarded child whose sensory organs are intact is stimulated during the development of auditory perception.

The child must be exposed to sounds and gain experience of sounds by hearing them. The more impulses, the more brain function is required.

The child should be able to separate sounds from any background noise that is present. If the child finds it difficult to differentiate sounds, the training should take place in a quiet room in the beginning, without background noise, and individually if possible.

As soon as the child has developed some capacity for auditory discrimination assisted by vision, try him with sounds alone.

Exercises. Listening and discriminating.
Get the child to notice all sounds in his surroundings, e. g.:

General discrimination:
  The telephone rings.
  Loud talking.
  Something falls to the floor.
  Car horn.
  Shouting in the street. Dogs barking.

Finer discrimination. Near sounds:
  Men's and women's voices.
  Rustling paper.
  A tap running.
  »Sit as quiet as a mouse. What do you hear?«
  The rain on the window pane, Peter sniffing
  and Jane eating an apple.

Finer discrimination. Distant sounds:
Here the child should disregard the sounds in
the room he is in.
  A radio playing upstairs.
  The vacuum cleaner being used downstairs.
  A bird singing in a tree.
  People walking by outside and talking.

In general:
  When the child goes for a walk with an
  adult, get him to notice all the different
  sounds. Tell me tomorrow all the sounds
  you heard on the way home.
  What sounds did you hear on the way to
  school today?
  The child tries to imitate the remembered
  sounds.

Discriminating sounds;
pitch, intensity, length and rhythm:
  Sort sound-boxes by pairs.
  Stamp when the music is loud, and tiptoe
  when it is soft.
  The child strikes three bells having different
  pitches, then shuts his eyes: »Which bell am
  I striking now?«
  Copy notes of different length (different in-
  struments).
  Copy easy rhythms on different instruments.
  Copy Morse code by clapping, hitting, etc.

Discriminating words and speech:
Here the speech therapist should draw up a
program which the child's family should follow
carefully and exactly. Later the child should be
able to understand speech, even when he cannot see the speaker's face.

At a later stage of development, if there is
sufficient intelligence, speech rhythms can be
practiced.

The next step is to clap or play on an instrument to show which syllables are stressed and
which are not in all the newly learned words,
e. g.:
  »Trumpet« (one stressed and one unstressed
  syllable).
  »The boy is crying«; unstressed – stressed –
  unstressed – stressed – unstressed.
This method in much more detail is used in
teaching the partially deaf, but can with advantage be used when teaching language to all
children. The procedure teaches speech
rhythm in a pleasant way and helps as well in
remembering new words.

Later in development the normal child can
discover for himself which words or sentences
have a given rhythmic pattern. But this is much
harder, and for most retarded children it is
quite impossible.

Auditory perception of direction and distance (localization)

How to locate a sound is learned by practice
and experience and depends partly on the
combined action of both ears, so the ability is
lessened if one ear hears poorly.

Exercises
  What direction is the sound coming from?
  Is the car coming nearer or going away?
  Which tree is the singing bird sitting in?
  Hide an alarm clock. Where is it?

Blindfolded:

The child tries to find the child who is speaking.

The teacher rings a bell, whistles, etc., in different places in the room. The child points towards the sound.

Two adults make sounds at different distances from the child. Which sound is nearest?

Auditory memory

To understand and remember spoken instructions or, perhaps, a little story, requires a certain level of neurological development, in addition to concentration and training.

Memory is often improved by and associated with comprehension.

Most children like to hear a little story before they go to sleep, at first perhaps one of only three or four short lines which can be easily understood by the child and is within his vocabulary. Let the child immediately retell the story in some way, perhaps by dramatizing, which the child enjoys. Gradually the story becomes longer. This may be called short-term memory.

Long-term memory can be practiced by asking the child to repeat the story the next morning and perhaps again some days later.

It is often very hard for the retarded child to remember something for a longer time, and repetition, perhaps many repetitions (over-learning) in various ways, is necessary.

Auditory memory is most easily trained in the retarded child if other senses are involved first. Most useful are sight, touch and kinesthetic sense. Later practice may be purely auditory.

Exercises

As always, it is an advantage to be able to teach the child by natural, everyday means, for instance by taking the child to a supermarket and telling him to fetch one, two and later more things from the shelves.

Artificial exercises, which most children enjoy, may be:

Take this book from the table, put it on the shelf there and shut the door (sight + hearing + movement). The adult points.

Take the book from the table, put it on the shelf, and shut the door (by hearing only).

Hop to the blackboard, draw a square, turn around three times and sit down on the chair.

Go to the grocer's and buy sugar, coffee and soda pop.

Later this becomes: 2 kilograms sugar, $\frac{1}{2}$ kg coffee and two bottles of soda pop.

The tasks can be made harder by telling the child to »buy« more things or by telling him to run upstairs and downstairs again on his way to the »grocery store«. He may meet another child on the way and talk to him and forget everything. Finally the child goes to a real grocery store without showing the list he has with him if this is possible.

Auditory memory can also be trained with the help of rhythmic patterns (see page 196).

If the child cannot remember what he is told, it is a great help to get him to picture whatever it is; if he is supposed to go to the bakery, for instance, ask him to image a large loaf of bread, or a carton of milk, or a cake with fluffy, white frosting – in short, get him to see with his mind's eye whatever he is supposed to remember.

The tactile senses or cutaneous sensibility

Sensibility: feeling.
Tactus: feeling, touch.
Tactile: perceived by the sence of touch.
Cutis: skin.
Cutaneous: of the skin.

The normal child

The tactile senses are located in the skin and in the mucous membranes which are in the nose and mouth among other places. The tactile senses comprise:

Sense of touch,
Sense of pain, and
Sense of temperature.
(Estimation of weight; see the Kinesthetic sense, page 93).

Sense of touch

The adequate stimulus of the sense of touch is a pressure on the skin so that it changes shape a little, stretches.

Sensibility to being touched is greatest where the sensory cells lie thickest, as in the tips of the tongue and fingers. On the back the sensory cells lie far apart, making it hard to decide, for example, whether one is being touched by one or two fingers.

As early as the first week of life the infant reacts to irritation of the skin by withdrawing his arm or leg (withdrawal reflex).

The seeking, sucking and swallowing reflexes are elicited by touching the skin or mucous membranes.

Later the child sucks everything, and eventually he can feel a difference between objects because the lips and tongue help in feeling.

A child is soothed by being stroked with gentle movements of the hand.

As the central nervous system develops further, feeling in the fingertips improves, the motor ability of the hand becomes better, and the child begins to feel things not only with his mouth but also with his fingers.

When the skin is touched, he knows where he is being touched and, later, what is touching him. There are several ways of touching:

a) Touching the child's body over a large area or at a particular point, e.g. with the flat of the hand or with one finger.
   This touching may be a strong, deep pressure, or it may be gentle and light.
b) The child touches an object. A firm touch by which, in connection with the kinesthetic sense, he percieves:

consistency, e.g.: holding a soft ball feels different from holding a wooden one.

A light touch by which he perceives:

surface and structure, e.g.: Stroking silk with his fingers feels different from wool.

By the help of the stereognostic sense (stereo: solid, gnosis: knowledge) he perceives without the help of sight, only by touching, the consistency and the structure of an object as well as

shape and dimension (size), e.g.: Your pocket contains different coins. Take out a dime.

Relation to motor ability and to other senses

The child moves up to a desired object, feels it, takes it up in his hand and examines it more closely. In the same way he feels with his tongue and other parts of the mouth the consistency of his food, its shape and surface texture. Motor ability thus plays a very large part in widening a child's tactile experience.

The sense of touch is supplemented by other senses, e.g.:

Sight: It can be both seen and felt that the table is smooth.

Hearing: When stroking sandpaper with the fingers, the coarse surface is heard as well as felt.

Sense of taste and smell: Different foods are recognized, visually and by touch, as well as with the help of taste and smell.

Kinesthetic sense: Estimation of weight.

Body awareness: The child must know his own body to be able to feel and say where he is being touched.

Perfection

An example of finely developed cutaneous sensibility is the quick and accurate reading of Braille by the blind. This skill is mastered only after a thorough training of the sense of touch.

The retarded child

Whole or partial loss of the tactile senses can, for instance, occur in some hemiplegics (paralysis on one side of the body) where cutaneous sensibility over the paralyzed muscles can be weak or entirely lacking.

Retarded children should be made to notice the sense of touch, even if sensibility is not lessened. Brief training can increase awareness of their own bodies or can encourage a child who drools to notice his saliva and swallow it.

Try not to say: »Don't touch« unless absolutely necessary. It is important that the child get as many tactile stimuli as possible.

Vocabulary

E.g.: Rough, smooth, fine, coarse, woolly, liquid, close, loose, thick, thin, pointed, round, angular, long, short, high, low, wide, narrow, etc.

When his speech development allows, he should practice the comparison of such adjectives as fine, finer, finest, using the sense of touch.

Samples of exercises
a) *Touching the child's body.*
While the child looks, try several kinds of touching. Then repeat with the child blindfolded. The child should now be able to distinguish several kinds of touch and also to feel on what part of the body he is being touched.

First press strongly and afterwards touch lightly

over large areas:
Rub the thigh with a rough towel.
Brush with a nailbrush.
Lay one hand firmly on part of the body.
Stroke with a soft brush.

On one point:
Touch with a finger.
Touch with a pointed object.
Touch with a brush or feather.

Distinguish two points.
Touch two places at the same time, e.g. left cheek and right arm.
Touch two of the child's fingers at the same time (difficult).
The distance between the two points may be great at the beginning and later less.

b) *The child feels an object.* Consistency. (The kinesthetic sense contributes here.) E.g.:
Hard - soft: The rubber ball is soft. The wooden one is hard.
Many different objects are used, so that the child does not get the idea that the words refer only to the first object named.
Stiff - flexible: The stick is stiff. The wire is flexible.

Elastic: Demonstrate with several kinds of rubber bands and pieces of elastic.

Liquid - solid: Water is a liquid. The table is solid.

Surface texture:

Several kinds of sandpaper and scraps of material can be used for sorting. First practice with and afterwards without the help of sight.

Smooth - rough: Notepaper is smooth, and sandpaper is rough, uneven.

Woolly: Fur, velvet.

Close - loose: Shirt-material contrasted with loosewoven fabric.

Thick - thin: Winter and summer clothes. Talk about their warmth.

Coarse - fine: Differentiate among several kinds of sandpaper.

Silk - wool - cotton - synthetic materials: What kind of material is your dress? See if it wrinkles.

Shape and dimension:

If the tactile perception of shape is poorly developed, visual form discrimination may be exercised first. The tactile perception of form and dimension can help the retarded child when he later learns figures and letters. The child must have a clear perception of an object's shape if he is to recognize the object without using his eyes, only by feeling.

The order of the exercises, first with the help of sight and afterwards without, may be as follows.

Large, three-dimensional objects. Playthings or similar objects.

Smaller, three-dimensional objects.

Large two-dimensional objects. Paper dolls, etc.

Smaller two-dimensional geometric shapes.

Smaller three-dimensional geometric shapes.

Large two-dimensional geometric shapes.

Small two-dimensional geometric shapes.

Later:

Figures and letters cut out in wood or cardboard. The thinner the cardboard the harder this is.

In a non-transparent bag put many different familiar objects. At first practice with rather large objects, later with smaller ones (cubes, beads, rings, keys, etc.) Without looking, the child puts his hand down into the bag, grabs something, names it and finally pulls it out and shows it (try both hands).

Investigation: the stereognostic sense

An investigation of 104 educable, subnormal children aged 9-18 years showed (Gamle Bakkehus, 1965):

At the beginning of the school year seven of the children did not show any stereognostic sense. At the end of the shoool year six had acquired it, and the seventh, after a year, could recognize shape, size, texture, and consistency without the help of sight.

It is important to improve the stereognostic sense with a view to later work in a factory. Foremen often complain that young retarded workmen cannot feel the shape of a piece of metal, for example, which complicates matters if they are supposed to put the thickest end down when inserting it into a machine.

Sense of pain

The normal child

The skin and almost all the mucous membranes are equipped with sensory cells which answer to stimuli with a pain reaction. The sense of pain is a protection and, if possible, causes that part of the body to be withdrawn from the cause of the pain. If the child pricks his finger, he draws his arm back.

From 18 months on, a child will hold the part that hurts, but only at about 4 years of age can he be expected to point and say where the pain is.

Relation to motor ability and to other senses

As already mentioned it is important to be able to move away from the source of the pain in certain circumstances. E.g. from the cat's claws or from stinging nettles.

Sight and hearing, as well as experience and memory can guide to the avoidance of pain. For example, the child hears the water boiling and understands that it is hot. The bee hums, the child sees and hears it, and knows that he must be careful not to get stung.

The retarded child

It is important to give the retarded child as much experience as possible with regard to possible causes of pain, so that he can afterwards try to avoid these.

On the other hand, the child must not be frightened unnecessarily. The child must be familiarized with many unknown things and situations, for the unknown is frightening, e.g.:

> If a child has to be x-rayed for the first time and will be afraid of the hospital, the doctors, etc., the mother should play »hospital« with the child, undressing him and laying him on a table, drawing a hanging lamp down over the child, lighting it for a moment and saying that the lamp represents a camera which will photograph the child's leg or some other part of the body.

It often seems that the sense of pain is less developed in retarded than in normal children. Whether this is really so has not been proved satisfactorily as far as I know. When the child seems insensitive to pain it may perhaps be because of the child's poor concentration, meaning that his attention is easily distracted from the pain.

Sense of temperature

The normal child

In the skin and mucous membranes there are also points which register hot and cold.

By experience the child gradually learns which things are hot and which are cold. Changing seasons and weather can, among other things, help him to notice various temperatures, and the child soon learns to know when he is freezing and when he is sweating.

As early as at 5 years of age child can regulate the bath water's temperature by himself.

Relation to motor ability and to other senses

It is useful to be able to move away from a burning bonfire or a hot stove if you have come too near. It also requires motor ability to be able to put on warmer clothes.

In judging temperature, sight can be a guide. E.g. there is frost on the window, and it feels cold.

Hearing can also be a guide. E.g. the kettle whistles, the water boils and the kettle is too hot to touch.

The retarded child

The retarded child must be guided, so that from experience he can learn to judge different temperatures, and to remember what is so hot or so cold that it is uncomfortable or may hurt.

If the child shares in all the usual housework, he will gain this experience in a natural way. E.g. he will understand the instruction: »the dress must only be washed in lukewarm water.«

Vocabulary

E.g. hot, cold, lukewarm, steam, liquid, ice, frost, freeze, sweat, boil, melt.

Later in speech development he learns the comparison of adjectives, e.g. cold, colder, coldest.

Taste and smell

The normal child

Sense of taste

This sense is located in the taste buds in the tongue. Children have also taste buds in the palate and the inside of the cheeks, which results in the child having a stronger sense of taste than older people, who have fewer taste buds.

There are in reality only four kinds of taste. Here are a few examples:

Salt: salty meat, salt water.
Sweet: sugar, cake, jam, candy.
Sour: lemon, unripe fruit.
Bitter: grapefruit, strong tea.

Sense of smell

The sense of smell is associated with sensory cells in the nasal cavity. The smell is stronger if it is sniffed up the nose. One can become accustomed to smells, so that familiar smells are not noticed so much as unfamiliar ones, even when the sense of smell is otherwise well developed.

The sense of smell can be useful in certain dangerous situations, for instance smelling something burning or gas, likewise smell and taste may prevent a child from drinking or eating something which smells bad or tastes horrid and may be harmful.

When eating, the sense of smell plays a much larger part than the sense of taste. What is ordinarily called taste is most often a mixture of taste and smell.

The newborn can both smell and taste. He turns away with distaste from a nipple that has been sprinkled with salt, while he will suck happily from one that is dipped in sugar.

As soon as the child can use his hands, he puts everything in his mouth - he sucks, bites, tastes and smells everything. At about 12 months he can remember smells and tastes for some time.

The child's range of experience widens. The cow barn smells differently from the pigsty. Hay smells good and flowers have different scents. Mealtimes become more interesting and important when the child knows the difference between various dishes.

Relation to motor ability and to other senses

Sense of taste: The muscles of the tongue, lips and cheeks bring the material to be tasted into contact with the taste buds, making the food taste stronger. The hands take the food and convey it to the mouth.

Sense of smell: To smell an object, you bend your head over it and your hands bring it up to your nose. If an odor is further away, you may bend your head back to smell better.

In both cases you sniff up; in other words, you inhale strongly through the nose, and widen the nostrils, so that as much air as possible can pass through the smell epithelium.

The sense of touch and of temperature as well as the kinesthetic sense help the child to recognize consistency, texture, and temperature of food, and assist the senses of taste and smell to distinguish what kind of food it is. Sight is also a help.

Perfection:

How good the perception can be, depends on experience and intelligence, in which memory plays a large part.

The ability to differentiate can be trained to an amazing degree, such as in specialists like wine and tea tasters, or, when only the sense of smell is used, in perfume manufacturers.

The retarded child

Even though the senses – the taste buds, the smell epithelium – are intact, the retarded child must be helped in learning to discriminate, to gain experience and to perceive also within these sense areas.

Vocabulary

Besides the words mentioned under varieties of taste, the child must learn many other words connected with taste and smell, e.g. liquid, thick, hard, and the names of different solid and liquid foods.

Exercises

What do you smell with?

Can you smell what we are going to have for dinner?

Is the applesauce sweet enough?

Here is a little game which children find amusing: First explain the game to the child, then blindfold him. Then the child tries to recognize by smell: coffee, tobacco, wood, leather, toothpaste, soap, oil paint, flowers, petrol, pine, etc. (Liquids and powders can be poured into small medicine glasses.)

Go for a walk with the child and get him to notice all scents (flowers, leaves, soil, etc.)

The kinesthetic sense

The word kinesthesis is formed from two Greek words:
kinein: move, and aistesis: feeling.
The term kinesthetic sense indicates that the movements of the body are experienced through this sense.
Another name for this sense is:
The proprioceptive sense: This term indicates that stimuli are received by the sense cells in the muscle itself (proprius = own), in its tendons and in the joint capsules.

The normal child

Sensory cells are located in muscles, tendons and joint capsules and interpret
   1) The strength of the muscle contraction as well as
   2) the position of the joints and the limbs in relation to each other.

1) The degree of muscle concentraction strength.
   Tension, relaxation and estimation of weight.

Muscle contraction is perceived by the help of the kinesthetic sense, which thus becomes the most important factor in relaxation treatment.

It is not easy to judge beforehand how strong a muscle contraction should be to lift a given weight. Experience, gained through the kinesthetic sense, informs us how much strength should be used (for instance, a table lamp, which looks heavy, may turn out to be light).

2) The position of joints and limbs

It is easy to know, even with the eyes shut, whether an arm is bent or straight, whether a leg is in front of, behind or at the side of the body or whether the back is bent or straight. Correction of posture is mainly based on the kinesthetic sense.

Ordinarily the child is not aware of the kinesthetic sense, but if new skills must be learned, instruction is usually given on how, for example, the fingers should hold the knitting needles, how to hold a racket, or how the feet should be placed for climbing up a rope. The method of holding and the movements are thus conscious for a time, until they become automatic through repetition.

Conscious movements have for many years been banned from physical education. In recent years, where relaxation exercises, correction of posture and technique of lifting – and not least Rudolf Laban's ideas – have opened the way to another viewpoint, the principles of gymnastics have changed greatly.

The so-called »educational gymnastics« has also helped to alter the viewpoint and to make gymnastics a more intellectual subject, where body awareness and conscious use of the body are prerequisites (see page 141). The child learns in this way to be aware of his body and its movements in space and time; he learns to judge and to accept his body and its abilities. This helps the child in general to understand and accept himself, thus making for greater self-confidence and development of his ego.

Relation to motor ability and to various senses

Coordination between the kinesthetic sense, knowledge of the body and a feeling of laterality are important for body awareness.

Sight can guide movements as well as the relative position of the limbs.

Touch assists in judging the weight of an object.

Time concept: Movements can be performed at different speeds.

Perception of direction, space and form can be reinforced by the kinesthetic sense (see Writing, pages 170, 176).

It often is easier to remember something experienced kinesthetically than visually or mentally. If something has been mislaid, it can perhaps be found by remembering a movement, e.g. arm-lifting, through which the object was hidden at the top of a closet.

Perfection

Some people are more aware of their bodies than others are because their kinesthetic sense is better developed.

A ballerina, for example, must consciously try to develop this sense. She trains for many hours each day in front of a mirror in order to develop beautiful arm movements. She must consciously let an arm movement begin between the shoulder-blades and feel it travel all the way down into the hand, before the movement can be perfect. The psyche plays a great part in the movement, but the instrument – the body, its movements and its technique – must be completely mastered before it is possible to convey the meaning of the dance.

In the same way a piano virtuoso must have his thoughts at his finger tips, he should not need to look at his fingers, but should feel their movements.

The retarded child

Poorly developed motor ability can be improved to a certain extent – corresponding to the development of the brain tissue – by systematic training, beginning with body knowledge and continuing with perception of laterality, direction, and space and developing the kinesthetic sense. Through this the child gradually becomes aware of his body and its movements in space and time – in other words, he learns to judge how much space his body

occupies, in what direction it is moving and at what speed. (See Educational gymnastics, page 142).

The normal child, living at home, gains many experiences with the help of kinesthetic sense.

For example, the child follows his mother into the kitchen and pulls all the saucepans and casseroles out of the cupboard. One is heavy, another is light, and two pots may be the same size but not the same weight.

The cupboard door is opened by a special arm movement.

The saucepan is taken out and pushed in again.

The child crawls up on a kitchen chair and jumps down.

The retarded child unfortunately often misses out on many of these experiences. Perhaps he is too restless for the mother to have him in the kitchen when she is cooking, or perhaps the child lives in an institution and seldom sets foot in a kitchen.

If a child is slightly paralyzed, it is important to stimulate both the tactile and the kinesthetic sense right from the beginning, in order, if possible, to get the muscles to function better.

An adventure playground can give a child many kinesthetic experiences, and an imaginative adult will know how to build on these. The more, different experiences the better.

For more about the kinesthetic sense, see under Gymnastics, page 142).

Vocabulary

The child learns many words connected with the kinesthetic sense, e.g. move, keep still, quick, slow, bend, stretch, tighten, relax, strong, gentle, lift, lower, hard, soft, press, let go, light, heavy, open, shut, pull, push, flexible, stiff, elastic.

An example of how a word can be practiced in relation to kinesthetic sense:

Light - heavy: The child lifts different things.
  a) Objects of the same weight, shape, size and color. E.g. two identical cans of food.
  b) Objects of different weight and size, but

the same shape and color. E.g. a set of kitchen bowls of different sizes.

c) Objects of different weight, but the same shape, color and size. E.g. a number of boxes looking the same, which can be arranged in pairs of the same weight (old shoe polish cans filled with lead). The child sorts the boxes.

d) Objects with different shapes, weights, sizes and colors are sorted by weight.

e) Later the same procedure with three objects, so that the child learns words of comparison by experience.

Light, lighter, lightest.

Heavy, heavier, heaviest.

Exercises

Feeling the strength of the muscle contraction.

Take a soft ball in the hand and squeeze it hard.

Stop squeezing and hold it loosely.

Draw a heavy, black line on paper, and afterward draw a light, thin line with the same pencil.

Lie on the back with arms by the sides and feet under the lowest bar of the wall bar.

Roll up into a sitting position. Can you feel it in your stomach? Repeat the exercise with hands folded behind the nape of the neck. Now you can feel it even more strongly in your stomach.

Walk around the room and stamp on the floor. Then walk so lightly you can scarcely be heard.

Lie on your back. Make yourself stiff – make yourself limp.

Stretch both arms up along the floor and make yourself really long. Relax.

Can you feel the difference?

(The sense of touch helps in most of these exercises.)

2) *The position of the joints and the limbs.*

Shut your eyes, don't move. Tell me how you are holding your arms and legs (e.g. the hip, knee and ankle joints are bent on the right side, the left hip is also bent, but the knee and foot are straight, the right arm is bent at all three joints, etc.)

Lay a book on the table a short distance away from you. Shut your eyes and pick up the book. (With the help of the kinesthetic sense one may succeed in putting the arm just far enough to the side to reach the book.)

Draw a circle in the air. Repeat with the eyes shut.

Play »statues«: The children move in time to music. When the music stops, the children must keep their positions. One of the children describes his position to the others.

Body awareness

The normal child

The mother tends the baby, at the same time talking to him and saying many small, apparently unimportant phrases such as »Now we wash the little nose,« »Now we put your arm in the sleeve« or »Now we lift your head a little«.

All this is repeated for many months, hundreds of times. These phrases and the whole caring situation are of vital importance for the child's development – also for his knowledge of his own body – with contact between mother, father and child as its basis.

The child feels the adult's touch, and himself touches his mother. At about 3 months he begins to play with his fingers, look at them and put them in his mouth, and later he does the same with his feet and toes, using all senses. The impressions the child thus gets may be regarded as the beginning of body awareness.

When asked, the child can point to some of the parts of his body when he is about 18 months old and later he learns to name them. He can later understand an instruction regarding his body, tell where it hurts, etc. This knowledge through experience will deepen his understanding of the use of the body, and is a part of body awareness.

When a child draws a man, this gives a good idea of how much the child knows about parts of his body. The child only draws what he knows about, not what he sees. Goodenough's »draw a man« test gives a good picture of a child's body knowledge.

Relation to motor ability and to various senses

The child perceives his body by all senses, particularly by the sense of touch, by vision and by kinesthetic sense, little by little as development proceeds.

Sense of touch: The mother touches the child, the child touches the mother and himself, and the child feels his surroundings with his hands or other parts of the body.

Sight: The child looks at his mother's eyes, face, etc. He looks at his own hands, feet, etc.

Kinesthetic sense: The child realizes his limbs' position and movements.

Hearing: The child hears what parts of the body are called, before he himself can name them.

Perfection

Examples are: Ballet dancers, acrobats and actors who all have to train their body awareness to perfection.

The retarded child

The retarded child has perhaps been so backward in development that he has not been able to receive the stimuli which the normal child benefits from while being nursed, talked to and babbled to by adults. A year or two later, when he might benefit from all this, he is so big that the mother thinks he should not be treated as a baby.

Yet the natural method, as described for normal babies, ought also to be used for older retarded children regardless of age, as long as it corresponds to their stage of development.

Older retarded children lacking body awareness

In the case of older retarded children, the following method has been shown to be useful in teaching body awareness. The method may seem somewhat detailed but the child should realize what is being dealt with or he cannot remember what he is taught.

1) »This is my elbow.«
2) »Can you point to your elbow?«
3) When the child knows the name, point to the elbow: »What is this?« The child answers »elbow«.
4) »How can you move your elbow?« The child straightens and bends and learns the words »stretch« – »bend« used for corresponding movements.
5) »Shut your eyes. Now, is your elbow stretched or bent?« (kinesthetic sense).
6) »When do you bend your elbow? (For eating, drinking, combing your hair.) When do you stretch your elbow? (Pushing, reaching, throwing.)«

Day by day go over all the joints of the body in this way carefully, one at a time and with many repetitions. Through this is acquired coordination of sight, touch, kinesthetic sense and speech, and *the child's brain function is developed* in the above-named areas.

A large mirror, where the child can see his whole figure, provides greater body knowledge.

To reinforce the child's memory, illustrate everything as clearly as possible. E.g.:

A box has a lid, to shut the box. You also have a lid, to shut your eye, it is called an eyelid,

Names that contain the words »over« and »under« may be hard for the child to understand. It helps if the words are learned through movement, kinesthetically: crawl over the table, crawl under the table.

In the same way practice the following:

Head: Face, eyes, eyebrows, eyelashes, eyelids, cheek, chin, mouth, lip, tooth, tongue, palate, forehead, ear, hair.
Neck: Nape.
Trunk: Chest, stomach, navel, hip, back, loin, rib, buttocks, penis.
Arm: Shoulder, elbow, wrist, upper arm, forearm, hand, palm (fingers, see page 98).
Leg: Hip joint, thigh, calf, knee, foot, foot joint, ankle, sole, toes.

The back of the body

It is difficult for a retarded child to be aware of the back of the body, because he cannot see it. Several senses must be systematically employed to train the back muscles and the hip-extensors. To swing one leg backwards with the knee straight, as is required in running, and, to a lesser degree, also in ordinary walking, is a movement that is only possible fairly late in development (see Walking, pages 28 and 128).

Fig. 41. Where did the hoop touch you? (normal child).

Buttocks and thighs (the extensors of the hip):

The child lies on his stomach on the floor. The adult lays his hand on each of the child's buttocks to stimulate muscle contraction (sence of touch).

1) Press your buttocks together – relax. Repeat several times, first with and afterwards without pressing with the hands (kinesthetic sense).
2) Turn your head and look at your leg. Lift it up towards the ceiling (sight). Repeat many times with one leg at a time.
3) The adult lays a firm hand at the back of one thigh. Lift the leg. Then do it without hand pressure (kinesthetic sense). Keep the hips on the floor (Fig. 42).
4) What did you do? (Ability to visualize and speech).

The back

A similar proceeding in the case of the back, but, as this is harder because the child cannot see his back, exercise the legs first. Perhaps show the child his back, with the help of two mirrors, before the exercise begins.

Lying on the stomach. The arms can be placed as the child wishes, along his sides or stretched out like an airplane. The adult lays a hand over the child's lumbar region. The legs are fixed under a bar or the like and the child tries to lift his body. When the child perceives his back there is a chance that the muscles will become more active, and little by little it should be possible for the child to, e.g.:

run with long strides,
make a running jump over a wide ditch, with one leg stretched forwards and the other stretched way back.

Finger awareness

Teaching children a finger rhyme while pointing to the fingers is not always sufficient.

A logical explanation is needed to assist the memory.

It is easiest to learn the names of the fingers in this order:

Little finger: it is little, it is the smallest.
Middle finger: It is the one in the middle.
Thumb.
Index finger: The one you point with.
Ring finger: On which a wedding ring is worn.

When a child knows his own fingers well, let him try on someone else. This is always a little harder.

Knowing the toes

Take your shoes and socks off.

You have five toes on each foot, count them. This requires that the child can count to 5. If not, only mention the big and little toe.

At a later time, when the child knows the ordinal numbers, talk about:

First toe = big toe.
second toe,
third toe,

Fig. 42. Stretching the leg backwards. Hip should not be lifted (normal child).

fourth toe,

fifth toe = little toe.

Proceed as for fingers.

Other exercises

To give the child a feeling of the body's size, place two children – of different sizes – in front of a large mirror.

Two children each lie on a piece of paper on the floor. Two other children trace around the prostrate children. Compare the drawings after the children have gotten up.

On a drawing showing the outline of a face, let the child place eyes, nose and mouth in the right places.

A hula-hoop is held upright at a suitable level for the child to crawl, walk or jump through. Where did the hoop touch you? (Hair, foot, shoulder, etc.)

If the child does not touch the hoop, cheat a bit, so it does happen (Fig. 41).

Hand dominance, laterality and right/left discrimination

Laterality (latus = side) is an inner feeling that the body has two sides, that there are two halves of the body and that these are not exactly the same.
The dominant hand: The best developed and most used (dominare: to control, to rule).
Right/left confusion: Uncertainty in discriminating right and left (confusio: mixing up).
Discriminate = distinguish, make a difference.

The normal child

Because the parts of the brain that control the right-hand side of the body are actually located on the left-hand side of the brain, a right-hand dominance will correspond to a left-sided brain dominance, and vice versa.

Some investigators think that there is an inborn, inherited disposition for a definite dominance. Others think that most people are right-handed because they live in a right-handed world. Unconscious imitation of parents can perhaps also play a part, so that cerebral dominance could be a result of, rather than a cause of, hand dominance. The matter is still open to question. The newborn infant has no hand dominance, but uses his hands at random until he is about a year old. Then the dominant hand will begin to cross over and take an object that is lying on the opposite side.

The hand that is best from the motor standpoint, and the easiest to maneuver with, will be the dominant one, unless there is paralysis.

To be able to perceive laterality, that the two sides of the body are not quite the same, and that one hand is used more easily than the other, is the beginning of right-left discrimination.

The child is only able to recognize right and left and to distinguish between the two sides with certainty at 6-7 years of age. Children in institutions usually learn it later, as they are not made to notice it so much as children living at home.

How important it is to know the difference between right and left can be illustrated by a few examples:

The teacher must know with which hand the child should write.

The child should be able to understand instructions as: »the second road on the right« and »the scissors are on the left in the drawer«.

Left-handed

Left-handed people usually find it harder than right-handed people to distinguish between right and left. There are more difficulties to overcome; for example, it confuses a child to be told to »shake hands« with his non-dominant hand. When writing, it causes difficulties to have to begin at the top left-hand corner of the paper and write from left to right (see Writing, page 173). In the beginning, the left-handed child needs much understanding and patience on the part of the adults.

About 7% of all normal children are left-handed.

Relation to motor ability and to various senses.

The child must first have acquired some body awareness before hand dominance and laterality can develop.

Laterality is experienced chiefly with the help of the kinesthetic sense reinforced by sight. This leads to the child's distinguishing right and left within himself.

Finally, awareness of laterality and right-left discrimination will help in perceiving body movements in space and time.

The retarded child

The retarded child learns later than the normal child to tell right from left, especially if the most suitable time for learning it has passed. This point in time varies with the individual, depending on intelligence and the extent of any brain-damage. Many trainable subnormal children never develop a clear dominance.

Even if the right time has been passed, practically all educable subnormal children will learn to distinguish right from left in themselves by round-about methods. E.g.:

You shake hands with your right hand.

You write with your right hand.

You have your wristwatch on the left wrist, etc.

The child thus acquires a sort of intellectual knowledge, but has no feeling of laterality.

The frequency of left-handedness is about 13% among educable subnormals.

Lacking hand dominance and awareness of laterality, the child often finds it hard to cope with traffic, has difficulty in writing, and has an incomplete conception of direction and space.

Vocabulary

In relation to hand dominance and laterality, the child must learn the words: half, side, two, the one, the other, right, left, both, etc.

Training of laterality and right-left discrimination

Several methods can be used with retarded children to prepare them for learning to write. Experience has shown that the following procedures produce good results.

I. The child has neither dominance nor awareness of laterality.

a) Two-sided movements:

The child lies on his back on the floor with a little cushion under his head, so that he can see what is going on. He puts his arms at his sides.

»Now I am drawing a line right through your middle, through your nose, navel and legs (a skipping rope can be laid over the child to represent the line).

How many pieces are you divided into?

Do you think the two parts are the same size?«

Afterwards play in this way:

Both arms are moved out sideways and then in again.

Both legs perform the same movement.

All four limbs move out and then in.

If the child finds it hard to perform the movements, the adult can help at first by touching the child's arms or legs (tactile). The next degree of difficulty is to point to the arms or legs (visual). The hardest is to perform the movements with the eyes shut, but this gives the child the strongest sense of making a movement (kinesthetic sense).

b) One-sided movements:

Move out – in. Only one arm or leg, alternately.

The exercise is made a little harder by asking him to move the arm and leg on one side simultaneously.

At the beginning there is often some movement on the non-involved side, too, but this will disappear if and when the child's motor ability improves. Do not try to hold the leg (or arm) still.

Until the words right/left can be understood, the adult can stand by the child's side and say »the arm on this side«. This is preferable to saying »near the door«, »on the window side«.

The exercise can be performed on another plane, by lifting the arms or legs one at a time upwards instead of out to the sides.

II. The child has shown hand dominance.

When the child himself begins to prefer one hand to the other, it will be advisable to investigate this more closely. There are many tests of dominance, e.g.:

Comb your hair,

Hammer in a nail,

Cut with scissors,
Draw, paint,
Throw a small ball.

Whether the right or left hand is dominant can also be seen by the development of grasp (see page 38). The hand which has the most advanced grasp can be considered to be the dominant one.

Daily observation of the child will reveal whether the child is right- or left-handed. It is important to make sure of this as quickly as the central nervous system will allow, and before the child learns to write.

With a retarded child it may take months before dominance is definitely established. The dominance is reinforced by, for example, placing all toys by the dominant hand or by playing ball only with this hand.

At the same time continue the »in-out« game in a slightly harder form. Again lay the skipping rope so that it divides the child into two parts. »All of you that is on this side of the rope is your right side«, using the word »right« for the first time (or left).

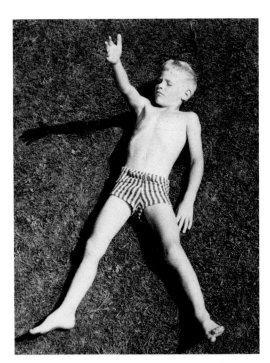

Fig. 43. A normal boy with quick reactions. Training laterality.

Until the dominance is sure, work only with the dominant side, e.g.:

Put your right arm out to the side and in again.
Put your right leg out – in.
Right arm and right leg out – in.
Right arm out and right leg up.
Repeat with eyes shut.
Afterwards, the child may sit up, so that he can see his whole body.
Show me your right shoulder, your right knee, etc.

Do not use the word »left«. It is advisable to advance slowly. Practice for a few minutes every day, half in play, and only when the child is willing.

When hand-dominance is quite established, by means of these exercises and many other small devices employed during the day, again work with both sides, and introduce the word »left«.

Finally, perhaps after many months, the child should be able to perform the following exercises.

Lying on the back: Right arm up and left leg to the side (Fig. 43).
What is this? (Left shoulder, right heel, etc.)
Point to your left cheek.
Move your left leg sideways, and turn your head to the right.

If you ask a child who has been trained in this way, which is his right arm, he will be able to say without hesitation. If you ask the child how he knows it, he will answer something like: »I don't know how, but it **is** the right«.

The child has come to perceive laterality and through this has fixed his dominance. He has also learned to distinguish right and left in his own body.

To distinguish right/left outside his own person

When the child is quite sure of right and left in himself, and he seems mature enough to progress further, the following kinds of things can be added to his daily activities:

Hang your coat in the left-hand closet.
Fetch the hammer that is hanging on top at the right, etc.

It may be pointed out to the child that right/-left still are in relation to himself, when he is standing in front of, e.g., a closet. Where is your right arm? The right side of the closet is on the same side.

It is a much more complicated task to find out whether the plate is on the left or the right of the cup, when the child himself is standing on the opposite side of the table.

To distinguish right/left on another person

The last and most difficult step which the educable subnormal child can learn by this method (but severely subnormals rather seldom) is to identify right and left on another person. The child must be taught that this is always in relation to the other person, not to the child himself. For example, the teacher stands with his back to the child.

Stretch out your right arm.

Take my right arm out with yours.
Now keep hold of my right hand with your right hand, while I turn around and face you. Where is my right hand now?
It is important always to give the child plenty of time to think.
To keep all this going, it is essential that the teacher as well as all the others who deal with the child really do use the words learned and do not say: »the arm nearest the window«.

Exercises

Hold a hula-hoop upright, a little above the floor.

The child crawls through it and if the hoop touches him, he says where it touches. Right heel, left ear, right knee, etc. (see Fig. 41).

»Signal-play« often amuses a child. He has to try to imitate various positions of the adult's arms. The signals should change as quickly as possible. Before the child has developed hand dominance, if the teacher stands in front of him, he will copy the movements as in a mirror. Later when he has developed further he will use his right arm when the teacher does (in this exercise, using a mirror would be confusing).

Investigation: right/left confusion in the educable subnormal child

An investigation (Gamle Bakkehus) during the school year 1965/66 gave the following figures: Did not know right from left:

	in himself		in others	
	1965	1966	1965	1966
20 children 9-12 years	14	2	20	17
84 children 12-18 years	28	5	50	20
104	42	7	70	37

35 children learned to distinguish right from left in themselves in the course of the 9 months.

33 children learned to distinguish right from left on another person. No attempt was made to teach the 20 youngest children this, but 3 learned by the example of others.

20 of the older children did not learn it, and this was no doubt because the right time for learning had already passed.

Perception of direction

The normal child

Even in the cradle the baby receives directional stimuli. Light comes from the window, but his mother comes in through the door on the other side. Or, the telephone rings in one corner, and the radio plays in another.

Later the child turns his head in all directions towards sounds, and when he can sit on the floor without falling over, he reaches for his toys in all directions.

In the crawling stage the child has a more conscious sense of direction, which is stimulated by a desire to investigate all his surroundings.

Walking gradually becomes directed and motivated because the child wants to get to a definite place.

At first the child thinks of directions with himself at the center. Later in development he can perceive direction between two objects, e.g.:

The toy car runs from child to mother.

The toy car runs from mother to child.

The toy car runs from the doll to the garage.

The directional movements later become more finely coordinated. When the child is learning to eat with a spoon, the contents will slip off the spoon until he learns to turn it correctly, and scribbling little by little develops into strokes made in certain directions and eventually into drawings.

The child can use directional words correctly in his speech by 3 years of age, e.g. up, down, forewards, backwards, sideways.

The child must know in what direction to read, before he can learn to read and write. Perception of direction is necessary to see the difference between »b«, »d« and »p«, that is, to see if the stroke in the letter goes above or below the line, or if the curve turns towards the right or the left. Furthermore, written letters should go in the same direction and follow a line.

To perceive direction is one of the prerequisites for finding the way in traffic, or on a walk, as well as for knowing the compass points and learning geography.

Relation to motor ability and to various senses
E.g.:

Hearing: The child hears a bell ring.

Sight: He looks towards the bell.

Kinesthetic sense: The child goes towards the bell and reaches out with his arms.

Touch: The child holds the bell.

The labyrinthine sense helps to register changes of direction.

Form concept is based partly on perception of direction and space. A triangle consists of three lines, each of which has its own direction. They enclose a form.

The retarded child

The retarded child can be encouraged to crawl on the floor, regardless of his age in order to be aware of all directions between himself and the toys, which are spread around on all sides. Walking in a given direction can be encouraged by asking him to fetch something from the closet or to carry something into another room.

In this training concentrate first on the center – the child himself. His body awareness, dominance and laterality must be built up, before he can perceive directions outside himself.

Vocabulary

It is an important part of the training that the child learn to use and understand the words that are related to the idea of direction. Kinesthetic sense is an important factor here, because words learned through movement are often remembered better than words learned otherwise, e.g.:

Up – down: Go upstairs – go downstairs. Put the book up on the shelf – put it down on the floor.

Out – in: Pull the drawer out – push it in. Put out your tongue – pull it in.

To the side: Stretch your arms to the side. Put your tongue out to one side.

Sideways: Go sideways on the beam.

Straight – slanting (sloping): Creep up the sloping plank. Lay the ruler straight on the table – slant it.

Forward – backward: Walk one step forward – one step backward.

Simon says: (»Mother may I?«)

Exercises

Reach for toys from different places.

When the child can sit by himself on the floor, place toys all around him.

Play with a ball, rolling it slowly, so that the eyes can follow it, from mother to child and back again. Increase the speed.

When the child can crawl, give him plenty of opportunities to do so.

Later in development (including vocabulary):

Spread many small paper flags on the table. Lay all the flags so that they point in the same direction.

The teacher draws a row of horseshoes turned in different directions and the child tells the direction of the opening.

The teacher lays a book in front of the child's feet: Jump with feet together onto the book, to the side of it, in front of it, behind it.

Walk one step forwards, backwards, to the right, backwards, to the left (give the orders as quickly as possible).

Shut your eyes and point to the window, door, table.

Draw on the blackboard: a straight line downwards (10-15 cm) and continue to the left, down, to the right, up, slanting down to the right, etc.

Go around the corner, to the baker's, back to school.

Draw a horizontal line (a large glass bowl half full of water is used to demonstrate that the surface of the water always remains horizontal, whether the bowl is held level or is tipped to one side or the other).

Hold a stick horizontally.

Draw a vertical line on the blackboard.

Hold the stick vertically (a plumb-line shows the direction).

Perception of space

The normal child

Perception of space means understanding an object's dimensions and place in space. So it concerns

estimating distance, and

estimating size (dimensions),

that is, the child's understanding of the three-dimensional space he himself moves in – from the room he is in, to the idea of outer space.

With regard to estimating the distance from nearer objects, see the chapter on visual estimation of distance, page 72.

In estimating the distance from objects which are far away, experience plays a large part. Distance is judged by how big a familiar object seems to be, and this is influenced by lighting and atmosphere.

Some examples of space perception:

An infant learns to know the size of his own body by looking at his limbs (visual) and by putting his fingers and toes in his mouth (tactile and kinesthetic). Later he realizes that adults are bigger than he is.

When the child can sit safely and lean and turn to all sides, he gets experience of the space near him and of the objects that he can reach from a sitting position.

Soon the child begins to crawl around on the floor, under chairs and tables, and he thus gets an idea of how much space his body takes up. He also learns that it is further to the ball than to the doll, for example, and later in development he realizes the distance between objects.

He widens his experience when he begins to crawl around all over the house. The child goes exploring, examines all objects and thus gains experience regarding their comparative size and position in the room.

At 15 months the child understands where an object was first placed, and where it disappears to when it moves out of sight, e.g. when a ball rolls under a sofa.

Many words, related to space perception, can be understood and used correctly by the 3-year-old, e.g.: in, on, under, over.

The child still has difficulty in comprehending more than one dimension, e.g. he can perceive length or width, but not both at the same time. It is as if he cannot take in both at once, cannot see the whole.

When shown two objects of different sizes the 4-year-old will say that one is big, the other is little, for he has not yet mastered comparison. Only towards the 5th year, depending on speech development, can adjectives be compared, and the child can judge one object as the biggest.

Perception of space is a requisite for finding one's way at home, in the street, in the gymnasium, in fields or woods; in short, coping with most of life's situations usually requires both motor ability and space perception, e.g.:

How far must my arm stretch out to reach the cup?

How much must I bend my knees and my back to crawl under a fence?

How hard must I jump to get over the ditch?

Can I get across the road before the car comes?

Perception of space is also necessary for using measurements and for judging volumes, etc. For example:

There is almost $1/2$ liter of milk left.

The tape is about 70 cm long.

When writing, all letters of the same type should be the same height and width.

Awareness of space is also a preparation for being able to learn geography and geometry and for gaining an idea of the universe.

Relation to motor ability and to various senses

To have body awareness and some sense of laterality and direction is necessary for perceiving something as being apart from oneself, and thus are preconditions for space perception.

Kinesthetic sense: Distances can be judged by movement, since different distances must be traversed to reach different goals.

Time: It takes more time to cover a long distance than a short distance, if the speed is the same.

Sight: The child sees an object, realizes its size and judges the distance to it.

Hearing: Sounds are understood as being near or far.

Touch: If the light goes out, you must feel your way. An object's size can be judged by feeling it.

The retarded child

Concerning perception of space, the retarded child must be stimulated to develop in the same way as described for the normal child.

Vocabulary

In order to understand speech, the child must also know the words that are used to cover the ideas inherent in space perception, e.g.:

Thick–thin: Show a thick and a thin pencil at the same time. Show several other pairs of things in the same way, to get the child to grasp the idea that the words »thick« and »thin« apply to other things, as well as pencils.

Later show two different objects.

Big–little: Play with the big ball first – then with the little one.

Long–short: Your bed is long–the doll's bed is short.

Narrow–wide: The table is wide–the bench is narrow. Crawl over them.

High–low: The table is high–the stool is low, sit down.

In the middle: Lay the hula-hoop on the floor, stand in the middle of it. Stand in the middle of the room. Draw a cross right in the middle of the blackboard. Lie exactly in the middle of the mattress.

Outside: Go outside.

Under–over: Crawl over the table, under the bench.

In: You are in the room. Put the blocks in the box.

Near to: The doll is near to you, take it.

Far away: The tree is far away from you, go to it.

Degrees of comparison should be practiced in step with speech development.

Big–bigger–biggest: three objects of different sizes, at first of the same shape and color, can illustrate this, e.g. 3 chairs, 3 cars, 3 blocks or 3 children.

Afterwards: The block is big, the toy car is bigger but the chair is the biggest.

At first use objects of very different sizes, later use finer gradations.

Nearest: Which house is nearest?

Exercises

The young child

How big are you? The child stretches his arms up and looks at them.

At the crawling stage the child should be allowed to move around the whole house, to go out into the kitchen, and to investigate the size and position of everything.

The older child

Mark the child's height on the wall. Compare the heights of two children.

Two children lie on the floor. Two other children trace their outlines, after which they get up. Look at the drawings. Who is the longest? Who is broadest?

Sit on the ground and draw a circle around yourself without moving from your place. How far can you reach? How big is the circle?

Notice the size of all objects present.

The relative size of objects.

Almost anything can be used. Spoons, forks, dolls, toy cars, stones, tree leaves, coins, nails, etc.

1) Sorting the objects. The same size.

   Take all the toy cars that are the same size.

   Find all the nails that are the same size.

2) Distinguish size. Two objects or persons.

   Which car is big?

   Who is the biggest, Peter or John?

3) Distinguish size. Three or more objects.

   Which block is the biggest? (Comparative adjectives come in here.)

   The Montessori long stair or similar material lies spread out on the floor:

   Which rod is the longest? Which is the shortest?

   Sorting four rods according to length.

   Sorting ten rods according to length.

Distances. The child as center:
The infant.

Put toys on the floor at different distances from the child.

Get the child to notice near and far sounds.

The ball lies beside the child, but suddenly it rolls under the bed.

The older child.

Which door are you nearest to?

Which of the other children is furthest from you?

Is the bakery further away than the grocery store?

Distance between objects.

Is Peter nearer to the doll or to the ball?

Which tree is nearest to the bench?

Draw a »ditch« on the floor. Can you jump over it?

Increase the distance between the lines. Can you jump over the ditch now?

Take a good look at the room, blindfold your eyes and walk around carefully. Feel your way to the window, closet, table, etc.

Jump over a rope, which starts by being 5 cm off the floor and later is raised a little more. Don't jump higher than you need to.

A stick is held at the height of the child's shoulder: Go under it without touching the stick.

Then hold the stick level with the hips and finally at knee height. The child must understand that he has to bend just enough not to touch the stick.

In this way the child learns to judge the size of his own body.

Concept of time

The normal child

The child realizes little by little that the course of an action takes a period of time, and that several happenings do not occur simultaneously, e.g.:

The infant cries, but it takes a certain amount of time before the mother picks him up.

The child crawls more quickly or more slowly according to how strongly motivated he is to reach his destination.

The child is fed first, and afterwards put to bed.

(See further examples under Vocabulary.)

Relation to motor ability and to various senses

Kinesthetic sense: You will have to walk a long way to get to the station.

Space: It takes longer to go to the bakery, for example, than to the grocery store (distance in terms of time).

Go around the house (dimension in terms of time).

Touch can also have a certain importance. The foot touches the ground repeatedly over a longer period of time and more times if the way is long.

Sight: The trees seem to rush past when the car is moving quickly.

Hearing: The car comes nearer quickly.

The retarded child

Time concept may be difficult for the retarded child.

Vocabulary

For the retarded child to learn to understand distance in terms of time, he must know the words that indicate time, e.g.:

Now: Now you are standing, now you are sitting and now you are walking.

Before: Before dinner. The day before your birthday.

After: After dinner. After school.

A day: From the time you get up until you go to bed.

A night: From the time you go to bed, until you wake. From the time it gets dark until it gets light.

Today: Today we had hamburger for dinner.

Yesterday: Yesterday we went to the movies.

Tomorrow: Tomorrow we'll go to the beach.

A week: Last Sunday you were home, today is Sunday again. It's a week since you were home.

A year: Today is your birthday. Can you remember what you got last birthday? That was a year ago.

Quickly–slowly: Run quickly to me. Go slowly back. Clap your hands quickly–clap slowly.

Walk around the room, keeping time to the drum. Now slowly, now quickly, and now even quicker.

Exercises

Lie on your side on the floor and curl up.
Now stretch out slowly and make yourself
very long.

Very slowly curl up again.

Stretch out quickly. Quickly curl up.

Go around the room at different speeds, but
I should be able to tell whether you are going slowly or quickly.

It often helps a child to understand time if he
can see on a stopwatch how many times the
hand goes around while he performs some
task. A stopwatch can be used for this purpose
if the child has not yet learned to tell time. To
use an ordinary clock with a large second hand
would, of course, be of more educational
value.

Preparation for learning to tell time.

Draw a circle on the blackboard. Divide it
into two equal parts down the middle.

Divide a layer cake into four pieces.

Draw a circle on the floor, and divide it into
four equal parts. Stand in the middle of the
circle, stretch out your arm as a pointer, and
make a complete circle, a half-circle, a
quarter-circle.

Quantity and number concepts

The normal child

Before the child can be expected to learn arithmetic, he must have developed quantity and number concepts.

At about 24 months a child can usually understand the meaning of the words: many–one–none, and a few months later he can place blocks in a row, which is the first step in understanding the cardinal numbers, 1, 2, 3, etc.

The child must learn to sort blocks and other objects according to size, color and shape.

When children are about 3 years old, their number concept usually goes up to 3, and at 4 years they know 4 as well. This does not mean that they can do arithmetic with the numbers, only that they know what each number means in terms of practical applications.

It may be mentioned that, even if a child can perhaps count up to 10, this does not mean that he understands the idea of all ten numbers, or that his number concept goes up to 10.

He must be able to move – to skip, clap, bounce a ball – a certain number of times, and should be motivated to count everything in his surroundings; cars, dogs, birds.

At about 5-6 years of age the child generally knows the number symbols 1–10, and at about 6-7 years he can write these numbers and has learned the first few ordinal numbers; first, second, third . . .

Relation to motor ability and to various senses

For understanding quantity and numbers, several senses are useful. A few examples:
Kinesthetic sense: The child jumps four times.
Sight: The child sees 3 cars.
Hearing: The clock strikes twice.
Touch: The child feels the big and the little ball, two balls.

Perfection

Examples of people who have acquired a well-developed number concept are mathematicians, statisticians and engineers.

The retarded child

If the child has no number concept, he must first acquire a concept of quantity. This should be taught as concretely and practically as possible, beginning at a very low level. For this, use things familiar to the child, such as toys, etc., and later use more abstract materials.

Vocabulary

Many words necessary for quantity and number concepts are mentioned under Exercises. Other examples: less, same, more, first, last, after, next, some, all, none, few.

Quantity concept (see footnote)

Big–little: A big mound of sand and a little mound of sand. Touch both of them and pat them.

As big as–the same as: Now put so much sand on the little pile that the two piles are as big as each other; they are the same size.

Big–little. A big mound of sand and a little mound of sand. Touch both of them and pat them.

As big as–the same as: Now put so much sand on the little pile that the two piles are as big as each other; they are the same size.

Many-one-none: there are many candies in the bag. Each child gets one candy, now there are none left.

Same-different: The two balls are the same (shape, size, color). The little red ball and the big blue ball are not the same, they are different.

Some-all: You may have some of the marbles, but not all of them.

Little-much: You can only have a little of the cake, so don't take much.

Number concept

The retarded child must learn to understand numbers, one at a time, and this number must not be connected with special things or a special shape, e.g.:

Learning the number 1:

Get out 1 plate, 1 cup, 1 saucer, 1 spoon and 1 glass.

The number must not be connected with a special color or particular dimensions.

Take 1 little red car, 1 big blue ball and 1 green block.

Take 1 long black stick and 1 short white stick.

The object's position, in itself and in relation to the child, must not be involved.

1 doll sits facing the child and 1 lies with its face turned away.

Here we are still only dealing with the number

1 (one). It must also be understood tactually and kinesthetically, e.g.:

Cut out several shapes and paste them on to a piece of paper. 1 triangle, 1 circle, 1 egg.

Draw 1 big red circle on the blackboard and 1 little blue square.

Number symbols:

The figure 1 can be learned in several ways, as for example:

Repeat the above exercises, laying the figure 1 beside each object, e.g.:

The child draws one shape and writes 1 beside it.

The child takes one object and lays figure 1 beside it.

The number 2:

E.g.:

1 red car and 1 blue car makes 2 cars.

Take off your shoes. You have 2 shoes.

Take off your socks. There are 2 socks and 2 legs.

Disregard shape, color, dimension and position, as in teaching number 1.

The child should also be able to abstract from the two objects' positions and movements, e.g.:

Put 2 cars beside each other and lay the figure 2 beside them.

Get 2 cars, one in front of the other, and lay the figure 2 beside them.

Get 2 cars, one on top of the other, and lay the figure 2 beside them.

2 cars run around in different directions.

In the same way teach 3, 4, etc.

To count

If the child has difficulty in counting, introduce it step by step.

For example, the child is asked to count 4 blocks which are lying on the table. First put the blocks in a row, because random placement makes the task more difficult.

1) The child picks up each block as he counts.

2) The child touches lightly.

3) The child points.

4) The child only looks.

The principle and some of the examples are taken from A. Brauner's film.

The cardinals 1, 2, 3, 4, 5, 6 . . . are learned first. Count everything; dolls, blocks, cars, flowers, etc., for practice.

The ordinals must also be mastered before arithmetic can be begun. Divide the toys into groups, e.g.:

In the first group put all the round blocks, in the second group the square ones, and in the third group the triangles.

The child must somehow experience the meaning of all the numbers, cardinals as well as ordinals.

When the child understands that figure 1 corresponds to **one** object, this understanding transfers gradually to easy sums, at a developmental age of about 5. E.g.:

The child has 5 coins and buys one candy for each coin = 5 pieces of candy.

Exercises

Each child fetches 1 ball.

Fetch 3 balls.

Count how many times I clap. Clap the same number of times.

2 children go to the beam, and 3 to the wall-bar.

Crawl on all fours.

Balance on 3 points (two legs and one arm).

Balance on 2 points (different ways).

Simon says (»Mother may I?«)

Crawl up the wall-bar and stand on the 5th bar.

Throw your ball at the wall 6 times.

Go 2 steps forward and then 2 more = 4.

Go 3 steps forward and 2 back (subtraction).

Skip 30 times.

Play dice.

Concentration

To be able to concentrate means:
> to be able to direct the attention towards something for a considerable time,
> to be able to finish something before attention wanders to something else,
> not to let oneself be distracted by changing, less important stimuli from the surroundings.

This requires, on the whole, a certain maturity: The relevant senses must be intact, especially sight and hearing.

Perceptual development must have reached a certain stage and the psyche must naturally harmonize with the child's general development, that is:
> the child must feel well,
> he must be motivated for the task,
> and not be bored by what he is expected to pay attention to. The task should therefore not be too easy, but do not overestimate the child's ability, or he may fail to perform the task.

The child's mentality may be the greatest obstacle to concentration, and therefore a psychiatrist and possibly a psychologist should be consulted if there are serious behavioral problems.

If the child is hyperactive, some authors advise arranging a little »office« for the child. This does not need to be an enclosed room, but can be done perhaps by turning the child's desk so that he is facing the wall. Unwanted stimuli from the surroundings are thus less distracting. This arrangement should not be understood as a punishment, but as helping the child and giving him more peace.

This method has been much criticized. It is my impression that the attitude of the teacher determines the success or failure of this method.

To teach this type of child in a classroom where the whole of one wall is a window, so that the child's attention is attracted by everyone who goes by outside, is just as deplorable for the teacher as for the child.

In many cases of poor concentration, it is poor sensory and motor development which is the primary cause, and the mental difficulties are secondary. Herewith a few remarks on such cases.

Causes of poor concentration

The normal and the retarded child

Some children are hyperactive, restless, easily distracted and greatly lacking in concentration and endurance compared with their general development. It is difficult to hold these children's attention for more than a moment at a time.

First it is necessary to find the reason for this condition, and there are many possibilities. Apart from the psychological causes, which this book does not cover, we may suspect the following:

Eye fixation
If the eyes wander restlessly, this will make visual perception very difficult. Before a thing has been viewed properly, the eyes start looking at something else, which distracts from comprehension of the first item (here it is not a question of nystagmus, but rather of large, uncoordinated movements).

Accommodation
In schoolwork and all close work the child will not see well if the accommodation reflex is not fully developed (see Sight, page 65). The child will give up concentrating on his task.

Visual acuity. Binocular vision
If something is seen indistinctly, the child can lose interest in the task right from the beginning. Talk to an oculist, if you suspect this (see Sight, page 66).

Shape and color recognition
If the child cannot distinguish form and color sufficiently well, picture books and much else will be incomprehensible and of little interest.

Figure-ground discrimination
Being unable to discriminate figures from their background can cause the child to be unable to select from the many stimuli which he receives constantly those which are important for the moment.

Auditory perception
Auditory perception can be lacking or late in developing.

Vocabulary
Vocabulary plays a large part. If the child cannot take in or understand the words connected with his task, he must give up.

Eye-hand coordination
If movement is required to perform a task, consider the child's motor development. If the task is too hard, he will give up.

Concentration training

Concentration training, or rather treatment, as will be described here, has the whole of this book as preparation. It is, however, the method of this training that is special, and which makes it concentration training and an effective help in making the child function at his level of intelligence.

Treatment should be undertaken only on the advice of a doctor, possibly in cooperation with a psychologist, and should be carried out by a specially trained psychologist, physical therapist, occupational therapist or educationalist.

The method needs a certain level of development in the child and is therefore most suited to normal children who have, for example, learning difficulties in school or for the slightly retarded, including the educable subnormal, but it can be modified for the severely subnormal.

Cooperation with the child's teacher will be an advantage in the treatment, which seldom needs to last for long. Twice a week for 2–6 months will have an effect also in many of the cases where the child's perceptual and/or motor difficulties have had a slight neurotic overtone.

It is best to begin individually in order to get to know each individual child and his reactions.

Later it is an advantage to collect small groups – as small as possible. To have to attend to the lesson and at the same time notice the others in the group, may be very difficult for the child; on the other hand, this is important for his social development.

The therapist's first task is to examine the child to estimate his level of sensory – motor development (see page 183) and through this to find the reasons for his lack of concentration.

The training consists in exercising attention and concentration.

1) Attention

The child must become accustomed to »listening« and to »seeing«, that is, to perceiving auditorily and visually.

The child only perceives what he attends to; for example, he does not hear if he does not listen.

On the other hand, the child cannot be expected to be interested in something he does not understand.

Stimulation should be given only when the child will be receptive to it, otherwise he will react dully to any stimuli that are tried. He must first be brought into a receptive condition; he must expect something to happen, so that he will »listen« and »see«.

Every lesson begins with something that immediately catches the child's attention. Everytime, think up a new idea for this purpose and change among the different senses with regard to the individual child, for example:

Take the child on your lap.

Take him kindly by the hand.

See, I have a black spot on my nose. Will you wipe it off?

What do you think is in this nice parcel?

Shut your eyes and listen. Did you hear what it was I dropped on the floor?

Or:

The material which you are going to use in the first exercise is put in the middle of the table, but covered over, so that the child becomes curious.

2) Concentration

When the child has learned to pay attention to what is going to happen, the next step is to keep his attention on the task.

The purpose of the exercises is that

the brain should continually be quickly functioning to receive and perceive stimuli and thereafter to translate them into action.

Later the child is stimulated to let each single action last longer and longer. Here it concerns all the small actions and tasks the child must master in order to keep up with his classmates in nursery school or school.

The duration of each exercise. No pauses:

In the same moment that the therapist notices that the child's interest in a task is diminishing, she should change to the next task without a pause, to prevent the child from being distracted by other, irrelevant, stimuli. Duration as well as difficulty of the tasks should be adapted to the child's level of development.

Each exercise or task is gradually »stretched« to last as long as the child is able to give it his full attention. Here we should warn against letting the child begin on one of his hobbies and continuing with it.

The exercises must be so varied that the child does not lose interest. Therefore the same exercise must not always be repeated at each lesson or, in any case, not in the same order. The child should be trained to take an interest in what will happen next, to consider and react to new and unexpected impulses.

Gradually the child will be able to occupy himself with the same task for longer periods each time, while the task is made more difficult, until at last he acquires the concentration which is required of a normal child at the same developmental age.

Duration of lessons. Mental fatigue:

The child must at no time feel stress, the speed must suit the individual and the treatment must take place in a cheerful atmosphere, so that solving the problem is a kind of sport for the child, and he is amused by it.

The duration of the lesson depends entirely on each child's ability. In the beginning it is advisable to take at most 15 minutes and to proceed slowly.

The idea is to continue almost to the point of fatigue. If the child cooperates well during a lesson of 30–40 minutes he will be tired mentally – and that is the purpose. The child must learn to concentrate more than he could do, or liked to do, when he was less advanced.

If the child gets tired unusually quickly, introduce ball play, skipping, etc., partly to give the child scope for his need for locomotion, and partly to increase the blood circulation, so that the brain can function better. These physically active exercises can be used profitably for a few minutes at the beginning of the lesson and can be repeated when about two-thirds of the lesson is over.

Concentration can be practiced by:
   a) Uncomplicated stimuli of one sense, and afterwards with
   b) stimulation of several senses at once, and finally, at a later stage, by
   c) exercises of a more intellectual nature such as writing, simple addition, etc.

The exercises given in this book can all be used according to the child's stage of development. Rhythmic exercises varied with non-rhythmic, sensory with motor, writing with easy additions, balance exercises and many others can be interwoven. The whole should be quickly changing, but without hurry.

Rhythmic exercises:

To listen and at the same time move in time to a given rhythm is an important element in this treatment.

The child must attend carefully to the changing rhythms, and at the same time he should listen to or look for changing commands.

The principle is that the rhythm should be played so softly that the child is forced to make an effort to hear it. Likewise no sharp, high sounds like a whistle or shrill voice should be used. The child should learn to listen.

The treatment makes demands on the child, and also on the therapist, who, as well as thinking up exercises, must, at the same time, observe the child and share his thoughts. Furthermore, the different kinds of exercises and tasks must have been chosen in advance, on the basis of the results of previous tests and examinations (see page 183).

III. Motor skills seen in relation to perception

Dressing, undressing and personal hygiene

The retarded child

If a child is to become independent, one of the most important requirements is that his hand movements are sufficiently developed, so that he can, for example, hold the soap, dry himself with a towel, and hold on to his stockings when they are to be pulled on or off.

In addition, the child should know his own body: hands, feet, behind, etc., visually and also tactually and kinesthetically.

He should know the names of the parts of the body, as well as all the words that have special reference to dressing and cleanliness, such as:

Temperature: hot, cold, lukewarm.

Smell: soap, urine, sweat, perfume.

Direction: out-in, up-down, and later: right side - wrong side, right-left, front-back.

Space: in front of, behind, through.

Names of garments and words such as: ribbon, knot, sponge, cloth, handkerchief, brush, button, draw, push, tie, etc.

At first the child should be placed where he can see what is happening when a grown-up is helping him. Afterwards he should try for himself. If he is allowed to dress and undress himself, even if it takes longer, this makes an important contribution to the child's feeling of his own capability, and it makes for self-respect.

As touch and kinesthetic sense become more developed, sight is not so important in the process. But it may be a good idea to glance at the mirror at the end.

It reinforces the child's learning if he is shown in detail, for example:

how the hands move when washing and drying them,

how to hold a brush or comb,

how to brush and comb hair,

how the toothbrush is held and used,

which way round to put on a shirt.

Clothes should be simple as long as the child has difficulty in handling them. E. g. there should be no buttons or zippers at the back, no laces or small buttons, and no clothes which are too tight or which are hard to put on or take off.

Playing with dolls helps the understanding and knowledge of these skills.

For older children and teen-agers the tasks become more demanding, and vocabulary grows along with the skills. To name a few:

Run the bathwater and bathe yourself.

Wash your hair.

Cope with puberty and menstrual periods.

Clean your nails. First hands, then feet.

Wash your own clothes.

Iron your own clothes.

Mend your own clothes.

Clean off stains.

Brush your shoes, wash your rubber boots.

Take your shoes to be repaired.

Put on make-up.

Shave yourself.

Cut and file your nails.

Use nail polish and change it regularly.
Pack a suitcase with everything you need.
Change underwear and stockings regularly.
Use deodorant.
Buy new clothes and know your size (size of shoes, dresses).
Choose the right clothes for different weather and changing temperatures.
Clean the wash-basin and bathtub when finished, etc.

(See also page 89: Surface texture).

Balance

The normal child

The ability to balance is related mainly to the labyrinthine senses and to the cerebellum, but many other factors enter in.

Cerebellum (little brain)

Cerebellum controls the coordination of all movements and thus has great influence on balance in general.

The labyrinthine senses (vestibular reaction)

The labyrinth is situated in the inner ear and from it originate several reflexes which partly influence the muscle tone and postural reflexes in the whole body (see page 10) and partly serve to orient the movements of the head and thus register changes in direction and speed.

The labyrinth is connected with the motor nerve cells of the eye muscles, and therefore there is some interplay between equilibrium and eye movements. This is called the vestibular-reaction or -sense.

Psychological factors

The psychological factors are important in balance training, and it is essential that the child feels secure. He may be assisted by an adult. The beam must be steady and, in the beginning, balance walking should be practiced on a stripe on the floor (or a tape) about 8 cm wide (the width of a foot). The supports of the beam should be shaped in such a way that the plank can be used as required, with either the narrow or the wide side uppermost. The child is led by both hands, so the adult must walk backwards, for in the beginning the child should be able to see that he is being supported. To support with only one hand gives uneven body balance.

Sight

Sight helps to orient the body in space and indicates where the foot can be safely placed to obtain body balance.

The kinesthetic sense

Among other things, kinesthetic sense registers the relative position of the parts of the body and therefore helps to equilibrate all movements.

Sense of touch and kinesthetic sense

The contact of the feet with the ground influences the upright position of the body through certain postural reflexes. Therefore it is preferable to do balance exercises barefoot. In summer, at the beach, balance can be practiced by walking on the sand without shoes.

Balance is also influenced by purely physical factors:

The size of the supporting area

The supporting area of the body is greatest when lying down, less when sitting and least when standing on one foot. So standing or walking with the feet apart gives a larger supporting area than standing with the feet close together. This is why the former position is preferable when working or lifting heavy weights.

The number of supporting points

More supporting points give a larger supporting area and greater stability.

The height of the center of gravity over the supporting area

Gradually, as the child grows, the body's center of gravity becomes higher in relation to the supporting area and balance becomes more difficult.

The shape of the foot

A strong, long and wide foot with movable toes which spread out naturally when walking, gives a good supporting area and in general a steady walk.

A crooked big toe (hallux valgus) or a knuckle protruding too much under the main joint of the big toe (the sesamoid bone) can make balance difficult.

The shape of the foot cannot be altered, but strength and flexibility can be trained and balance thus improved.

Stages in the development of balance in chronological order:

Eye control.
Head balance; lying, sitting.
Body balance when sitting. The falling (Parachute) reflexes develop.
Crawl on the stomach around on the floor,

under chairs and tables.
Crawl on all fours; hands and knees.
Play crawling on four limbs, on three, on two.
Bear-walk on hands and feet.
Get up and stand, with support.
Stand unsupported.
Walk with support.
Walk unsupported.
Jump supported by both hands.
Kick a ball without losing balance.
Jump with the feet together, unsupported (flatfooted).
Go, stop, change direction, vary speed.
Walk on a line 8 cm wide.
Walk on a low 8 cm wide plank.
Springy jump.
Jump over a »ditch«.
Walk on a 6 cm wide plank.
Hop on one leg, the dominant one.
Hop.
Jump over a rope.
Dance.
Hop on the non-dominant leg.
Stand on one leg. Dominant and non-dominant. On the dominant first. (The legs should not touch each other.)

The retarded child

The same conditions prevail in the case of the retarded child.

The program of exercises should be adapted to the individual child, since no phase in the development of a normal child should be omitted. Every step may take months or perhaps years, but experience shows that this is the only possible way.

Exercises
The area of support is diminished, the center of gravity raised, fewer supporting points:

Lie on your stomach and lift your head, supported on your elbows.
Lie on your stomach, lift your head, supported by outstretched arms.
Lie on your back, lift your head, roll over onto your stomach, sit up.

»Push over« exercise. From the sitting or the kneeling position the child is pushed over, so that he learns to save himself with out-stretched arms and hands (Falling reflex).
Crawl on your stomach under the chair and over to the wall.
Crawl on all fours (hands and knees).
Stand on four, on three, on two.
Kneeling down, walk on your knees.
Ordinary walking.
Walk on your heels. Small steps.
Walk on your toes.
Hop on one foot.

Increasing the degree of difficulty of the balance exercises:
Stand on one leg with support – without support. (The legs should not touch each other).
Walk on an 8 cm wide line (the width of a foot).
Walk on a plank laid on the ground.
Walk from one wooden block or brick to another.
Walk on an 8 cm wide plank, 5 cm high.
Walk on a 6 cm wide plank, 15 cm high.
Go sideways (both ways) and backwards on the beam.
Ball play and other exercises while balance walking.

Eye movements and focusing:

Eye movements must be controllable, and the fixation reflex must be developed, or balance is lost. Here one sees reciprocal action. With poor balance, good focusing can help, because the glance quite instinctively is directed to the beam or the line on the floor. On the other hand, good balance will be affected if the eye movements are restless. Here eye fixation may be taught and the child can be shown that the balance exercises will be easier if he tries to fix his eyes on the beam or on a fixed point on the wall. See pages 65 and 199.

Before the child can be expected to »walk the plank«, he must be able to stand on one leg. If the eye movement are restless, it often helps if the child looks at a vertical line (a stripe on the wall), if the glance cannot be fixed on a certain point. If the eyes move sideways, this especially hinders balance.

The grade of difficulty of balance exercises where sight assists can be increased as follows:
Ordinary walking through a room while focusing on a point on the wall.
Walking backwards, still focusing on the point.
Walking on an 8 cm wide stripe, looking all the time at the stripe.
Walking on an 8 cm wide stripe looking at a cross on the wall ($1/2$ meter above the floor).
Walking on an 8 cm wide stripe, looking at a cross at eye level.
Walking on an 8 cm wide stripe, looking around the room while walking.
All these exercises can be repeated on a low 8 cm wide beam.

Before it is possible for a child to balance with arms hanging loosely, he should lift his arms – »like the wings of an airplane«.

The adult should always have a piece of chalk in his pocket. On paths or in the playground, draw a line, a »snail« or hopscotch squares. There is no need to call the children, they come at once and imitate the adult, who, on his way across the playground, walks round the »snail« or hops through the squares.

Changes of direction and speed (Labyrinthine senses)
The child runs around the room to a rhythmic accompaniment. Running quickly at quick rhythms, walking slowly at slow rhythms. Stand still when the music stops. Go-stop-go in different directions; forwards, backwards, to the left, etc., at command.

The child must be able to spin round and to turn a somersault without getting dizzy.

Play

The normal child

A child who develops normally will learn to crawl, walk and run in the course of his first years of life, and this will lay the foundation for the child's further motor development and for the numerous skills which he needs for joining in other children's play and for generally holding his own in daily life. In this connection it must be pointed out that each new movement, each new skill, must be practiced before it can be mastered.

Up to 2 years of age, »play« will mainly consist of sensory-motor development. It may be questioned whether »play« is the right word. To the adult it may look like play, but for the child it is serious; it is a great, exciting work into which he puts all his energy. He practices each skill over and over again until he is quite sure of it and then he begins on new skills.

When the child is 2 or 3 years old, play is still individual. All the same, in this period children can play side by side and enjoy each other's company in this way. However, day nursery and kindergarten children are often seen to communicate and to do things together even at this age, though only for short periods.

At this period, playing with adults plays a large part in the child's development, not least in the development of speech.

After 3 years of age imitative play begins, and gradually becomes more constructive. From the time the child is 4 years old he gradually enters more and more into playing with other children.

At about 5 years, interest in group play becomes greater, but only when the child is about 7 is he able to cope with the social problems involved in playing with other children. Play thus becomes an important part of the child's social development.

Play is made up of stimuli to all the senses: it helps to develop mind as well as body and can give a natural outlet for the child's need for activity, and for his thoughts and feelings.

The normal child's development is not entirely spontaneous. He sees how other children behave in different situations, and is encouraged to try for himself, possibly supported at first by siblings and parents. Stimulation is needed and adequate perceptual and motor development, as well as help and practice.

A child's persistence can be unbelievable. For example, a 9- or 10-year-old boy can go on and on practicing a certain kick which he has seen his big brother use brilliantly on the soccer (football) field. The child can continue practicing the same skill until he has mastered it, even though it is exhausting, and thus he builds up capacities which can be important later in life.

Play is thus a natural preparation for adult life and work.

The retarded child

Learning to play

It may be difficult for the retarded child to take part in this natural life-expansion. Consider how many kinds of play the child is excluded from if, for example, he cannot jump. The child will be unable to run properly, jump over obstacles, play hopscotch, skip, etc., and will therefore be isolated and will not, through play, get the physical and mental development suited to his abilities. It is thus not enough to give the child a chance to be with other children, for often this procedure has the opposite result, as the child is encouraged to take part in something which is too advanced for his stage of development. He fails and suffers another defeat, and perhaps will never have the courage to try the game again.

The retarded child must be given a start deliberately by the adult or else he will sit motionless and withdrawn in his own narrow world. At best, he will play for only a short time. It requires much imagination and understanding on the part of adults to succeed in motivating and activating the retarded child, and it needs much thought and intuition to put oneself on the child's level and help him from there.

Thus it is important to analyze closely the components of a game before encouraging the child to take part. For example, to play marbles requires the following:

to understand the object of the game,

to be able to crawl around on the ground in different positions (motor ability),

to be able to distinguish the marble and the hole from their surroundings (sight and figure-ground discrimination),

to be able to focus on the hole and the rolling marble,

to have considerable ability to judge direction and distance,

to have good manual dexterity,

to have a certain degree of eye-hand coordination,

to have developed color perception (your marble is blue),

to be able to judge the strength of the flick (kinesthetic sense).

This game is demanding and the adult should estimate beforehand what aspects will cause difficulty, and whether it will be at all possible for the child to learn the game, and, if this seems

possible, the adult should prepare the child by helping him practice. Only then will the child enjoy taking part in the game and become more competent in all the skills required by the game.

By helping the child, teaching him to play, teaching him the basic elements of the game, we render the retarded child an invaluable help towards self-expansion, towards gaining confidence and self-reliance. In this way, the adult is helping shape the child's future life.

In the following pages some of the most common skills will be described in more detail, with suggestions for preparatory exercises. Unless otherwise indicated the description applies to both normal and retarded children.

The springy jump

The normal and the retarded child

To jump is a prerequisite for running, hopping, skipping, wandering in fields and woods and generally taking part in other children's play.

The small normal child and the undeveloped older child jump, on the whole, flatfootedly. They cannot easily leave the ground, and they have neither the muscle strength nor the ability to coordinate for such a complicated movement (Fig. 19).

Later one often sees older children jump on their toes with straight ankles. If such a stiff jump is made down from a gymnastic apparatus or the like, it may injure the foot and cause pain. Therefore it is important to teach the child a springy jump, where the toes touch for only a very brief moment but the heel, immediately after, reaches the ground at the same time that the knee- and hip-joints bend flexibly.

The physical education teacher may have difficulty in teaching this to a normal child if he is a little stiff in the joints, but this jump usually develops naturally, little by little. It is best not to let the child jump down from a high apparatus until the jump is satisfactorily developed.

When it is a question of jumping, more attention must be paid to the retarded child, because he often knows nothing about his feet and their movements. Experience shows that this is not always due to faulty brain development, for in many cases the springy jump can be learned quite quickly.

The exercises listed below will promote foot development.

All exercises begin, continue and end with the feet parallel, that is, there are equal distances between the heels and the toes. The feet-together position is not used, for this position makes no use of the muscles on both sides of the leg.

The hip joint may be so shaped that the child must be allowed to walk with the legs turned slightly outwards, but this is rare.

Exercises

When the child is sitting he holds the toes of one foot and bends them up and down (body awareness). Say the words »up«, »down« at the same time.

Bend the toes up and down without the help of the hands.

Finally repeat with the eyes shut (kinesthetic sense).

Repeat the same with the ankles. Sitting

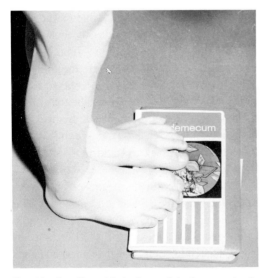

Fig. 44. Standing with the front of the feet on a book. The book should be thick enough that the heels can only just reach the floor.

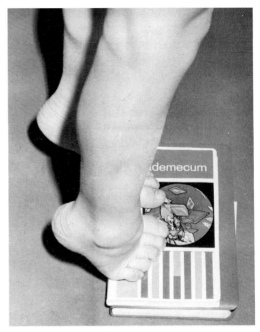

Fig. 45. Raising and lowering heels.

with the legs outstretched; bend the feet up and down at the ankles.

When do you think you bend your ankle up and down in the course of the day? (When walking, running, jumping, etc.)

Standing. Slowly raise and lower both heels with support.

Repeat without support.

A single gentle jump (only one jump at a time, to avoid a stiff jump).

Jump forward with feet together, slowly, lightly.

Walk on tiptoe. The toes should be spread out on the floor at each step. The steps should be quite small and tripping, and the toes pointing straight forward.

With the front of the feet resting on a book, raise and lower the heels slowly (supples the ankles and strengthens the calf muscles) (Fig. 44/45).

Walk on your heels. Feet parallel, toes straight forward and the whole front of the foot lifted.

Barefoot walking on sand and soft earth.

Jump over a »ditch«. Gradually increase the width.

Jump lightly down from a step.

Jump down from higher steps, boxes, chairs, tables.

Jump over a rope. Increase the height.

Jump and make a mark on the wall as high as possible.

One child swings a rope around himself in a circle, and the other children jump over it.

All kinds of high- and long-jumps.

Pushing off with the toes of the hindmost foot when walking, so that the adult can see the whole sole of the child's foot from behind when the toes are out on the floor. Support the child with one hand. Balance is difficult, for the exercise must be done slowly, before it can become quick and natural (Fig. 20).

Fig. 46. Boy with good hipmovement. He can run with a long stride.

Running

The normal child

Running is jumping ahead. With a faster run the steps become longer, and frequency – the speed with which the leg movements change – increases.

One of the prerequisites for being able to run is that ankle, knee and hip joints are flexible, for the long spring necessitates bringing one leg forwards at the same time that the other is being stretched backwards (Fig. 46).

The muscles must be strong, so that the take-off can be powerful and the jump long. When running, the body rises into the air for a moment, and both feet are off the ground at the same time. Muscle strength is necessary, especially in the thighs and calves.

The running should be springy, and the heel should touch the ground for a moment during each stride. Only in very fast running, sprinting, does the heel not touch the ground, because the speed is so great that there is no time to put the heel down.

The retarded child

To practice running with the retarded child is much the same as with the normal child who is at the same stage of development, only it must be practiced more thoroughly, taking account of some special circumstances.

Joint flexibility, muscle strength and the springy jump are practiced, consideration being given to the child's stage of development, which, as described, has great influence, especially on the movements of the ankle.

Added to this, many retarded children have no concept of the back of the body and so do not use the muscles situated there (see page 97).

Exercises

Lying on the stomach. Turn the head and look at one leg, which is lifted (body-knowledge).

Lying on the stomach. Repeat the exercise, but without lifting the hip (suppleness). If a sandbag is placed on the leg, more strength is needed.

Lying on the back. Lift one leg with the knee straight, while the other leg is stretched out on the floor (suppleness).

Lying on the side. Bring the one leg far forwards and the other far back. Keep both knees as straight as possible (Fig. 46).

Run from wall to wall 10 times back and forth, quickly (training respiration).

Running jump over »ditch«. The ditch is made wider little by little.

Let the child jump over the ditch many times until he gives up. This amuses the child and is good training.

All kinds of running games.

Hopscotch

Normal and retarded

To play hopscotch a child must be able to:

Jump on both feet springily.

Hop forward.

Stand on one leg.

Hop, stand still, hop, stand.

Hop and change direction.

Distinguish lines (sight).

Find his place in the squares (perception of direction and space).

Kick a stone while hopping.

Learn the rules of the game.

It is thus a complicated task which can be difficult enough for the normal as well as the retarded child. Girls often have an astonishing expertise in this, while boys sometimes think this is not a game for them and therefore do not make an effort. Boys sometimes find it harder to hop and kick than girls do, because of their later motor development.

There are so' many educational benefits in hopscotch that it is well worth the trouble to help the retarded child to take part in this game. As well as balance, it trains the leg and foot muscles and gives a surer eye-foot coordination – all skills which can be useful in the child's daily life.

At first the adult should perhaps hold the child's hand while he hops around the room – without squares or stone – or a stick can be used as support. Later he hops without support and with a stone.

Skipping rope

Girls especially enjoy skipping rope; they can skip from morning to night in season. Boys unfortunately think that skipping is something only for girls. Lately, however, this occupation has become fashionable among athletes, who skip rope to warm up.

Skipping rope requires good coordination of arm and leg movements, as well as a certain amount of endurance and is therefore a good exercise for all children. Skipping does not need as much space as many running games, and can therefore be performed indoors the whole year round.

But it is easier to skip while running than when standing in one place, and it is usually easier to skip with a running step than with feet together.

It is often easier for younger children to skip with a hula-hoop than with a rope. It may be necessary to show the child how to turn the hoop in his hands. The overhand grasp should be used.

When skipping with a rope the child often begins by swinging the rope in such a way that the hands nearly meet over his hand, leaving no room for him to jump through, as the loop becomes too narrow or the rope is twisted. Therefore, let the child watch himself in a large mirror while he skips.

At first the child jumps while the rope is still high up in the air. By swinging it forward over the head, and letting the rope lie on the ground in front of the feet before he jumps, the child soon gets over this difficulty.

Preparatory exercises
(Possibly before a mirror).

Running jump forwards and on the spot (without a rope).

Jump on the spot with feet together.

Skip, running with a hula-hoop.

Skip with the hula-hoop, with feet together.

Demonstrate the arm movements to the child, who copies them without a rope. (Bent elbows, small light movements of the wrists, the same for both arms).

Daily skipping practice with the whole class. Some use hula-hoops and the more advanced use ropes. Both boys and girls take part.

When the whole class has learned to skip, the

exercises can be varied in many ways and used as a stimulating part of a physical education lesson.

It should be noted that if the arm movements are large, they will restrict respiration somewhat.

Climbing trees and fences

To climb up a rope or a tree, to hang on a branch or to scramble over a high fence requires the child to be able to lift his own weight by the arms and hands. In addition to muscle strength, some ability to balance and some endurance are necessary. The child has to learn to hold on for some time.

Before the child can lift a heavy object a certain number of times and hold the same object up for a certain time, he cannot be expected to lift his own body (Fig. 31).

To have to crawl up the wall bar frightens many children. The child must never be forced to practice such skills, and when he does dare to make an attempt he must be quite sure of the adult's support. A firm and quiet grip on the child's hips when he is climbing gives confidence, as long as the child understands that the hands will not be removed unless the child says: »I can do it myself«.

The daring to go up the wall bar is often best encouraged at first by letting the child turn his back to the wall bar so that he can look around, at the same time helping him by supporting his hands while he tries to reach up as high as possible. »Lift one knee and put your foot down again. Lift the other knee – then down again. Try to lift both knees at once. I will keep hold of your hands«. A single attempt the first day is enough. Next time it will be easier, and it usually doesn't take long before the child, without hesitation, scrambles up the wall bar with his face towards the wall.

After this, the climbing apparatus in the playground or in the gymnasium will also become attractive.

An inactive child becomes more active when he knows he can manage the tasks.

Preparatory exercises
Lift a sandbag up to your chin with both hands.
Weight to be lifted and number of repetitions are increasesed gradually (Fig. 31).
Two children hold a stick firmly with both hands. The one tries to pull it from the other.
Hang on the bars briefly (if the child is not overweight). Begin with 10 seconds.
Push-up (standing on hands and toes with body and legs in a straight line. Lower yourself to the floor and push up again so as to be able to push your self up on a fence).
Heave oneself up by the arms on the wall bar or a beam.

Other skills

The retarded child

Bicycling

Bicycling is a good method of transport for all, also for many retarded children. If the general balance is poor, balance should be practiced beforehand (see page 123).

The movements of the legs and steering can be learned on a tricycle, or possibly practiced on a stationary bicycle. Also practice getting on and off.

If the child is very nervous, in the beginning the adult may run beside the bicycle. The bicycle, by the way, should be so low that the child can easily put his feet on the ground.

Swimming

The child's enjoyment in playing with water is naturally followed – where there is opportunity for it – by paddling and by playing with boats and sand, and the child begins in this way to be at home in the water.

The retarded child must learn swimming right from the basic movements, for it is quite difficult to coordinate the motions of swimming. In some cases »dog-paddle« can be sufficient but, if possible, the child should learn to swim properly.

Begin with preparatory exercises, arm and leg movements separately. Arm movements can be practiced standing in front of a large mirror and afterwards lying on the ground, where leg movements can later be added. Some children can with advantage be trained in »dry-swimming«, lying over a stool or bench.

Swimming is not only a practical safety measure, but is also enjoyable and pleasant, and splendid exercise for the whole body.

Athletics

Literature on athletics should be referred to. It must, however, be strongly stressed how valueable it can be for young retarded men and women to take part in athletics and sports, both for social reasons and as training for physical work. Not least, membership in a sports club can also solve many leisure problems.

Riding

Many retarded children can enjoy riding, even if only at a riding school. It is also pleasant for the child, who learns among other things to become friends with animals. Riding gives training in balance and in use of the leg muscles.   .

Perhaps the most important aspect of riding is that it gives the child more self-confidence.

Playgrounds

It is desirable that an adult systematically introduces each new child to all the apparatus and play opportunities. Retarded children often overestimate their own abilities or do not dare to try anything new.

Natural playgrounds are the best; fields, woods and beaches.

Children in towns are sent to man-made playgrounds, which also can give the children a wealth of opportunities.

On a playground there should be possibilities for many

Activities,

including:

Rolling, crawling.

Playing with sand or water.

Jumping, walking, running – on level and on uneven ground.

Balancing: on lines, on planks, etc.

Climbing, hanging.

Playing ball. On firm ground and against a wall.

Hopscotch, skipping.

Balancing on movable objects: swings, seesaws, roller skates.

Riding bicycles and tricycles.

Reaction ability – playing ball, etc.

Training respiration and circulation (long racetracks or bicycle paths).

Obstacle course.

Apparatus and facilities for practicing every skill should be available, and preferably so that each skill may be practiced in many different ways.

The whole playground should not be level

It is an advantage if the whole area is not level, for it does the child good to run over uneven, perhaps sandy, and somewhat hilly ground. The child can hide behind small hills and run, slide and roll down them (the sand can be renewed time to time at comparatively low cost).

Climbing frames, trees, etc.

Climbing apparatus of different grades of difficulty should be provided, and the ground under them should be soft.

Hopscotch

Part of the playground may be cemented, so the children can draw outlines for hopscotch.

In the case of retarded children, one hopscotch design can be drawn beforehand, as a pattern for them to copy.

Swings and seesaws

It is pleasant to swing, it makes your stomach tickle and it is fun to soar over the heads of one's playmates.

The child can swing sitting, standing or kneeling, and develop daring.

A seesaw gives some of the same experience

as a swing and, furthermore, the child has to learn to avoid bumping on the ground. However, seesaws can be dangerous.

Seesaws teach children something about the properties of levers, and both pieces of apparatus exercise the labyrinthine senses (see pages 10, 123) as well as eye-focusing while the body is moving.

The ground underneath should be sand or soft earth.

Merry-go-rounds and revolving platforms
stimulate the vestibular sense, but can be dangerous in a playground where there is no supervisor.

Percussion devices
Children love to make noise, and for this purpose a metal drum can be hung up horizontally, so that it can rotate on its axis. It is filled with something noisy, such as stones or gravel.

The world can have many colors
A transparent disc (of plexiglass or the like) painted different colors, in segments, is mounted on a stick, so that the disc can turn around and the world can be observed through different colors.

Tires
Old tires can be placed on edge and fastened in cement holders in a row on the ground with a distance of a step between each. They should be arranged near a fence, so that the children have something to support themselves by, when they step from ring to ring.

Tires can also be hung up on ropes and used as swings or they can be used as hoops for rolling along the ground.

Slides
Sliding is fun and can give a child self-confidence.

Wall space for playing ball
It is important for both girls and boys to practice throwing a ball up against a wall, for that promotes excellent eye-hand coordination. Therefore there should always be many high,

smooth walls or high fences in every playground.

Various possibilities for balance-walking

Space for roller-skating and skipping rope

A covered area for playing, in wet weather
One wall here could consist of a large blackboard for drawing on.

Equipment

Durable, steady carts
for small children to hold on to while learning to walk.

Scooters, tricycles and soap-box cars
are grand playthings for children, and furthermore they act as preparation for riding a real bicycle. These can also be used in traffic games, if the playground is big enough to be marked with streets.

Also:
Roller skates.
Large and small balls.
Hula-hoops.
Skipping ropes.
Chalk and hopscotch stones.
Stilts (fine for balance training).
Nine-pins.
Lawn bowling.
etc.

Playing ball and ball games

The normal child

When an infant reaches for an object, this is the prelude to ball play. The object is held and shortly afterwards released.

The next phase appears in the period around 8 months of age, when the child enjoys throwing everything on the floor and also playing »give-and-take«.

Development of hand grasp and of eye-hand coordination leads to handling of a rolling ball.

In general, playing ball can be divided into catching and throwing.

Catching

At first, catching a large ball consists only in holding the hands and forearms forward and waiting for the adult to throw. When the ball touches the arms, the child bends his elbows and draws the ball in towards his chest (Fig. 47).

Later, he should be able to catch a large ball with his fingers spread out and with a hand on each side of the ball (Figs. 48 & 49).

If it is a small ball, the hands at first make a bowl-shape for the ball to fall into. The touch of the ball on the palms of the hands stimulates the hands to hold onto the ball. If the reaction is not quick enough, the ball falls through between the fingers.

Some children hold their hands far apart and try to close them on the ball, which method usually fails because there is an opening on both sides of the ball between the hands.

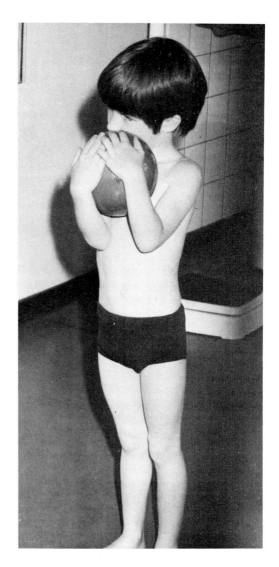

Fig. 47. Immature grasp of ball.

Fig. 48. The ball cannot be guided with the fingers held together.

Fig. 49. Outspread fingers give better control of the ball.

To catch the ball the hands ought to be in the same position as for making a snowball (Fig. 50).

If the ball is to remain in the hands, the grip must not loosen. Here we must remember that an intentional, static (continuing) muscle contraction represents a later stage of neurological development than a short, dynamic muscle contraction.

Throwing

Throwing is difficult, because the object (the ball) should be projected in a certain direction and for a certain distance.

Coordination is difficult, because the ball should be released suddenly and at the right moment in the arm movement. Engaging the whole body in the movement in order to get more power behind the throw is also difficult.

The 21-month-old cannot direct his throw. He stands with his feet apart, facing what should be the direction of the throw. First he runs forward, then he stands still and throws, then he runs again. Running does not help throwing, and the legs, trunk and shoulders do not take part in the movement.

When the child is a year older, he begins to be able to throw more or less in the desired direction, and the arm is drawn back a little, but otherwise the trunk is held as before.

At 4-5 years of age, the whole body begins to take part in the movement, which is thus better coordinated, but it is only towards the end of the 5th year that his throw gains more strength by the help of weight transfer and rotation of the body.

It is best to begin with underhand throwing, as this is the easiest to control.

An »adult« overhand throw with the right hand, starting from a walking position with weight on the back (right) foot, goes on to rotate the trunk to the right and lift up the throwing arm. Then comes the actual throw. The body weight is brought forward over the forward foot at the same time as the trunk sud-

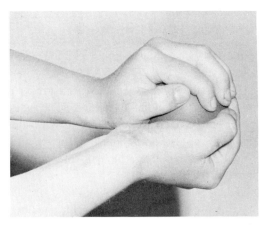

Fig. 50. Holding a small ball can be compared to making a snowball.

denly and strongly turns in the direction of the throw, and arm and hand go with it, so that the muscles here help to give extra speed to the ball. The back foot is lifted during the turn and is brought forward, while hand and arm seem to follow the ball on its way.

Almost all the senses are involved

Sight: Eye-focusing, because the eye follows the ball's movements. Hand-eye coordination.

Hearing: The sound of the ball hitting the wall or the floor warns that it is on its way back.

Touch: The ball touching the palms stimulates the fingers to close on the ball.

Kinesthetic sense: Estimation of the force of the throw and of the position of the limbs when trying to throw and catch.

Perception of direction: In which direction the ball should be thrown, and in which direction it will rebound from the wall.

Perception of space: How far should the ball be thrown?

Body balance: Running and jumping must be done to catch the ball and to follow it on its way.

Speed and ability to react.

Time concept: E. g. in kickball a child must judge how many bases he can run before the ball reaches him.

Children play ball all over the world. It is enjoyable and it gives them an outlet for a great deal of their energy, and as already observed, it aids development in many respects.

Think how many hundreds of hours most children spend playing ball in some form or another while growing up, and how much training they get, as well as enjoyment. Girls mostly play against a wall and attain by this great sureness and speed, whereas boys, for example, prefer throwing the ball over the next-door roof, i.e. to show how far they can throw it.

By this, boys miss the chance to develop eye-hand coordination, which is so important for learning to write, among other things. This could perhaps be practiced in another way, but

there are few games where eye-hand coordination is so effectively practiced.

See further, under Handgrasp, page 34.

The retarded child

To be good at ball games requires, as described, a well advanced development of the central nervous system. The task is difficult, because it needs a well developed perception in so many different fields in addition to a well advanced motor development.

A remark such as: »You are stupid, you can't catch a ball, so you can't play with us« can make a retarded child creep into himself and never want to touch a ball again.

Help and stimulation at a suitable time would in some cases have spared the child this defeat.

Some children find it easier to catch with one hand than with two, since reciprocal coordination between the hands may be difficult. If the child is to enjoy playing ball, he must learn to play with one hand as well as with both.

When playing against a wall it is usually easiest to catch the ball when the distance from the wall is short, i. e. less than 1 meter. Children with coordination difficulties, with slightly weak sight, or with slow reactions often manage better when they stand about 2 meters from the wall, so that they have more time to see and to react.

Beginning with the easiest preparatory exercises will soon reveal how far the child can advance without stress, that is, how far the central nervous system's development has reached.

To be more precise, it may be noted that the educable subnormal can usually learn to handle a ball remarkably well and will be able to take part in many ball games, if he does not start learning too late. On the other hand, the severely subnormal, because of the above-mentioned factors, will have difficulty in learning to play ball, and many will never develop so far that ball games should be attempted – apart from rolling a ball and easier play with a large ball. Yet others, by persistent training for several years, will attain unexpected and sur-prising proficiency in ball play.

The most elementary exercises in handling large and small balls will be described below in different developmental phases, because the order of the exercises must depend entirely on which fields of perception are developed first in each child, whether the grasp is secure, and whether the child can run.

Exercises
Ball play with a large ball
Basic exercises, using both hands and in-creasing in difficulty:

Sitting on the floor: Roll the ball to the child and the child rolls it back (using both hands).
Standing: The child learns to hold the ball with his fingers spread out (if he cannot spread his fingers, this movement must be learned first).
Standing close to an adult: The ball is thrown to the child, who tries to catch it with his fingers spread out. Increase the dis-tance.
The ball is thrown back to the adult.
The child throws the ball to the ground and catches it again (here the ball bounces back along the same path).
Standing near a wall: Throw and catch. This can be difficult to work out, as the path of the ball depends on the angle at which it strikes the wall.

It also makes a difference how well the ball bounces, so begin with a rather soft ball. The force of the throw also makes a difference.

At first the child should always use an un-derhand throw against the wall, because this will return the ball at a better level for catching than will an overhand throw. The latter throw may be the most forceful, but the return is quicker and the direction is more difficult to predict.

Learn proficiency: Catch the ball ten times in succession.
Practice speed: How many seconds does it take to throw 10-20 times against a wall from a fixed distance?
Two children practice different throws to-

gether: The ball is thrown at the ground for the partner to catch.
High throw: The ball is held over the head with both hands.
Throwing from chest height: Both hands push the ball forward quickly.
Side throw: Both hands on the same side of the body.

Ball play with a small ball
Basic exercises:
With an ordinary small ball (a tennis ball), preferably not too smooth, practice in the same way as with a large ball. Remember to practice »making a snowball« first. The domi-nant hand should be below, ready to throw, and the elbows bent.

By bouncing the ball on the floor the child learns to catch with one hand, first with the dominant one and later with the other. Catch from below first and later from above.

Playing against a wall also teaches the child to catch with one hand. Use an underhand throw first.

Gradually increase the distance from the wall. Increase strength of throwing and finish by throwing overhand.

If necessary, correct the position of the legs and trunk, so that the whole body is used when throwing. The left foot is forward when throw-ing with the right hand. The child should not stick to one place, but should move freely ac-cording to the path of the ball.

When the child is quite at home in all these ordinary exercises, he will be able to enjoy playing ball with other children.

Exercises: First with a large and later with a small ball.

Draw a circle on the ground or use a hula-hoop. Throw bean-bags into the circle. In-crease the distance.
Throw a bean-bag or a ball into a waste-paper basket;
increase the distance.
Set up nine-pins in various groupings and knock them down with a ball.

Bouncing a ball on the floor: Large ball

(»Dribbling« = bounce the ball repeatedly and catch it each time, and

»Bouncing« = knock the ball against the ground repeatedly with one hand – do not hold it).

»Dribbling« – standing, walking and running. Bounce the ball 20-30 times with the dominant hand, then with each hand in turn and finally with the non-dominant hand.

Run, bouncing the ball.

Bounce as fast as you can (bending at the knees).

Bounce to music.

Throw the ball in the air and catch it again (standing, walking, running).

Bounce the ball, turn around once and bounce again.

Bounce while changing position: sitting, kneeling, standing, walking.

A small ball against the wall:

Draw chalk circles of different sizes and colors on the wall, and throw a ball into the circles. Increase the distance.

Throw, clap and catch.

Throw and catch, with both hands, with right or left hand.

Throw and catch. Change from overhand to underhand, from right to left.

Throw, turn around once and catch (turn both ways).

Two children play together with a large ball:

It may be difficult to do something with other children, to play with the ball and at the same time notice the reactions of the partner.

Sitting opposite each other with legs apart. Roll the ball to partner.

Standing facing. Bounce the ball on the ground and partner catches.

Throw to each other. Throw in different ways.

The children stand opposite each other about 1 meter apart. They take turns bouncing the ball, once each, and go on as long as possible.

Two children each have a ball. Both throw their balls at the same time against the floor, and catch each other's ball.

Various ways of playing ball with a partner, standing, running.

Playing ball to music.

All these exercises can be used to teach counting, as the child counts the number of catches or the number of times he can bounce the ball without stopping.

Group games

To get the whole group to play without losing the interest of the most inactive players can be difficult. If the basic skills have already been taught individually, it is usually easier to get the children interested in playing together. Refer to literature on ball games.

Preparation for various ball games

To take part in kickball, soccer (English: football), basketball and other games, the details of the game must be mastered and the rules known. Only then can play begin.

This seems obvious, but it is unfortunately difficult to observe in practice, for children are impatient to begin playing since they are not – like serious players – accustomed to practicing the basic movements first. Retarded children, in particular, do not get much out of taking part in a game unless each detail has been practiced beforehand so that they can be fairly competent, especially when the play goes fast.

In kickball, for example, such a child easily stands aside if he does not feel equal to the situation. The child will perhaps drop out, or the other children will not want him to join in.

With this in view, training for soccer (English: football) is described in detail.

Most of the preparatory exercises can be practiced in the gymnasium in winter, and the inventive teacher can make the drill seem like play – or perhaps better, like a sport.

Only the basic principles and grades of difficulty are described here. For more information see relevant handbooks.

Soccer (English: football)

Preparatory exercises without a ball:
Training in running.
Training in various jumps.
Practice the watching position (legs apart with slightly bent knees and hips).
Moving to all sides in the watching position.

Preparatory exercises with a large soft ball:
At first some children are frightened of a hard soccer ball or football, and it is easier to practice with a soft ball, e. g.:
Kick with the inner edge of the dominant foot (forefoot) and then with the other foot.
Kick with the outer edge of the toes (dominant foot, other foot).
Each child can practice by himself against a fence, or five or six children, with the teacher, can form a circle and kick the ball around the circle.
Stop the ball.
Kick the ball over a bench.
Zig-zag run, kicking the ball between ninepins.
Goal kick.

Preparatory exercises with a soccer ball:
Repeat the same exercises with an ordinary soccer ball.
Two children kick the ball to each other while running down the field.

Practice heading the ball, using a soft ball first:
Practice heading in different ways. The ball should strike the edge of the scalp.
Five or six children stand in a row in front of the teacher, who throws the ball:
Heading the ball back to the teacher.
Heading to the player at the side.
Go through the rules of the game, and when all the exercises are mastered sufficiently, begin the real game.

It is useful to continue preparatory practice at the beginning of each lesson. The children thus discover how much help they get from practicing the separate skills, and through this they have a chance of becoming good soccer players and possibly members of a team.

Other games

Ball-tag, volleyball, basketball, badminton, table tennis, and many other games can be similarly analyzed to suggest various preparatory exercises.

Gymnastics

The normal child

The words »gymnastics« and »physical education« do not cover anywhere near all that this subject should include during the years at school. At any rate, this subject can be divided into three main branches. I have called them:

    Educational gymnastics,
    physical training, and
    athletic training.

Educational gymnastics

Five- to seven-year-old children no longer move just for the sake of movement – they have learnt to crawl, walk and run – but to perform an action. Movements have thus become motivated. Gymnastics should therefore be motivated as much as possible, and appeal to the child's intellect. The English term »Educational gymnastics« covers this quite adequately, in that gymnastics for children of preschool age is a stimulation of sensory motor development. This stimulation should continue during the first years of school.

Teachers of gymnastics should therefore be cognizant of infantile reflexes and primitive movement patterns, to avoid working against the natural development of these reflexes and thus perhaps causing bad habits of movement (see the chapters on Motor Development).

Physical training

At this stage the child needs general training; any weak points should be strengthened and skill in using gymnastic equipment should be practiced. In addition, he should learn the correct technique for lifting and carrying.

Athletics and sports

For those in the top classes, things change again, for here it is a matter of training for athletics and sports, including learning the principles of various ways of building up strength, circuit training, interval training, etc. It will also be useful to give practical training in correct motions to use when doing work (in factories) and in the technique of lifting.

Rhythmic and dramatic play, etc.

All the above can be mixed with play, rhythm, mime, drama, jazz-gymnastics, etc., according to the age of the children and the teacher's preference and ability. The lessons can thus be so comprehensive and varied that most of the class can find something that interests them.

Gymnastics should be an intellectual subject

For all age groups it is an advantage to give the subject as much intellectual content as possible, corresponding to the child's stage of development. By explaining to the children the effect and object of an exercise, and by giving the children individual problems which need thought to solve, the subject can be made more interesting even for those who are not very fond of activity.

E. g.:

> A boy may be asked to find out for himself the elements making up the game of football, which skills it would be useful to practice, or which groups of muscles should be trained so as to gain proficiency in playing. The effects of training on the functioning of the heart and on respiration can be explained and monitored by the children themselves with the help of the »steptest« (see page 164) or the bicycle ergometer.

To teach gymnastics is a very demanding and comprehensive task. The teacher should have enough knowledge of anatomy, physiology and kinesiology in order to understand what each exercise or game involves. He should also know and follow closely the normal child's perceptual and motor development, stage by stage.

Within the subject of gymnastics itself, the teacher should familiarize himself with the main ideas of different systems and trends, especially if these were not included in the Training College curriculum. More possibilities for variety are of great advantage to the teacher, for groups, even of the same age and background, may have quite different abilities, interests and aims.

Furthermore, it should be borne in mind that every new trend in gymnastics will, in the nature of things, emphasize points which earlier systems did not sufficiently stress. However, this does not at all mean that all the old ideas are useless.

Educational gymnastics for preschool children

The normal and the retarded child

Educational gymnastics, a main subject

Educational gymnastics should be a main subject for preschools and infant schools because it includes all the basic elements of the subjects the children will learn later at school.

Among other things, here they learn body awareness, perception of direction, space, shape, and color, as well as the concepts of time and number. Likewise, dominance can be established, and the vocabulary within all these areas enlarged. Everything is made clear through movement, so the child can more easily remember what he has learned because he understands it better.

The teaching of gymnastics must, of course, be concurrent with and coordinated with the training of perception in the classroom.

Close cooperation between the physical education (P. E.) teacher and all the others who deal with the child is most important, so that they can reinforce each other's teachings.

The exercises in this book can evidently all be used as sensory-motor stimulation in some form of educational gymnastics for normal as well as retarded children.

As a further inspiration to the readers who may not already be acquainted with it, I shall briefly describe the system of educational gymnastics which has been used for many years in England in many nursery schools as well as in primary schools.

The principles were laid down by Rudolf Laban, and English P. E. teachers have adapted them for small children. I shall try to give an idea of their essentials:

During the first few months at school (at 5 years of age), the children learn body awareness and the use of equipment. Afterwards there are no real exercises, but small, simple tasks involving movement, which the children themselves must try to solve. While they are making the movements which are required in solving a task, the teacher consciously aims at teaching the children to realize:

1) WHAT is moving,
2) WHERE in space,
3) HOW the movement is made.

1) WHAT *is moving:*

Which *part of the body,* the whole, or perhaps only one arm?

Where does *the weight of the body* rest? On the back, on the feet, on the buttocks?

How is *the weight transferred* to other parts of the body?

Exercises

Transferring weight.

Stand on the whole foot, on the toes, on the heels.

Sitting with legs outstretched. Walk on your buttocks.

Sitting on the floor with knees up (hook position). Press both hands on the floor, lift your buttocks and walk on hands and feet.

Sit »side-saddle« with feet first on the right, then on the left.

Lying on the back. Lift both knees high and roll up on your neck. Return to sitting position.

Standing with feet apart. Transfer the weight from foot to foot.

Standing. Lean forward, bending the ankles until you fall (one foot will instinctively be put forward at the last minute and the weight will be transferred to it).

2) WHERE *in space does the movement take place?*

Standing *in the same place.* E. g. can one foot stay still while the body and the other foot move, or the child can *move around in the room.*

A movement can take place *at different levels.* E. g. the arms can move at floor level, at hip level or up over the head.

Direction can change. Forwards, backwards, to the side, up, down.

Exercises

Stand with feet apart. How far can your arms reach out in all directions and at all levels (you are allowed to bend your legs and to move one leg.

Move around the room in different ways, low or high (low may be crawling on the stomach, and high can be on tiptoe).

3) HOW *is the movement carried out?*

a) Is muscle contraction strong or weak?

Is it a powerful or a light movement? Part of the movement can be powerful and part light. Suitable contraction of the muscles used for a given movement shows good coordination and this should be practiced.

Certain parts of the body are taut while others are relaxed? Which parts are taut?

Exercises

Clench your fist and raise your arm hard up towards the ceiling, then let it fall loosely down.

The children can think up other forceful movements. Draw large, flat figures-of-eight in the air with the whole hand, as if you were painting with a big brush with soft sweeping movements. Think out other soft movements for arms, legs or the whole body.

Walk and stamp – walk softly.

Throw the ball hard – throw it gently.

Practice tightening and relaxing.

Lie as if you were asleep, quite relaxed – go stiff as a board and then relax again.

b) The time factor.

A movement can be slow or quick, sudden or hesitant, and the speed can increase or decrease.

Exercises

Lift both arms slowly upwards – pull them quickly or suddenly down again.

Think up some more exercises where you vary the speed.

Walk slowly to the wall and run back.

Keep with the beat – slowly – getting quicker – getting slower. – Stop when the music stops.

The child thus finds out how movements can differ in many ways. The body is an instrument, but to use it with skill you must know its possibilities.

In order to use his body and understand its movements, the child is given tasks which he has to think through in order to solve.

This will improve his ability to evaluate, his independence and his self-reliance.

Examples of tasks

How many different ways can you stand on two of your limbs?

How many different ways can you crawl?

Run around the room without bumping into others:

Run in different directions, alter the speed and sometimes stop suddenly (at first the teacher can order the changes, but later the children themselves should clearly and consciously change their movements, choosing among the many possibilities).

Tuck the end of a bench into a climbing rack so that the bench slopes down to the floor. How many different ways can you go up the bench? (Each child tries his chosen method.)

Which way was the easiest, the quickest, the most risky?

How many different ways can you jump? (On two feet, on one foot, over a ditch, down from a step, from a chair, from a platform, forwards and backwards, from a rope to a mattress.)

It is seen that with the help of this method the children little by little are able and willing to move freely and to dance individually to music.

A child is not born with graceful, harmonious movements – they must be learned. Some children learn them apparently spontaneously while growing, and are well-coordinated for their stage of development, but this is far from true in all cases, especially not in retarded children.

The retarded child

Some directions for teachers

Besides what has already been mentioned, a few special conditions may be noted which concern the sensory-motor education of retarded children.

Do not let the child go on doing only those things he can do already; instead, encourage him to start something he cannot yet do, but which he has a chance of learning at that particular time.

The lessons must be adapted to each child's sensory-motor level and explained in relation to this. Every project is discussed, considered and several solutions are tried. In this way gymnastics tends to become *an intellectual subject:* educational gymnastics.

It simply cannot be stressed strongly enough that even retarded children should be given an explanation for why they should do this or that, or the brain will not be sufficiently stimulated, the child will see no reason for his actions and will lose interest.

This needs plenty of imagination and inventiveness on the part of the teacher. Here, as in all other teaching of retarded children, the child must never be underestimated, or he will lose interest. On the other hand, do not expect too much, so that the child feels inferior and may »forget« to come to the next lesson. The program must be so arranged that the child feels all the time that he is making progress, and that what is required can be achieved by energetic practice.

The child must learn to rely on and to use his body purposefully, and so gain confidence in his own abilities, so that any nervousness can be replaced gradually by a mature evaluation of the situation and by greater self-confidence.

The exercises for which the teacher has to give commands should not come in the same order or be the same each time, because this can produce conditioned reflexes so that a certain command or a certain tune produces a certain movement. This method has been much used in gymnastics for healthy people to fix the movements and make them automatic. In the case of retarded children, this must not

be the only procedure, because it is so important to get as many areas of the brain as possible to function. The child, as well as seeing and imitating, should learn to:
Listen and think and put what is perceived into motion. These are brain functions which we must try to develop also in retarded children.

It is not desirable that the teacher should do all the exercises himself. He would be physically overtaxed, he would not be able to supervise what the children are doing and thus would not have a chance to help and correct them. What is worse, the teacher would eliminate the necessity for the children to think out how to do the required exercise. (An exception must be made if dealing with children with a very low I. Q., e.g. the most severely subnormal).

Each lesson should be planned in advance, although the program should be so flexible that it can be changed as required, according to the mood of the children and any sudden inspirations.

There can, however, be a set purpose in each lesson, something the teacher has decided to teach the children that day, e.g. variations of speed, practiced in every possible way.

The thoroughly planned lesson means that there are no pauses and therefore fewer disciplinary problems. The children do not get tired after an hour's exercise – or more – if different groups of muscles are used and if energetic exercises alternate with less energetic ones and educational tasks alternate with free movements in games or dancing to music.

One of the difficulties that occurs in normal practice is that the classes are often very uneven in ability, but it is just here that educational gymnastics allows the exercises to be performed in groups, or even individually.

The retarded nursery child

Educational gymnastics for the retarded nursery child has many purposes:
   To amuse the child,
   to satisfy the child's need for movement (the active child),
   to encourage the child to move about (the inactive child),
   to give variety and motion during sedentary schoolwork and thus increase the circulation both to the brain and other body parts, so that the child does not fall asleep during the next lesson,
   to stimulate the child's perceptual and motor development in a natural context, and thus to prepare for actual school subjects,
   to teach the child various games (ball play, hopscotch, skipping, etc.),
   to stimulate the child's self-reliance, and
   to stimulate social contact.

Educational gymnastics every day

It may be questioned whether the normal child only needs gymnastics twice a week, but there can be no question that the retarded child should have educational gymnastics every day, in an attempt to prepare him for school.

It is unbelievable that only very few places in the world have acted on this knowledge. Samuel Kirk writes in 1964: »Since the time of Séguin (1846) nothing has happened in the sphere of physical education where it concerns treatment of retarded children«.

This is not quite true today, for a great deal has happened, as this book, among others, tries to show. But these ideas are not yet generally used.

Even in cases where the child never manages to learn to read and to think abstractly, what the child has learned through educational gymnastics will in any case be a help in his later ordinary development.

Physical training of older children

The sensory-motor stimulation is followed up during the first years of school and is combined little by little with more special physical training of skills, strength, respiration, circulation, balance and hand-eye coordination, as well as the correct way to lift things, etc.

Social development

In the nursery school the exercises and tasks

Fig. 51. The right way to lift from a low level. (By permission of Margit Eklundh, »Spare Your Back«.

Fig. 52. The right way to lift in a gymnasium (From Margit Ehlundh.)

are arranged in such a way that each child works by himself, but later the exercises should require two children to work together, and finally a group should try to cooperate.

Physical training of the retarded young man or woman

Finally a few words about the retarded young man or woman, whose work opportunities are usually confined to manual labor, often rather strenuous.

It is necessary in advance to train the strength of these young people, which, on average, is less than that of the more gifted. Girls, especially, need training for strength, as housework can be physically demanding.

As regards the older classes, training of strength should be continued, and speed as well as quick reactions should be drilled, e.g.:

Down on your stomach, over on to your back, up to the top of the climbing rack, down, run, turn.

All exercises should consist of changing movements with quick and, for the pupil, unexpected commands.

Quick ball play between two or more pupils.

In addition, hand movements and manual dexterity must continue to be practiced.

I would finally add that a physically well-

trained person looks and feels better than an untrained one and does not tire as easily.

Work-movements and the technique of lifting

Work-movements and lifting technique are so large a subject that I can only refer to the relevant literature.

Fig. 53. The wrong way to lift.

Young retarded men and women during their time of growth should be trained in natural working-movements, and the correct way to lift heavy objects. If they injure their backs, they cannot fall back on lighter office jobs. Therefore, early training is essential.

After they have learned throughout their schooldays to lift the gymnastic equipment and other heavy objects correctly, it will be advisable in the oldest classes to practice other kinds of working-movements and lifts, e.g. to lift trunks, boxes, crates, children, furniture and furthermore, to practice shoveling snow, digging, pushing a wheelbarrow, etc. (Figs. 51, 52, 53).

The gymnasium

A brief note on what a gymnasium for retarded children and for all younger children should contain.

Wall bars (climbing racks)
It is a good idea to paint each bar a different color, so that the teacher, when teaching a class, can easily tell the pupil to put his feet or hands on, for example, the yellow bar. As the paint soon wears off, it is advisable to only paint 10-15 cm at each end.

A low bench
The bench can be used to jump down from, and the children can vault from side to side, supporting themselves by placing both hands on the bench.

One end of the bench can be hooked over a bar on the rack to give an opportunity to practice various kinds of crawling up the sloping bench.

Painted lines on the floor
can be used for balance-walking, traffic play and as a »ditch« to jump over.

Balance beams
The beam must be steady, so that it does not shake and make the child nervous. The lowest beam should only be a narrow plank laid on the ground. A beam 10 cm high could come next.

The width of each should be the width of a foot, about 8 cm.

Wall space for ball play
This is unfortunately lacking in most gymnasiums.

Mirrors
One or more large mirrors will give the children more body awareness. In learning many of the exercises, such as skipping and the technique of lifting, it is a great advantage to be able to see one's movements.

»Footprints«
For children who walk with uneven steps, or for those whose feet turn out, it is useful to have painted footprints throughout the entire room. The toes should point straight forward and there should be two or three different lengths of strides.

Ladder
Lay the ladder on the floor so that children who have a shuffling walk can walk between the rungs and learn to lift their feet.

Trampoline and mattresses
A trampoline is a delightful apparatus and can help to give good body balance. If there is not enough money for a trampoline, a thick foam-rubber mattress can be used to jump on (or a couple of old bed mattresses).

Climbing frames
of several grades of difficulty are useful for

developing a stronger hand grasp and for increasing self-reliance.

Beam

When the child can hang for 1 minute on the wall bar and can lift himself up by his arms, that is, can raise his trunk up a little between his arms, then, but only then, can he practice moving himself along by his hands while hanging from a beam.

Rope

can increase the strength of hands and arms if there is already some strength. Nervous children may enjoy swinging on the rope.

Weight-lifting

Lifting bars with weights at each end (barbells) is uneducational, because children and retarded young people should be taught to lift with the back straight. When lifting a barbell, the first part of the lift is performed with a rounded back, which can only be allowed if the back is strong, has been trained for lifting, and is well »warmed up«.

Small hand weights can be used if the child's disposition is favorable.

Sandbags and boxes with sandbags in them are greatly preferable when training and teaching correct lifting technique.

Bicycle ergometer

ergon; work, meter; to measure

An bicycle ergometer is a stationary bicycle which measures the effort used, as several kinds of brakes can be applied or taken off. The pulse is carefully measured and should not exceed 160-170 in older children. The pulse is taken at the neck, because the arms move somewhat when bicycling. After the effort the pulse should quickly return to normal – how quickly depends on how much effort has been exerted. This bicycle can be used for strengthening the legs and for general physical conditioning (see page 163) and children enjoy riding it.

But the bicycle must be used with care by retarded children and the following points are important:

Does the child have a heart defect? If so, a doctor must be consulted.

The child must first learn to pedal evenly.

Training must be gradual, as the retarded often have poorly developed respiration and heart function (see page 163).

The pulse must be watched carefully, especially at the beginning.

Equipment

Skipping ropes

which, besides being used for varieties of skipping can also be used for, e.g.:

Jumping high jumps (many children are afraid of jumping over a stick), and

two ropes can be used to make a »ditch« for a long jump.

Balls

Large and small balls in many colors (also for practicing color discrimination.)

Musical instruments

An inventive teacher can make the lesson pleasant and valuable by accompanying the children's movements on an instrument. Consider the child's stage of development, for if he only sits and rocks in time to the music it is not so helpful (see page 151).

Bean-bags

can be used as balls for small children and for foot exercises. The bags can be picked up with bare feet. Long throws can also be practiced with bean-bags.

Hula-hoops

in different colors. Can be used for jumping through, skipping, instruction in body awareness and dominance, etc. (see pages 97 and page 100) (Fig. 41).

Many small words can be learned through movements done with a hula-hoop (see pages 104, 106).

Sandbags

of various weights – from 1 to 10 kg – can be used for many purposes. The bags should not be too full, for then they slide off if they are put on a leg, for example, and are to be lifted during muscle training.

Sandbags can also be used for increasing the strength and duration of the handgrasp (Fig. 45) and for teaching the technique of lifting.

Medicine ball

A medicine ball is a large, heavy ball (2 kg is usual) which is excellent for strengthening arm and shoulder muscles.

Bouncing ball

The large bouncing ball, which when blown up looks like an animal with long ears, is fun for children and trains balance as well as leg muscles.

Rhythm and rhythmics

The normal child

Rhythm and joy of movement

The Greek word rythmós means undulating movements. By rhythm is understood a regular alternation of strength, speed and duration which may be motoric, visual or aural.

Rhythm of movement is an alternation between contraction and relaxation and may be strong or weak, quick or slow, accelerating or diminishing in speed, sudden or hesitant and of differing durations.

Rhythm of movement is something living; it is a natural expression of each individual's mood and being. Rhythm of movement should not be confused with beat or meter, it cannot be counted, but must be experienced, perceived.

This perception of rhythm of movement, along with the quickened circulation caused by the movement, evokes joy of movement, which is the chief purpose of gymnastics.

Rhythmic movement

Even as an infant the child experiences rhythmic movements – he sucks in a certain rhythm. Later he crawls, walks and runs rhythmically, just as when writing, the movements are rhythmic.

All these rhythmic movements vary more or less from individual to individual, under the influence of such factors as: perception and reaction, comparative length of limbs, temperament, and momentary frame of mind.

Intelligence as well as mental and physical condition and characteristics thus determine the child's inherent, individual movement rhythm, which is susceptible to change only as influenced psychologically. A quicker or slower rhythm from a musical instrument can be followed briefly but soon the child returns to his own individual rhythm.

The cooperation of different senses

Rhythm can be perceived through various senses:

Hearing: Auditive rhythm is noticed in music, in speech, in the waves beating on the shore, etc.

Kinesthetic sense: Kinesthetic rhythm is felt in movements, such as breathing, walking, running and dancing.

Touch: Rhythm can be felt through touch, which is used in teaching the deaf where, for example, piano music's rhythm is conveyed through the floor to the child (kinesthetic sense is also involved here).

Sight: Visually, rhythm is experienced by seeing the movements of people and animals, trees bending in the wind, the ripple of the waves on the surface of the sea. Rhythm can also be observed in the arrangement and relation to each other of colors, lines and shapes in landscapes, painting, sculpture and architecture.

Sense of time: The length of notes and the duration of intervals can be observed.

Rhythmics

The word rhythmics means the science of rhythm, which can also include studying the rhythm of movement.

However, the word as used in ordinary speech means the many different ways of producing rhythm and rhythmic movements, such as:

Copying simple rhythmic patterns, which really means copying metric forms (meter: measure of verse or music) of accented or unaccented elements by beating on instruments, or by clapping or stamping. When doing this, the children usually sit in a circle around the teacher, but this gives no opportunity to move the whole body.

As training in hearing and concentration, this kind of rhythmics can be an excellent preparation for learning speech rhythms as well as for performing other kinds of movements to music.

For example, the teacher can produce simple rhythm patterns, which the children try to follow while moving around the room, or the teacher can put a record on and let the children follow the music while moving more or less as they wish.

Finally we can speak of the rhythmic, harmonious total movement, where, for instance, the teacher's lively piano playing gives the impulse and stimulation and thus inspires and calls forth the children's natural movement-response to the music. In short, a mutual interaction between the musician and the pupils, between music and movement.

Individual teaching is impossible in practice, but difficulties in class teaching can be avoided to some extent if each group consists of pupils as similar as possible in understanding of rhythm and in body size. If the children easily feel the beat and rhythm of the music, they move naturally and rhythmically in time to the music. Often this is not the case, however, so it is best if the teacher himself can arrange the groups.

P. E. teachers all over the world have used movement to music – or music to inspire movement – in many forms. From Germany came, among others, Jacques Dalcroze's eurhythmics. (See also page 142: Rudolf Laban and Rudolph Steiner). In Denmark, Helle Gotved and others have worked with music and movement for adults, inspired by the Medau system. The idea here is for the music to follow the pupil's movements in the interaction between music and movement, so Helle Gotved created a form of gymnastics for ordinary people who have no special qualifications either in music or movement.

The Dane Astrid Gøssel, has introduced a kind of rhythmics which from primitive movement patterns leads on to natural, relaxed movements.

Drama and mime

Several kinds of drama and miming, either with or without musical accompaniment, have become fashionable lately and can be both enjoyable and beneficial for children.

Jazz-gymnastics can also be used as an enjoyable form of physical education.

The retarded child

Most kinds of rhythmics can be used with retarded children – possibly in a modified form – but the teacher must remember what he is trying to accomplish:

to give the child pleasure,

to train the child in freer, more natural movements so that he can experience the joy of movement,

to promote the ability to concentrate (listening exercises),

to prepare the child for singing and music lessons and

to stimulate speech training (see page 52).

The teacher must understand thoroughly the normal child's neurologic development in order to meet the retarded child on that level of development which he has reached and, furthermore, the teacher should be able to judge whether the child's movements are normal for his stage of development.

Supporting the child in his motor development involves helping him grow out of his primitive or abnormal patterns of movement. Abnormal patterns of movement, such as continual rocking, as a rule should not be encouraged, even though the child is able to perform these movements in time to music. In such a case the child is simply not ready for rhythmics. These stereotype patterns of movement can occasionally be allowed, in order to quiet the child if no other means can be found. Continually allowing the child to abandon himself to these movements denies him the chance to possibly react to other stimuli.

Remember that the normal child rocks to music before he is a year old, so the often praised »musical ability« of older retarded children corresponds in many cases to a very low stage of development. For example:

A 12-year-old imbecile boy has arm movements corresponding to the arm pattern of a 3-month-old (not to be confused with the movements of a psychotic child); both arms are bent simultaneously at all joints and afterwards are simultaneously straightened at all joints. The midline is never crossed. In ordinary walking and in accompanying all kinds of music, the arms move in this pattern at different speeds. Possible explanations are:

1) The boy's central nervous system, as regards arm movements, has developed to only the 3-month level, so nothing can be done.

2) The movement has become a habit, which no one has tried to correct, even though the level of development may permit correction.

3) Through late development of the brain tissue, the child is now in a position to advance a little further in the development of his movements.

In cases 2) and 3) the child should be trained out of the 3-month stage, by practicing using one hand at a time and crossing the midline. The Parachute (falling) reflex should be stimulated and movements like crawling on the stomach and on all fours should be practiced in a cross-pattern, followed by running and walking.

Only then will the child possibly be ready to take part in rhythmics.

It is necessary to observe the retarded child's individual rhythm of movement as well as his ability to comprehend rhythms in order to decide whether he has developed sufficiently to take part in group exercises in which the speed and rhythm are regulated by music.

Rhythmics are no substitute for the sensory-motor training of educational gymnastics (see page 142), but the skillful teacher can use rhythm as a pleasant variant.

Drama and mime

Dramatizing of events and phenomena of daily life can also be enjoyed by retarded children, but only if they understand what it is all about and the situation which they are expected to reproduce. The child's level may be too low and his vocabulary and ideas too undeveloped.

The retarded child must have experienced and seen the situation in real life, have learned the words connected with it, and have thought the thoughts, before he can be expected to act and dramatize the required situation.

One must also take into account that the retarded child has suffered so many defeats that he is afraid to ask the meaning of a word, a sentence or an idea which he does not understand.

Relaxation methods

Those who are specially interested in the subject of relaxation can be directed to Edmund Jacobson's progressive relaxation method, in which the kinesthetic sense is developed so as to teach the patient to perceive tension and relaxation.

These relaxation exercises are not psychologically profound, nor do they require special training before the teacher can use them with children. Some of the exercises are described briefly in the chapters on Speech, Kinesthetic Sense and Writing.

Relaxation treatment involving depth psychology is quite outside the scope of this book and may, on the advice of a doctor, be undertaken by a specially trained physical therapist or psychologist. Such relaxation treatment affects the psychic mechanisms, and much insight and experience are needed to keep it under control.

Schiultz's method is one of these. In addition to relaxing the muscles, it can also influence respiration, capillaries and the functioning of the heart.

Flexibility of joints

To be able to move around freely, all joints should move normally. Imperfect joint movement is more common in retarded children than in normal children. This may be congenital or may be caused by too little exercise or perhaps by late motor development.

On the other hand, some children's joints move too freely (hyperflexibility), principally because of too little muscle tone (hypotonicity). (Specific pathological conditions lie outside the scope of this book.)

In all cases the doctor and a physical therapist should be consulted and their advice should form the basis of possible treatment or training, which, under their supervision, can be performed in many cases by those who have the daily care of the child.

It should be pointed out that even though ordinary walking, for instance, does not need full movement of the hip joints, the hip joints should be movable to the full extent if walking is to be graceful and free. Ordinary movements always use the mid-position of the joints, for movement at the extreme of the range is somewhat uncomfortable.

Limited movements of joints

Limited movement can have many causes, only the most common of which will be named.

Psychic causes

Mental tension is transmitted to the muscles by impulses from the central nervous system. Muscular manifestation of mental tension can only be altered mentally, by altering the impulses sent from the brain.

Relaxation therapy can be useful, perhaps in conjunction with changes in the child's environment and possibly psychotherapy.

Limited movement in the joints themselves

The joint may be formed in such a way that full movement is impossible, or the joint capsules and ligaments can be too tight. The joint cannot be altered, but in some cases a long period of treatment can induce the capsules and ligaments to stretch slightly.

Shrinkage of the connective tissue

A muscle consists of muscle fibers and connective tissue. The connective tissue is not elastic, but it can be affected to some extent by continuous stretching over a long period, as mentioned above. On the other hand, the connective tissue can shrink if it is never stretched, and if the joint is never fully moved.

The influence of stiff joints on daily movements

A few examples:

Stiff joints in the spine may sometimes be accompanied by lumbar lordosis and round shoulders, i.e. too large a curvature. In other cases an almost straight spine is seen, i.e. too little curvature. If the back is stiff, all body movements will seem stiff.

A stiff hip joint hinders free walking movements.

A stiff ankle can disturb the whole balance of the body when standing and also impedes walking and running.

If the big toe cannot bend sufficiently upwards, the foot cannot articulate when walking and the result will be that the child waddles on flat feet.

A stiff wrist, especially with limited backwards bending, hinders a good grasp of tools.

If the fingers cannot freely spread, the hand becomes a poor means of holding things.

Opposition of the thumb (adduction and inward rotation) is necessary for fine motor skills (Fig. 26).

Fig. 54. Be careful with this and similar exercises where quick forward bending is combined with twisting.

Treatment of stiff joints

Treatment of stiff joints depends on the doctor's opinion and on the individual case. If, for example, there is a tendency towards contracture (shortened muscles), the treatment should begin as early as possible in the child's life and be carried out by a physical therapist, or, in lesser cases, under supervision of a physical therapist.

Passive movements, i.e. another person trying to move a child's stiff joints, is only occasionally permissible. The exercises must never be painful, nor should they cause soreness afterwards. Since a retarded child does not always notice pain, passive movement is inadvisable. With active movements, which the child himself performs, there is no risk.

It must be strongly emphasized that a stiff back should not be stretched by bending far forward, especially when the trunk is being twisted at the same time, for this movement can cause a slipped disc in persons susceptible to this, and one cannot know beforehand who they are. The exercise in Fig. 54 should not be used, for it starts with arm-swinging from an outstretched position and ends with bending forward, twisting and stooping suddenly. It is impossible to stop this movement before it is too late, even if it is hurting. The corresponding exercise performed when sitting with the legs apart is also not recommended.

The following exercises can be used instead, increasing the flexibility by extending the range of motion.

Hip joint:

The hip joints are made supple by extreme movements in all directions and will do no harm, e.g.:

Lying on the back. Lifting one leg at a time with the knee straight.

Lying prone. Lifting one leg at a time with the knee straight.

Lying on the side. Lifting the upper leg, with hip and knee stretched.

Sitting with legs apart. Rotating of both legs – inwards and outwards.

Sitting with legs apart. Spread the legs as much as possible.

Sitting cross-legged.

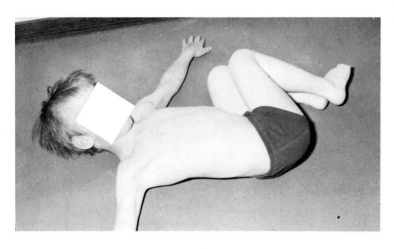

Fig. 55.
Practicing rotation of the spine.

The spine:
A stiff back should be made supple by gentle small movements in all directions and without great strain. For example:

Lying on the back. Roll along the floor, allowing the spine to rotate (Fig. 12).

Crawl on the stomach (Fig. 13).

Lying on the back. Draw up one hip, and then the other (making the other leg »long«).

On all fours: Sway and round the back (make a cat's back).

Sitting astride a chair or bench. Hands behind the head and back erect. Sideways bending on all planes, i.e. straight to the sides coupled with rotation in a slow and gentle movement. Bend as far as possible each time.

Sitting on a chair. Pelvic rocking (sway back and round back alternately), while the upper part of the back and the shoulders are kept still.

Lying with the knees pulled up to the chest. Move the legs together from side to side with bent knees. The shoulders and arms rest on the floor (Fig. 55).

Long-sitting (legs outstretched) »walking« on the buttocks.

Lying prone with the heels under the lower wall bar. Bending the trunk backwards with arms at the sides (so as to bend as far as possible).

Lying prone. Put the hands flat on the floor just under the shoulders. Stretch both elbows so that the back is bent backwards without lifting the hips.

Lying on the back with feet under a wall bar. Roll up to sitting position, raising the head first, then the shoulders and last the back.

Roll back in the reverse order (this cannot be done if the lower spine is very stiff).

The ankles
Sit on heels, so that the ankles are fully stretched. Do not turn the foot. The toes should be pointing straight backwards.

Stand with feet parallel with the front part of the feet on a book. The heels should remain on the floor. Raise and lower the heels without protruding the buttocks. This exercise supples the ankles and strengthens the calf muscles (see Fig. 44).

Standing ski-movements with feet parallel and slightly apart. Heels on the ground. Low knee-bending, so that the buttocks touch the heels, if possible. Stretch both arms forwards so as not to fall backwards, or perhaps hold on to a bar.

The wrists
Standing on hands and knees. The fingers should point straight forward and be spread a little. Lean the trunk forward over the arms so the arms incline forwards, bending the wrists sharply.

With the hand and forearm resting on a table, bend the wrist sideways towards the thumb (Fig. 30a).

Hyperflexibility

(Loose joints)

If the joints are loose this is usually caused by poor muscle tone and slack joint capsules.

No treatment has yet been found for such children, beyond trying to strengthen the muscles in order to stabilize the joints as much as possible.

All the same, it does not help much, for instance, to let the child with hyperflexible hip joints lie for 8 hours every night in a »frog position« (lying on back or stomach, hips and knees bent about 90 degrees and turned out to the sides, resting on the underlying surface), or to let the child sit cross-legged for most of the day. The newborn should be laid on his side when he is going to sleep and any other time he assumes the »frog-position«; in the end this may become a habit for the child, so that the characteristic walk with turned-out legs may be less marked.

Poor muscle tone in the shoulder joints (e.g. in mongols) may hinder the infant's development of head balance when lying prone, for the child cannot lift his head and support himself on his arms because his shoulders are too slack and his arms slide to the sides. If the child's arms are supported he will lift his head at once, provided that he has reached this stage of development.

It would be interesting to investigate whether establishing better sleeping and habitual positions produces any improvement. Experience seems to indicate that this does help.

Muscular strength

The normal child

Muscle contraction: muscle tension.
Muscle stretching: the muscle is stretched, becomes longer (can be roughly compared to stretching an elastic).
Spinal column or spine: backbone.

Dynamic muscular work

Dynamic muscular work is the least fatiguing. A muscle is tightened and loosened alternately, and the circulation of the blood is improved. E.g.: An arm is raised and lowered alternately. This movement can be performed for a long time without causing fatigue.

Static muscular work

In static muscular work the muscle is tightened to hold a joint in the same position for a longer time. The muscle has no chance to rest, and the circulation is restricted. E.g.: Lift an outstretched arm to shoulder-height and hold it there for some minutes. The muscles of the shoulder work statically and tire quickly.

It may here be pointed out that the ability to perform static muscular work is trained by static exercises, while ability to perform dynamic work must be trained by dynamic exercises. The same muscles may be involved but the way the muscles are innervated (see Strength training) is different.

The ability to perform certain kinds of static muscular work seems to be developed later than the ability to perform dynamic work.

Strength training

In training a muscle the following is part of what occurs.

The innervation is trained

(Innervation: the impulse from the central nervous system through the nerve pathways to the muscle.)

The innervation is trained, as a response to stimuli, to send adequate (suitable) impulses through the central nervous system to the muscles required for the desired movement, e.g.:

The child sees an apple on the table, reaches out and takes it.

Here it is a question of the strength of the innervation, i.e. how strongly the muscle should be stimulated to facilitate taking the apple and bringing it to the mouth. If a heavier object is to be lifted the innervation must be stronger and involve more nerve cells.

To adjust the length of the innervation is also practiced. In order not to release the apple too soon, the muscles must receive impulses as long as the apple is to be held.

New blood vessels are formed

New blood vessels are formed in a muscle during training, and result in better nourishment of the muscle.

Strength is increased

If an exercise can be performed in the same way 8-10 times in a row at the same pace, this exercise will maintain the present strength of the muscles but will not increase their strength. Muscle strength can only be increased by increasing the load (the resistance to contraction), so that the muscle is forced to work at near its maximum ability. This can be done:

by increasing the length of the lever, or

by increasing the weight (resistance) with sandbags, pulleys, etc.

To train dynamic as well as static muscle strength, all exercises should be performed both ways. This can be done by performing the strength-training exercises dynamically, but now and then holding a static position for about 10 seconds.

No painful muscles

Muscle training should not cause pain during the exercises nor produce painful muscles the next day, for then the training has been too hard. When a muscle is overloaded it becomes painful, and it is not healthy to overstrain the muscles. Therefore training should progress slowly. When training takes place in groups, this may be difficult, but it can be regulated by letting the pupils perform each exercise the number of times which suits each of them.

In many ways it is an advantage to let the children help each other in pairs during strength training, e.g. by holding each others' feet when training the abdomen or the back (which is necessary if there is nothing to tuck their feet under). This gets the children to cooperate with each other and they take more interest in the exercises.

The retarded child

In most retarded children it is possible to train their muscles even if they have very low intelligence.

The improvement usually applies to pure muscle strength, not to motor ability. It is the motor development which is most important; muscle strength comes second, except in cases of paralysis (see the first chapter of this book regarding motor development).

With regard to muscle strength it will be a great advantage, in the case of a retarded child, if the child is examined thoroughly by a physical therapist first and then, for a shorter period, has individual training of any relatively weak muscle groups. The child should understand why he should be trained and so be motivated for it. Five to ten minutes daily can in many cases cause a formerly inactive muscle to come into use and often quite quickly become stronger, provided the physical therapist succeeds in making the muscle work naturally in the child's daily movements. For example:

A child who always has his hip joint slightly bent and whose hip extensors are weak must be trained by resistance exercises. This training results in the child knowing and feeling the back of the hips and legs (body awareness and kinesthetic sense). At the same time, the child practices stretching his hips well when running, long-jumping and walking. Hip-stretching must enter into the child's daily movements before there can be any lasting improvement in muscle strength.

The more cooperation the P. E. teacher can give the less the physical therapist needs to do.

Examples of muscle-strengthening exercises

The normal and the retarded child

Strengthening exercises can be arranged in different grades of difficulty, so that the teacher as well as the pupil can easily observe the effects of the training. Every exercise should be performed easily 8-10 times running before the next grade of difficulty is introduced.

Do not hold your breath while exercising.

Fig. 56. Training the back.

Back

Trunk-lifting; lying face down with the thighs on a footstool and the feet under a wall bar. The movement begins with the forehead on the floor.

a) Hands at the sides.

b) Arms stretched sideways (Fig. 56).

c) Hands under the forehead, palms down.

d) Arms stretched up, along the head.

e) Sandbags in the hands and arms stretched as in (d).

Front

Sit-ups:

Lying on the back. Roll up to sitting position, head first.

a) Feet held under the 3rd or 4th wall bar. 90° bending of hips and knees with arms stretched up beside the head. The arms draw the trunk upwards while quickly swinging them forwards.

b) as a) but with arms folded on chest (Fig. 57).

c) as a) but with hands folded behind the neck.

d) Hanging with the back against the wall bar. Lift the knees high, so that the lumbar part of the back is rounded.

e) as d) plus stretching the legs out horizontally.

Knee-stretching

Deep knee-bending and -stretching.

a) Get up on a stool or bench and then down. At first use a low stool, graduating later to one the height of the shinbone. Straighten the knees completely each time.

Fig. 57. Exercising stomach muscles.

Fig. 58. From bent-arm position the body is lowered so that the feet touch the ground.

b) Stand beside the wall bar and support yourself with one hand at hip level. With feet apart as if walking, bend the knees until the front knee is bent 90° (not right down. This is a preparation for the technique of lifting, and it is almost impossible to rise from a very low knee-bending position if a heavy weight must be lifted).The feet should point straight forward and the heel of the front foot should not be lifted from the floor (Fig. 51).

c) as (b) but without using the wall bar.

d) as (c) and with a sandbag on the back.

e) When (d) can be performed easily with 5-10 kg on the back (see footnote) perform knee-bendings on one leg with support of the wall bar, and without extra weight. The free leg is stretched forward and the child stands on a stool, to give the leg room. The pupil must not drop down into maximum knee-bending. If he does, he is not ready for the exercise. (Children prone to water on the knee should never perform this exercise.)

Arm bending

a) Standing. Lift a sandbag 20 times (Fig. 31). The weight is gradually increased.

b) Stand on the lowest wall bar, facing the wall. Start with bent arms, drop the feet, and lower the body slowly (Fig. 58). Do not go so high on the bar that the feet cannot reach the floor at the end of the exercise. Walk up again. The child should not drop down suddenly, for that may injure the shoulders.

c) as (b) but stop and count to 3 when the arms are bent 90° (static).

d) as (b) but only go down to 90° arm bending and lift the trunk again.

e) Start with arms stretched and pull the trunk up by the bent arms; sink slowly again.

Arm stretching

Push-ups:

a) Stand on hands and knees. Bend and stretch elbows slowly with the weight well forward over the hands.

b) Lying prone, hands against floor, under shoulders. Stretch arms and bend them again. Hips and legs remain on the floor during the exercise.

c) as (b) but the knees and shins remain on the floor. The hips are stretched and lifted.

d) as (b) but balance on hands and toes. The whole body is lowered, keeping a straight line from head to feet.

e) as (d) with a sandbag on the back.

No one should lift very heavy weights before bone growth is quite complete i. e. at about 20 years of age.

Physical fitness

The normal child

Physical fitness includes many factors, the most important being:
    Mental balance,
    respiration (breathing),
    heart function and circulation,
    muscle strength, and
    neuromuscular coordination.

Respiration (breathing)

Respiration, a reflex action, is quicker and more uneven in a newborn child than later in life. Superficial breathing alternates with some deeply-drawn breaths. Frequency of respiration in the 1st month can vary greatly, with an average of about 60 per minute.

Frequency of respiration (the number of breaths in and out in one minute) decreases during childhood and is lowest in athletic adults. In a child of 5 years it lies around 20-30, in an adult it is about 18, but in an athletic adult it can be as low as 12 or less. These figures give frequency at rest. During strenuous work it can rise to 30-40.

Respiration develops as a result of all the child's movements, right from the infant's kicking in his cradle to more advanced movements later.

Physical fitness chiefly means to train the ability to transfer oxygen from the inhaled air around to the working muscles.

Physical fitness means training the respiratory muscles, for the body needs more oxygen when moving, and respiration will therefore automatically become deeper – more oxygen at each inspiration – as well as quicker. A physically fit person, even when resting, will have a deeper respiration, and so it will not be necessary to breathe as quickly, and frequency of respiration will be less than before training.

Respiration is influenced also by the psychological factors making up the individual's mental state.

Heart function and circulation

The pulse in the first month of life usually averages about 125; it rises somewhat in the course of the first month and then falls consistently during childhood. Here are average pulse rates:

1- 3 years	ca. 120
4- 5 years	ca. 100
9-12 years	ca. 88
16 years	ca. 80
adults	60-80

These figures are pulse rates when at rest. When working or moving, the pulse increases, because working muscles require more nourishment than when resting, which means quicker blood supply. Pulse rates at rest and at work can be influenced by training.

However, the maximum pulse rate, i.e. pulse rate when working as hard as possible, is not dependent on condition, but on age. Young people can have a maximum pulse rate of as much as 200, while the maximum pulse rate for middle-aged people averages about 160. This should be taken into account when training different age groups.

It may further be pointed out that pulse rate is influenced also by the individual's mental state.

Strength training

A worker's endurance depends on whether the muscles have a surplus of strength available in relation to the work in question. Without this reserve the person soon tires.

Effective physical conditioning must place a just under maximum demand on the ability of the muscles. Sandbags and weights can be used.

Neuromuscular coordination

The child must first learn the exercises which will later be used in the physical fitness program and repeat them so often, more and more quickly, that they finally become automatic.

Forms of training

In training for physical fitness, speed is important, i.e. the exercises should be performed quickly and without long pauses. Good forms of condition training are running, bicycling, swimming, rowing and skiing done quickly over moderate distances.

Different forms of gymnastics, e.g. circuit training, can also be used. Here also the tempo should be quick, and the muscles should be loaded to just under their maximum ability. However, the exercises should last long enough to tire the pupil, and the training should take place at least every other day.

Testing physical fitness

To check on the effect of training, fitness should be tested before and after the training period. This can be done in several ways, one of which is with the help of the bicycle ergometer.

This is a stationary bicycle where the tightness (the resistance) of the wheel can be adjusted, and the amount of effort is calculated according to the amount of resistance and the number of revolutions. The pulse rate before and after the exercise and the duration of the exercise are recorded. The method is based on the knowledge that a person with poor physical fitness – doing the same work – will have a higher pulse rate than a physically fit person

Without special equipment various »step-tests« can be used, e.g. the Harvard steptest and others, some of which can be carried out simultaneously by a whole group.

The test can be modified according to the subjects and the requirements. It is most important that the test be carried out in exactly the same way each time, and that it is easy to use in the daily program.

The Harvard steptest

Used for adults, the test is as follows:

The pupil steps up onto and down from a 47-50 cm high footstool for 5 minutes with a speed of approximately 30 times (up and down) a minute, if he can manage it. Then the pupil sits down, and the pulse is counted three times, at 1-1.5, 2-2.5 and 4-4.5 minutes after the end of the exercise. The three figures for the pulse rate are added together (pulse beat) and the points are calculated by this formula:

$$\text{Points} = \frac{\text{working time in seconds} \times 100}{\text{Pulse beat} \times 2}$$

Results: 90 points = very good
over: 75 points = good
less than: 50 points = poor

The pupil must be in top form to get 90.

The retarded child

Partly because of late development, partly

because of lack of movement and training, older retarded children may retain an infantile respiration, which is still quick, superficial and sometimes irregular.

In addition, these children often have too quick a pulse rate for their age, and in some cases it may be a little irregular, but without signs of a heart defect. The heart function and, with it, the pulse frequency thus seem to be due to the child's general late development.

If the child gets out of breath after even a short run, he stops running, and his physical fitness is not improved. If the child is used to giving up quickly in any physical effort, he will perhaps be inclined to give up in any kind of work, including schoolwork. The child is not used to persisting in doing anything which has ceased to be amusing or pleasant, and therefore he has difficulty in completing a task.

The retarded child's condition can, however, be trained with good results, and the above-mentioned defective respiration and too rapid pulse rate can be improved. In certain cases a formerly irregular pulse can be made normal.

It is important for this training to be carried out during most of the child's schooling.

Strenuous exercise, e.g. 15 minutes twice a day, will *increase the supply of oxygen to the brain* and facilitate every kind of learning in school. This is a purely physiological phenomenon, which Rudolf Steiner schools have been able to utilize, but which is generally not made use of sufficiently other places.

Testing physical fitness

The Harvard test can be difficult to carry out with retarded children, and therefore less demanding tests should be used. These tests are less exact, but very suitable in daily work with the children. The following two tests are suitable for subnormal schoolchildren as a minimum demand of condition:

1) The child rests lying down for 3 minutes, and then steps onto and down from a stool (the height of the child's shin) 50-100 times as quickly as possible.
   Decide on the number of times

beforehand, taking into consideration the abilities of the group to be tested. Time the test using a stopwatch.

The child now lies and rests again for 3 minutes with the legs lifted a little (see page 166).

The pulse rate should then be the same as before the test.

If the pulse is usually very rapid, or is faster after the exercise than before, the child needs training. Take into account the length of the time taken. The frequency of respiration should also be noted.

2) A less exact measure of endurance, but pleasanter for the child if he can skip, is to get him to skip rope 100 times and take his pulse when he has rested as above (1).

Incidentally, the better the child is at skipping, the less effort he will need to make. The duration of the exercise will partly reveal this factor.

After a few month's training, test again; the pulse rate after resting, as well as the respiration, should have decreased.

Notes on fitness training

If a child has a heart defect, first get a doctor's permission for the training. The exercising in such a case must proceed cautiously, with careful observation of the child, who must not get too breathless, not become blue at the lips or change in the color of his face. On the other hand, the child must learn to live with his handicap and, when the doctor allows, be trained to the limits of his capacity.

Given that the child has no heart defect, and that there is no other medical contraindication (warning against treatment), the training ought to take place once a day and be strenuous enough to make the child properly breathless.

During training, the pulse rate should not exceed 160-170, but this is unfortunately impossible to test without special equipment. However, retarded children seldom over-strain themselves, and the few who are inclined to do this should be observed and calmed down a little.

The duration of the lessons depends on the teacher's time and the amount of space available. Ten to 15 minutes daily is better than nothing, as long as the children exert themselves sufficiently. An hour would be ideal.

When the child has become tired and breathless, he should be told not to stand still just after making such an effort, but that he can get his breath back either by walking slowly around the room or by lying on his back with his legs slightly raised. If this is not done, the child risks becoming dizzy and, in extreme cases, he could faint, because all the blood vessels in the body are expanded after exercising; standing still will cause much of the blood to run to the legs, leaving the brain insufficiently supplied.

It is usually not advisable to make the child conscious of his breathing, and giving special breathing exercises often causes confusion. Strenuous physical training, because of the greater demands it makes on respiration, will gradually, indirectly, cause the respiration to become more adequate.

Exercises

Training all the larger muscle groups against resistance at just under the maximum and in rapid tempo, without long pauses (the exercises on page 160 can be used).

Run 10 times from one wall to the other. Increase the number of times.

Run up and down stairs. Increase the number of times.

Run to music.

Run, jumping over small obstacles, ropes, etc.

Run, skipping, with a hula-hoop or rope.

All running games requiring fast running and allowing only short pauses.

Low jogging (running in place with exaggerated articulation of the foot, such that the toes never quite leave the floor).

High jogging (run with small steps, lifting the knees high and exaggerated articulation of the foot).

Running at half speed, i.e. in even time at the child's own discretion.

Afterwards practice alternating running and walking, for longer and longer distances, preferably outdoors.

How many times can the child skip with a rope in 1 minute?

Long, brisk walks.

Long, fast bicycle rides.

Running at full speed (sprinting)

Sprinting should be done for only short distances, less than 30 meters.

Interval training

Training in running can be done as interval training, i.e. alternating hard and easy periods of 2-5 minutes each. Begin moderately, gradually increasing speed and effort. E.g.:

Change many times between: running at $\frac{1}{2}$ speed for 1 minute, then running at $\frac{3}{4}$ speed for 1 minute, and finally walking normally for 1 minute. The pauses should not be too long compared with the length of each period of movement.

Circuit training

Suggestions for circuit training technique and scoring can be found in sports manuals.

Results of physical fitness training in educable subnormal children

Twenty-seven educable subnormal children (aged 12-16 years), who were exceptionally physically untrained, were given physical conditioning for 15 minutes three times a week for 2 months.

The training consisted of running twice a week and riding the bicycle ergometer once a week.

Result:

Average fall in pulse rate during the same exercises was 15% for the boys and 13% for the girls.

IV. Readiness for reading and writing

Readiness for reading and writing

The normal child

More than 10 % of normal children in primary schools have learning difficulties to some extent. The strain of not being able to keep up with the others could perhaps have been avoided in many cases by previous purposeful perceptual and motor training. Nursery schools should be able to prevent this unhappy circumstance, especially if the cause was an environment with too little stimulation. Readiness for school does not always come naturally; sometimes it must be created. The principles enunciated in this book can help just such children.

Especially regarding learning to write, where the motor factor is so important, many children starting school are not developed enough to learn this skill, but nursery schools and kindergartens should intentionally help children to be ready for school. This will make school easier and pleasanter for many children.

The later neurophysiological maturation of boys (the reason for which is not yet known) is noticed also in writing. Not only do girls develop faster in general, but their preschool activities probably are better suited to developing the eye-hand coordination needed in writing; they sew, thread needles and play for hours throwing balls against walls, etc.

The retarded child

Regardless of the teacher and the method used, normal children eventually succeed in learning to read and write. How difficult this task is for the child depends to a large extent on his intelligence, but how developed and prepared he is beforehand is also fundamental.

For the retarded child, careful preparation is absolutely necessary if he is to have any chance of success, and therefore all areas of perception must be used, and all methods employed, according to the child's needs.

As many difficulties as possible must be cleared away beforehand, if reading and writing are not to seem unattainable skills. How far the child will progress after he has learned the most elementary forms of reading and writing is another matter, and is not easy to predict.

For many retarded children it would be better to use the time to give them as much experience as possible of the ordinary activities of daily life, rather than to begin teaching them reading and writing before they are ready.

Which stage of motor and perceptual development should the child have reached before he can reasonably be expected to begin learning to read and write?

Mental attitude

Motivation, the wish to learn to read and write, must be present, and should not be spoiled by making the task too difficult. If the child experiences progress and success in his work, he will be motivated to continue.

Psychological difficulties in general will not be described here, but it can be noted that they may have arisen as a consequence of the child's perceptual and motor difficulties and in such a case they often will disappear when these do.

Hand dominance

Dominance must be established before writing can be begun (see page 100).

Motor development

The child's handgrasp must be observed to determine the appropriate writing tool and position of the hand (see pages 34, 172). If necessary, finger dexterity should be trained according to the stage of motor development. Even if the right moment for training has already passed, in most cases some improvement can still be achieved.

To spare the child unnecessary motor difficulties, the movements needed for writing must be trained at the kindergarten level. A single example is given here, taken from Montessori materials.

The small knobs on the cylinders (the original blocks. There are many poor imitations) are of a thickness and height to be most easily held with three fingers, (i.e. the three fingers used in writing), when inserting the cylinders in their places. The knobs are so short that the three fingers have to be held level, which corresponds to an adult hold when writing (see page 172).

Later, fitting the geometrical forms into the holes of the pegboard, requires finer hand and finger coordination, but always the same three fingers are used.

A normal 5-year-old who is trained by this or similar methods can easily and naturally use an adult grasp on the writing tool, employing both hand and finger movements without unnecessary tension, and thus is free to concentrate on shaping figures and letters. The task of learning to write has thus been made considerably easier for the child.

Eye-hand coordination

Eye-hand coordination is a matter of development as well as of training (see page 77).

Sight

Eye focusing must be sure and quick without jumping over words or lines, and can be practiced, for example, by »reading« a series of pictures, row after row.

At the beginning it is natural for a child to point with a finger; this gives him visual and motor practice in following the lines across the page, and also strengthens his uncertain eye focus. See exercises, page 70.

Perception of shape, direction and space influence on:

> Estimation of the size of the blackboard or paper in relation to what should be drawn or written.
> Recognition and forming of letters. For example, b, d, and p are made up of the same elements, but does the stroke go up or down and does the curve turn to the right or left?
> Reading and writing direction.
> Comparative heights of letters.
> Width of letters.
> Size of spaces between words.
> Slant of the letters.
> Placing of letters on the line.
> Reversals (see page 177).

Hearing

Auditory perception must be well developed. The child must be able to listen, discriminate and recognize sounds and words, and also remember them.

The kinesthetic sense

By first »writing« large, with gross motor movements, the shape of the letters is learned through the kinesthetic sense, which is a great aid to memory.

Many small abstract words gain meaning for a child only after they have been learned through movement (see page 105).

Touch

A well-developed sense of touch can be a help in learning letters, e.g. by using sandpaper letters, clay, modeling wax, etc.

Speech

Ths child should be taught to speak properly. Good enunciation, pronouncing words completely, is a priceless possession, while careless speech means poor reading and spelling. Vocabulary should be as large as possible, and understanding of words should be precise, not only the names of concrete objects (house, man, dóg, etc.) but also the more difficult, abstract words.

As English is unfortunately not a phonetic language, there are great differences between how a word is written and how it is pronounced, and this makes it very difficult for retarded children.

Number concept

Number concept is also necessary for learning to read and write, e.g. to decide how many loops there are in the letter »m« and how many letters or syllables a word contains.

The child must be ready to learn to read and write

To ensure that the child will not be frustrated in the school situation, it is necessary to take account of all the above circumstances. Usually one finds in any one child several different defects which must be improved before the child's whole level of development can be raised, and reading and writing readiness attained.

Writing viewed from a motor standpoint

The normal child

There are many things to pay attention to before writing can actually be begun to be taught:

Distance of paper from the eyes

The normal distance between one's eyes and a book is 30-40 cm. If the child sticks his nose in the book this may indicate an eye defect, but it may also be just a bad habit. Or perhaps the accommodation reflex (see page 65) is not yet fully developed. As long as the child seems to have these difficulties it is better that he learns from a blackboard than always from a book.

The blackboard

The large size of a blackboard is advantageous, as the gross motor movement of the shoulder, elbow and trunk help the child, through the kinesthetic sense, to better realize what shapes he is drawing or writing, which makes it easier for him to master them and then to remember them.

It is therefore useful to have large wall blackboards (see Fig. 37) which are adapted to a child's requirements, i.e. the blackboard should extend from the height the child can reach to nearly down to the floor. Many children, for instance those with poor balance, like to kneel down when drawing or writing. Since all the children in the class should take turns using the blackboard, it should be many meters long and possibly cover more than one wall, so that the children can revel in drawing with templates, improving their fields of vision, eye-hand coordination and free drawing skills.

When standing, the child should learn to place himself directly facing the blackboard, not too near, and in a well-balanced position with feet apart, which facilitates natural arm movements and also gives the best view of what is being written.

Writing at a table

The table should be large enough for the child to rest both arms on it, and the height should allow him to lay his arms on the surface without having to raise his shoulders. The chair should be low enough for him to rest his feet on the floor. If it is not, the child will naturally maintain his body balance by wrapping his legs around the legs of the chair.

Lighting must be good, and placed in such a way that it does not reflect off the paper. The chair should support the lower back, and the child should be allowed to rest both arms on the table to relieve the muscles of the back, since during growth, strength does not always keep up with bone growth. Chairs fixed to tables should not be used as they prevent the child from changing position, which is bad for the circulation.

Size and placement of the paper

To begin with, the paper should be large enough to allow gross motor movements, e.g. newspaper is excellent for painting and drawing, as long as the colors are bright enough to stand out.

On the table, the child learns for himself to place the paper so that the drawing or writing is done out from the midline of the body.

When the time has come for writing figures and letters, the position of the paper must be considered further. For upright script the paper is placed more or less parallel to the table edge; for slanting writing it is placed at an angle to avoid too much backward bending of the hand.

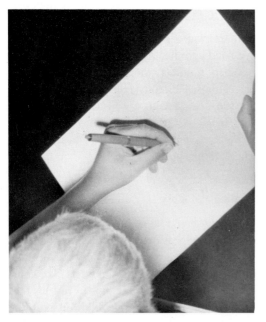

Fig. 59. Writing position and placing of paper for the left-handed.

An even script is attained most easily by always placing the paper at the same angle to the table edge.

Writing with the left hand

If the child is left-handed, the paper should slant in the opposite direction. To avoid rubbing out what has just been written, and to allow the hand an unhampered position, it is advisable to slant the paper so much that a line from the left top corner to the right bottom corner is almost at right angles to the child's middle and to the table edge. In this way the hand is pulled toward the body, which is an easier movement than pushing it from left to right (Fig. 59).

Writing implements, position and movements of the hand

Chalk
Development of the grasp determines the writing implement. Thick chalk is suited to a turned-in cross grasp. Later, when the finger grasp is used, ordinary chalk can be used. The adult supine (turned-out) grasp, which is used later when writing with pencil or pen, is not really suitable for writing at the blackboard; instead, a finger grasp, preferably a turned-in grasp (as used for a paintbrush), is the best.

The chalk must be used comfortably in drawing before figures and letters may be attempted. Large blackboards encourage drawing practice.

Brush
To further improve hand movements and produce a light grasp of writing tools, the child should be encouraged to paint with watercolors, but it is necessary to teach the child the technique of using the whole brush for thick lines, and only the point for light, fine strokes, and to rotate the brush for wavy lines and when changing directions.

Pencil
Free finger and hand movements when writing are furthered by holding the forearm at an

angle of 45° in relation to the table top, i.e. the forearm should not be turned inward too much.

Many children support their chin on their free hand, either because their backs are tired after sitting still for so long, or because of poor head and eye control. Supporting the head on the hand helps eye focus.

The child usually holds the pencil near the point, especially if he begins to use an adult grasp too soon. However, this hand position causes the fingers to hide what is being written, and the child is inclined to put his nose right down on the paper next to the point of the pencil. The fingers should be back further on the pencil.

If the child's grasp has developed naturally, perhaps by suitable educational toys, the child should be able to hold a pencil loosely and easily when he begins to use the »adult« grasp. The writing tool should not be held so tightly that the teacher cannot easily pull it out of the child's hand when he is writing. Therefore a soft pencil should always be used, so that it is not necessary to press down very hard.

The pencil rests on the middle finger and is guided by the index finger in the downward strokes and by the thumb in the upward ones. The fourth and little fingers support the hand and rest gently on the table.

When the writing movement begins, the wrist should bend a little forward and, as it moves across the line, it should bend backwards a little. This is repeated with each 3 cm of writing and at the same time the arm moves gradually sideways. At least $^2/_3$ of the forearm should rest on the table to give a firm base for the movement of the hand.

None of these movements can be performed freely if the writing arm is supporting the body because the child is leaning on it. The non-writing arm should support the body, while that hand holds the paper and now and then draws it to the left so that the writing is always done opposite the midline of the body.

If a child has not developed a natural writing technique, but tightens and clutches at the pencil, so that the index finger looks like it is going to break, then a thick, triangular pencil can often be of help. There will be less tension and the child will also discover that the three writing fingers can each hold one side of the pencil. All three fingers should hold the pencil at nearly the same height, i. e. the thumb cannot be bent as much as the long fingers. This in itself wants coordination.

With regard to the position of the hand there is no point in being too particular, so long as the grasp looks natural and the hand does not get tired or sore from writing. The grasp described above may be considered the most suitable from the motor aspect, and will make writing the easiest for the child.

Ballpoint pen
After he has used an ordinary six-sided pencil for some time, the child is ready to write with a soft ballpoint pen. A general rule for the thickness of a writing tool, seen from the motor aspect, is that long fingers need a thicker writing tool than do short, thick, stubby fingers.

To my knowledge, previous studies have not described using ballpoint pens in teaching writing. In some ways ballpoint pens are easier to write with than the fountain pens used previously, since they, like pencils, can be moved in all directions without having to be turned in the hand. On the other hand, most ballpoint pens are thin and smooth – for no known reason – and therefore more tiring to hold. Furthermore, ballpoint pens must be held more upright than other writing tools and require greater pressure.

Writing with the left hand

Many theories have been advanced concerning the hand position when writing with the left hand, but few have considered the purely motor aspect.

To draw a line, a child who writes with his right hand will draw the line from left to right with a pulling motion, whereas the child with left-hand dominance will draw the line in the opposite direction – in any case until he has properly established the direction of writing – for it is easier to pull than to push. It is therefore always more difficult for a left-handed person to write in the direction generally used in the western world.

Left-handed people also have a tendency to write »mirror writing«, which automatically gets them into a natural pulling movement from right to left. Thus mechanics play a part in writing, whatever other factors may be important. The left-handed child is usually left to find a way to solve the problem by himself, often by writing with an over-bent wrist, which physiologically is a difficult and awkward position. The retarded child usually does not write for so long at a time that this aspect matters much, but it is a difficult position in which to *learn* to write, because it needs constant static contraction in the muscles which bend the hand. From the purely motor standpoint, mirror writing would be the preferable solution, but as this expedient is not acceptable, a normal hand position, as is used by right-handed people, is recommended. If the child practices this hand position from the start, his only difficulties should be those which arise from the awkwardness of writing from left to right with the left hand (see Fig. 59). However, the paper should be turned towards the right, so that it makes an angle of 45° with the edge of the table. By this, the child avoids erasing with his hand what he has just written. Therefore he always has to keep his hand beneath the line.

It would be interesting and valuable for people with a left-handed dominance if a writing experiment was done to compare left-handed children who have always written with an extreme, forward-bent wrist and those who use the same grasp as right-handed children, only mirror reversed. Former writing experiments are now of no value, a steel nib can not be pushed, and a fountain pen behaves differently than a ballpoint pen does.

Preparation for writing

The retarded child

In free drawing the hand grasp is practiced as well as eye-hand coordination. Of great importance is the mental enjoyment of creative drawing.

Writing, however, is something quite different. The child has to learn to copy a set of constructed forms, the letters, so preparation by free drawing alone is not enough, especially in the case of retarded children.

Below are a few examples of how to lead a retarded child towards the goal of writing-readiness.

All the exercises are performed first with chalk on a blackboard, later with a brush on large sheets of paper, and finally with a pencil.

The extent of the blackboard and of a sheet of paper

The child must first be made familiar with the surface; he should be able to discern its extent and shape, whether he is using a blackboard or a sheet of paper.

To progress from the stage where only the details are noticed – the actual drawing – to the stage where the size of the drawing and its position on the paper can be judged, is difficult. However, some ability to do this is one of the requirements of writing-readiness. Realization of the extent of the surface is not developed as spontaneously by retarded children as by normal children, and it is therefore a great help for the child to be made to notice it.

The young child first practices purely motor realization of the extent of the room by crawling and later by walking all around the walls, crossing the floor, etc. This prepares him for being able to realize the extent of the blackboard or the paper, and ought to be done from the time the child has achieved self-locomotion.

Practice on a blackboard comes later.

Exercises
Draw a line around the whole edge of the blackboard, draw a cross in the top right-hand corner, draw a cross in the middle.
Divide the board into two equal halves by drawing a vertical line,
and then in four by also drawing a horizontal line.
Draw the diagonal.

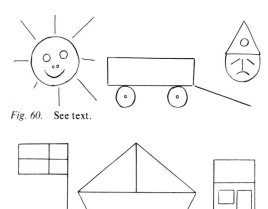

Fig. 60. See text.

Fig. 61. See text.

Fig. 62. See text.

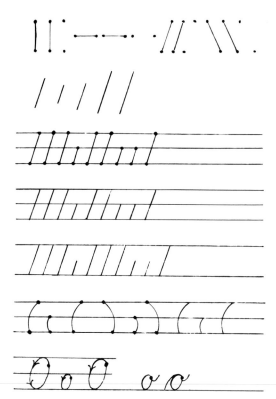

Fig. 63. See text.

Repeat the same exercises later on paper of different sizes.

When perception of shape has begun to develop, build on it by, for example:
Combining lines and geometrical figures in different ways (Fig. 60).
Copy simple drawings as exactly as possible (Fig. 61).
Finish incomplete drawings (Fig. 62).
Do »reading« from left to right and quick visual perception exercises (see pages 104 and 80).

The shaping of written letters require much motor practice. It is not so easy to write letters in a straight line with the same slant and the same height and width. To begin at the beginning, use the child's own scribbles:
close the curves, so that they make circles or ovals (printed or written script).

Preparation for writing can be carried out in various ways, but the important thing is that the retarded child learns to »see« all the small details forming numbers and letters. The teaching cannot be too detailed.

Preparation for written script may be as shown in Fig. 63.

Preparation for printing is similar, but with vertical lines and circles instead of slanting lines and ovals.

The order of the exercises is as in Fig. 63:
1) Join the dots, making strokes in all directions. The order is: vertical, horizontal, slanting.
2) Draw lines parallel to what has just been written. The length is less important here.
3) On the double lines draw from dot to dot, long and short strokes. The ratio 1:2 is the easiest for a child to remember.
4) As in 3) but without dots.
5) Repeat on single lines.
6) Draw curves. Practice in both directions. The difference between a straight and a curved line may be practiced as follows: Draw a short, upright line and make two dots on it. Join the dots with a curved line.

Repeat on the opposite side (leading to »b« and »d«).

7) Round or oval in the same way. Writing of the letters »a«, »o«, »d«, etc., is made much easier if the child learns from the first to begin at the place marked on the drawing and go in counter-clockwise direction.

When the child has mastered this on a blackboard and has also improved the clarity and placing of his drawings, then he should practice the same thing using a brush and watercolors, still very large and on lined paper. Finally, practice with a pencil on paper with wide lines.

Writing numbers

The retarded child

Numerical symbols

The actual teaching of reading and writing is outside the scope of this book, but since writing numbers comes at the kindergarten stage, it may merit a brief comment, as the effect that neurophysiological and perceptual development have on writing may be considered at an early stage, especially in the case of retarded children.

After the preparations I have described, the preschool child should be reasonably able to master the motions of writing, to understand the relationship between double and single lines, and to distinguish between straight, sloping and curved strokes.

The next stage is to learn the shapes of the numerical symbols (see also, Number concept, page 111), again starting with chalk at the blackboard. To »draw« numbers with gross motor movements is not the same as being able to do ordinary writing with small, finely coordinated finger movements, but perception of the shapes is reinforced in this way with the help of the kinesthetic sense.

The shape of the numbers should be simplified and the children should notice that they consist of strokes and of circles or semi-circles (printed script) or ovals (written script).

The numbers can be divided into three groups in order of difficulty, since each group contains figures which resemble each other:

a) 1, 7, 4 consist of straight lines,
b) 0, 6, 8, 9 consist of circles, and
3) 3, 5, 2 are the hardest, especially 5 and 2, which consist both of semi-circles and of straight lines.

With regard to reversing direction along the vertical axis (reversals; e.g. 4 for ⅄), the problem seems to be minimized by using the following sequence.

Examples of how to teach each number:
One model number, about 30 cm tall, written on the blackboard or on a large sheet of paper, is traced with the three writing fingers, while the number is said out loud.
Sandpaper numbers, 8-10 cm tall, are traced with the fingers and named (Montessori). The numbers are written large in the air with the three writing fingers, and this is repeated with the eyes shut, still naming them out loud. The children practice in pairs writing numbers in the air for the partner to read.
Numbers, 8 cm tall, are written in sand (on a straight line), *not copying* but from memory. A number is written on the blackboard, on double lines. The same number is written 5-6 times.
The child stands back to view what he has written, and himself criticizes the direction, slant, height, width, etc.
The child then rubs out the worst figures and writes in new ones instead. Finally he adds three »excellent« numbers.
To be able to see his own mistakes is much more satisfying, more instructive and less embarrassing for the child than if the teacher corrects him. There is also more fun in writing this way, and the child learns to see the whole, which, as mentioned, is difficult in the beginning.

Copying stops as soon as the child is sure of the shape. Writing may be a conscious shaping from memory, combined with the sound of the number (or letter). The child should learn to »see with the inner eye« at the same time as the hand movement little by little becomes automatic. Besides, copying is boring, and as the retarded child has little ability to concentrate, it becomes an unnecessary compulsion and makes writing neither interesting nor meaningful for the child.

As soon as the child can write the first numbers, he should also try to use them, e.g. the whole class can count the tables, chairs, books, etc., and write down the numbers.

In the first numbers workbook there must be plenty of room, so that the numbers the child himself must write in can be at least 2 cm tall. It is quite enough to have to work out the answer; writing the numbers should not be made difficult by allowing too little space.

By careful preparation, and by never going on to the next step until the present one has been mastered, the writing of numbers need not be difficult for the child to learn.

A few remarks about writing the alphabet

The retarded child

In writing, the retarded child should aim at a script that can be read easily and that does not obviously differ from that of a normal schoolchild.

When he writes in large letters on the blackboard, his eyes follow closely the movements of the hand, but as normal handwriting is smaller and faster, for this the eyes play a more subordinate role. The fast rate of perception that is required here can seldom be attained by the retarded child.

Whatever teaching method is used, the child sooner or later should learn to write letters, and a few perceptual and motor aspects should be mentioned.

Triple guidelines

The old method with triple lines is a motor, psychological and practical help to the retarded child, because he always knows beforehand how tall each letter should be, and where it should begin. The ratio of 1:2 between heights of the tall letters and the short ones is the easiest.

If there are no guidelines it can often be difficult for the child to begin writing. The possibility of being able to write letters anywhere on the paper confuses the child, as does having to decide the relative size of the letters.

The problems can be simplified by using only two heights of letters, i. e. letting »t«, »l« and the large initial capitals all be the same height.

Details

It reinforces the retarded child's perception of the shapes of the letters to be told to notice various details. A few examples from written script:

The oval is used in »a«, »o«, »d«, etc.

»i« and »u« are pointed, but »m« and »n« are rounded at the top.

»i« is half the height of »l«.

Reversals

Letters can be turned on the horizontal axis (n-u, M-W) or on the vertical (b-d, p-q). Reversals in the order of letters or syllables also occur (but-tub). Here it is the word picture that is not yet clear.

Reversals are common up to a certain stage of development. They usually are beginners' difficulties and can occur with all types of script, both in reading and in writing, until perception of shape and direction is better developed.

Similar letters

It helps the child if the letters are learned in groups according to similarity and type. It is an advantage if the groups overlap, so that the same letter comes in several groups – in the case of the written script, for example:

1) *e, l, b,*

2) *i, u, t,*

3) *a, o, d, g,*

4) *n, m, v, r,*

5) *a, p,*

6) *l, h, k,*

7) *s,*

8) *g, z, y, f,*

and finally finish with the more infrequent letters *q, x, z.*

If the first letters learned are »e«, »l« and »b«, the words »bee« and »bell« can be written. Thus the combination of letters can be practiced from the beginning, and the space between words is more easily explained. Both words belong to the child's vocabulary and can be demonstrated by objects, pictures and sounds. The words can be pronounced and repeated in many and different short sentences.

These examples are chosen from written script. Similar ones can be taken from printed script, where the arrangement of the groups of letters may be slightly different, as well as the degree of difficulty – and therefore the order of teaching varies.

In both cases it is important that the child, as mentioned above, should stand back from his writing and scrutinize it in order to practice taking in the whole. Otherwise, the child sees only the letter he is engaged in shaping, and his writing becomes uneven. The child criticizes and corrects his own work, finishes with a few finely executed words or letters and looks forward to the next lesson.

Writing lessons should continue all through the child's school career, partly to keep up the standard, and partly to take advantage of the central nervous system's full productivity, because retarded children often mature much later than do normal children.

Types of script seen from the motor standpoint

The normal child

Through the years, many investigations have taken place to find out which script is the easiest to learn. To date, as far as I know,

equally good results have been obtained for printed and for written script. This suggest that the shape of the letters is of no importance in learning to write. As described above, the primary factor is writing readiness.

Types of script have been judged using the criteria of ease-of-reading and speed, but, so far as is known, they have not been judged from an anatomical and motor standpoint, or from the standpoint of the structure of the hand and its kinesthetic possibilities. It would quite obviously seem more natural for a long hand with slim fingers to write written script, while the round, printed script suits the strong, short hand better. It would be interesting to see the results of an investigation along these lines.

A normal child learns little by little *to read* six different alphabets:

Printed capital (Roman) and small letters.

Printed script, capital and small letters, and in some cases, written script, capital and small letters.

Of these the child learns *to write* at least two alphabets, i. e. capital and small letters in either printed or written script, but they may chance to get a new teacher and perhaps have to change from one kind of script to another. This does not, however, present the normal child with special difficulties.

The retarded child

Each teacher is allowed to choose his method of teaching and his preferred type of script. It is usually advisable to respect the individual teacher's wishes, but with retarded children this can create difficulties for both the teacher and the child.

The teacher's difficulty is that the child can have learned several kinds of script from previous schools or teachers. According to his grade in the school, the pupil either changes over to the script current in the new class or he keeps his own, depending on how well he has learned it. In the case of a retarded child, either course can present the teacher with many problems.

The retarded child has difficulty learning

something new, and, after having learned one alphabet with much effort, to learn a new way to form letters can result in his mixing all the alphabets together and finally becoming so confused after changing teachers a few times that he refuses to learn to write – or, more or less consciously – pretends that he cannot.

Compared to reading, writing requires good motor ability, more precise perception of shape, and a better memory, all of which are difficult for a retarded child. First he learns to talk. He learns words and sound-symbols. After that he learns symbols for these symbols, written signs – of which there are six different kinds!

Choice of script

The child's first written letters are usually the large Roman capitals. To let the child stick to these letters is usually only an easy way out, quite apart from the fact that they are harder to read, especially for a slow reader, e. g. HANDKERCHIEF.

No matter what script the normal child learns later on in school, eventually he will be so practiced in writing that his script will be quick and sure, even when he prints.

The retarded child usually never gets this adept at writing, and therefore his writing will not alter much after he leaves school. Educable subnormal young people often complain that they have not been taught to write »like other people«, by which they mean their closest relatives, often their parents. The cause of this is partly that they do not have enough skill in writing and partly that they have been taught printed script. In both cases their script is not the handwritten script that their 40-year-old elders use. One advantage of teaching retarded children to write rather than print is that the written script, even in its unpracticed form, looks more flowing and adult.

If the fashion in all schools shifts over to printed script, this will no longer be a problem. It is necessary here to keep up with the times and possibly even anticipate changes. Or, better yet, to agree on some form of modified printed or written script.

The heart of the matter is that the retarded child should learn only one type of script, although he needs to learn to read more than one.

In choosing a type of script it should be taken into account that the small child's primitive scribbles are carried over into writing, and it is difficult to stop and begin again. The retarded child has the same difficulties to contend with, so some kind of connected script would be preferable.

The retarded child's difficulty in leaving spaces between words will be lessened when the script is »flowing«, as there will be more difference between the end of a letter and that of a word. »Flowing« here means that within a word, each letter is connected to the next one.

To have chosen the script beforehand for a whole school would be an advantage for the retarded kindergarten children who will later attend that school, so that the children, when drawing, can gradually be persuaded to draw either upright or slanting lines, circles or ovals.

These examples are chosen to show how many small – but for the child great – problems are involved in teaching writing. By understanding the problems in advance, by trying to simplify them, and by preparing the child properly, the teaching of writing becomes considerably easier.

V. An example of a sensory-motor evaluation form

A sensory-motor evaluation form

Educationally sub-normal at school age

To get a picture of the child's level of development in all aspects it is useful, together with a psychological test, to use an evaluation form which covers motor ability as well as perception. Such a form has many advantages, for it can be used as:

a basis for treatment and teaching,

a help towards evaluating the treatment and teaching,

a reminder, so that no aspect is forgotten,

a means of enhancing cooperation between all those who deal with the child.

The program given on the following pages has been used for some years for testing educable subnormal children of school age, but could be used for all children with learning difficulties, as well as for children in preschools.

Depending on the child, the various items can be made easier or harder, but naturally must remain constant from one evaluation to the next.

The evaluation form is comprehensive, but the child must be examined carefully, if he is to be helped.

The examination cannot be done in just one session; it must be done in two parts, so as not to tire the child. It would be best if the forms are completed by the relevant specialists, as noted at the bottom of each form.

Lacking some of the specialists, a team of available adults can try to judge the child little by little. In any case, it pays to complete all the forms as they give a comprehensive view of the child's abilities and possibilities. Many circumstances which otherwise seem puzzling will find their natural explanation in a study of the forms, where it can be seen clearly that *all the different aspects are interconnected.*

Many items can be completed during daily observations of the child.

The forms have space for four examinations so that any progress can be noted.

Do not always follow the order on the forms, but allow for the child's momentary inclinations. Leave a few easy items to the last, so that the child finishes with a feeling of success.

The examinations that require the child to undress should usually be left to the last. Often the child needs to be coaxed to take off his clothes, for example »Take off your socks for a moment, so that I can see how well you use your feet«.

As an example, the initial examination (all 12 forms) can be completed by an experienced examiner in about an hour and a quarter, if he is dealing with a subnormal child. With a brighter child it will be quicker.

How often the child should be tested depends on how quickly he progresses. It is advisable to check on a child once a year. The second examination will be noticeably quicker.

It is useful if the examiner writes a short summary of the whole result, mentioning only those points in which the child needs daily practice.

These forms give only the minimum requirements for any attempts to begin teaching the child to read and write, but say nothing about whether the child will be capable of the abstract thought which is needed to get any benefit from reading.

Explanation of the evaluation forms

Form 1

To show how to use these evaluation forms, a sample is given for a boy, Peter, who is 11 years old and has an intelligence quotient (I.Q.) of 60 (the normal I. Q. is 90–110).

Reflexes. A minus (–) for reflexes shows that they are under control, which they should be at Peter's age. The reflexes are tested by a doctor or a physical therapist, but all those who deal with a child ought to know what reflexes indicate in a child's development and by what age they should be inhibited (controlled).

Legs. Peter's legs are of equal length and do not need any kind of raised heel or special footwear.

SENSORY-MOTOR EVALUATION

Name: Peter   School:

Date of birth: Jan. 2, 1964; (11 years old)

DIAGNOSIS FROM   No sign of cerebral palsy
MEDICAL REPORT   No heart defect
                 Slight brain damage

Date	Jan. 13, 1975		
I. Q.	60		
Weight	30 kg		
Height	136 cm		
Babinski, r.	–		
l.	–		
Sym. T.N.R.	–		
Asym. T.N.R.	–		
T.L.R.: supine	–		
prone	–		
Leg – cm shorter	–		
Shoe heel, increase of height	–		
Special footwear	–		
Other remarks	–		
Examined by			

nat. = natural
r. = right
l. = left

Form 1: completed by doctor or physical therapist

Form 2

Rolling is undeveloped, since Peter rolls hips and shoulders at the same time without being able to rotate his spinal column (see page 190).

Crawling is undeveloped. The ankles are bent. The arms are turned outwards, so that the wrist is not bent as completely as it would be if the fingers pointed straight forwards. It follows that Peter's wrists are rather stiff (agreeing with Form 4, bottom).

Walking. There is no rotation of the back when walking, and so a free arm swing cannot be produced spontaneously. The stiff back when walking corresponds to the inability to rotate the spinal column when rolling and crawling. The flat feet without sufficient movement of the foot joints correspond to the undeveloped leg pattern when crawling. The legs are turned outwards at the hip joints, which corresponds to the great degree of outward rotation at the hips (see Form 4). Normal outward and inward rotation should both be 30°.

Jumping. Peter has no spring in his jump. He jumps like a young child, flat-footed and without stretching the hip joints, which could also be expected from his crawling and walking patterns.

Running is a little more relaxed than walking, especially in the arms, but the legs cannot perform a more complicated movement (see page 28). As might be expected, the legs are turned slightly outwards in this movement also, and they are not carried backwards sufficiently, so the running steps are short. The feet do not articulate enough, and the foot muscles are not strong (see Form 5) so that Peter cannot really »glide« when running.

Playing wheelbarrow. Peter is good at playing wheelbarrow. He stretches his arms well, which shows that his falling reflex is functioning and that he can carry a good part of his body weight on his arms.

Somersaults. Peter is not afraid of turning somersaults, which shows, among other things, that his back is flexible enough (see Form 4), even though he does not rotate his spine when rolling or crawling. This is not necessarily due to a stiff back, but instead can be due to either psychological reasons or merely to a too primitive movement pattern. However, if this primitive pattern is allowed to continue, his back may become stiff.

NAME: Peter   BORN _____

Date MOTOR	13 Jan. 75		
Roll: total or	+		
with rotation	–		
Crawl: on the stomach arm pattern	nat.		
leg pattern	nat.		
other remarks			
Parachute reflexes: arms: forward	+		
to the sides	+		
backward	+		
Crawl: hands and knees arm pattern	turned out		
leg pattern	ankle bent		
other remarks	stiff spine		
Walk: arm pattern	shoulders stiff		
hips	backward swing		
feet	flat poor articulation		
spinal rotation	–		
other remarks	legs turned out		
Jump: ankle	stiff; flatfoot		
hip joint	bent		
springy	–		
Run: arm pattern	nat.		
hips	no extension slightly turned out		
feet	poor articulation		
other remarks			
Wheelbarrow:	+		
Somersault:	+		

Form 2: completed by physical therapist

Form 3

Skipping. Peter can skip with a hula-hoop, but not with a rope. There is no point in trying to teach him this before he can jump properly, with more articulation of the feet.

Recording how many times a child can skip consecutively – if he can skip – gives a good indication of the assurance and coordination of his movements.

The number of times skipped in 30 seconds indicates the level of coordination and the speed. If the child is moderately good at it, he can usually skip 30 times in 30 seconds.

Lifting. When lifting a heavy object from the ground, Peter's back is rounded and his knees are straight. It is not too soon to begin training Peter to lift heavy toys, gymnastic equipment and other loads from the floor, using the correct technique (see Figs. 51, 52, 53).

Respiration (breathing) is regular and of mixed (chest and stomach) type, but too frequent for a boy of 11, even a retarded one.

Pulse. The pulse is fairly normal for an 11-year-old before exertion. Three minutes after exertion consisting of mounting and dismounting a stool 50 times Peter's pulse should not still be 96 but should have fallen to 88 again. Also, Peter took too long to do the exercise. 50 times should not have been strenuous at that speed. Peter is not accustomed to exerting himself.

Posture should be investigated by a doctor or a physical therapist. His stomach is pendulous, which is also to be expected, as the hip extensors and the stomach muscles are weak (see Form 5). These two groups of muscles should normally control the pelvic tilt and prevent a sagging stomach.

Flatfoot and *valgus* are also to be expected, since Peter turns his feet out when walking and therefore leans on the inner edges of his feet.

Knee. Knock-knees cannot be dealt with directly. Indirectly, worsening may be hindered by correcting the position of the legs and feet when walking.

NAME: Peter   BORN

Date	13 Jan. 75			
Skipping: hula-hoop	+			
No. of times in succession: rope	–			
No. in 30 sec: rope	–			
Lifting heavy weights	round back straight legs			
Respiration: type stomach-chest-mixed	mixed			
frequency	28			
regular	+			
Pulse: before exercise	88			
exercise = 100 skips or 50 steps	50 steps			
duration of exercise	2 min. 38 sec.			
after exercise	96			
regular	+			
Posture: at ease	pendulous stomach			
pelvic tilt	increased			
Flatfoot: r. + l.	slightly			
Valgus: r. + l.	slightly			
Knee: r. + l.	slightly knock-kneed			

Form 3: completed by physical therapist

Form 4

Examination of flexibility of the joints and of muscle strength, which should form the basis for treatment and training, should preferably be left to a physical therapist. Something should, however, be known about these subjects by the teacher (especially the P. E. teacher) as well as the others who deal with the child.

Flexibility of the joints
Bending forward with his legs straight, Peter cannot touch the floor with his fingertips. In this case this is due not to back stiffness but to stiffness of the hips, which normally should be able to bend at right angles. The muscles at the back of the thighs are too short.

The spine: Flexibility of the spine is normal. Peter did not use this mobility in rolling, crawling or walking because of his primitive motor patterns.

Hips: Peter's hip joints can rotate outwards 40° but inwards only 20° (it should be about 30° to each side), so the natural mid-position is slightly outward, which is why he walks like he does.

Peter is quite unused to extending his hips (moving the leg backwards), he has no body awareness of his back.

Hand and finger movements are difficult. Here, too, he lacks body-awareness (Form 6).

NAME: Peter   BORN

Date	Jan. 1975							
FLEXIBILITY OF JOINTS	r.	l.	r.	l.	r.	l.	r.	l.
Distance of fingers from floor, cm	12 cm							
Spine: bending forward	nat.							
bending backward	nat.							
bending sidways	nat.							
rotation	nat.							
Shoulders: arms raised:	nat.							
Hip flexors: knee straight	70°	70°						
Hip flexors: knee bent	nat.							
Hips: abduction	nat.							
inwards rotation	20°	20°						
outward rotation	40°	40°						
extension	unused restricted							
Ankle: bending up	nat.							
Toe-joints	nat.							
Forearm: outward rotation	nat.							
inward rotation	nat.							
Wrist: towards the little finger	nat.							
towards the thumb	stiff							
Thumb on ball of little finger	– rotation							
Fingers: spread and close them again	stiff							
Thumb: touches all finger-tips in turn	slow and unaccustomed							
Wrist: bending backwards	60°	60°						

Form 4: completed by physical therapist

Form 5

Values for muscle strength as follows:
  5 = normal muscle strength,
  4 = the part of the body in question can be moved in spite of some outside resistance, and
  3 = the part of the body can be moved, but only if there is no outside resistance.

Muscle strength

The two halves of Peter's body are symmetrical, since the figures are the same for the right and left sides. Strength, however, is lacking, especially in the stomach, hip, foot and hand muscles. This corresponds with the unsatisfactory movements in the same areas.

»Elbow flexors; sandbag: 8 times × kg« gives the exercise for finger and elbow bendings as in Fig. 31. Peter performs the exercise 8 times with a sandbag which weighs 4 kg, and this is acceptable.

NAME: Peter   BORN

Date	13 Jan. 1975							
MUSCLE STRENGTH	r.	l.	r.	l.	r.	l.	r.	l.
Strength (0–5) (5=normal) Stomach muscles:	3	3						
Back muscles:	4	4						
Hips: adductors	5	5						
abductors	4	4						
inwards rotators	4	4						
outwards rotators	5	5						
extensors: with bent knee	3	3						
extensors: with straight knee	3	3						
Flexors bent knee	5	5						
straight knee	4	4						
Shoulder blades adductors	5	5						
abductors	5	5						
Knee extensors	5	5						
Knee flexors	5	5						
Ankle flexors (upward)	4	4						
Ankle flexors (downward)	4	4						
Hanging on wall bar	10 sec.							
Elbow extensors: a. b. c. (c = best)	a							
Elbow flexors sandbag: 8 times	4 kg							
hanging as in pull ups: 8 times down								

Form 5: completed by physical therapist

Form 6

Body awareness. Worst regarding fingers and legs, corresponding to the lack of motor development in the same areas (see Forms 2 and 4).

Kinesthetic sense
Eight identical containers, for example old shoe-polish cans, are filled with different amounts of lead, so that there are 4 pairs, both cans in each pair weighing the same.

Sense of touch
A bag with familar objects in it: In a non-transparent bag put, e. g. a key, a cube, a marble, a coin, a ring, etc. The child has to take an object from the bag and name it without looking at it.

Surface and texture: Distinguish 3 grades of sandpaper without looking.
Consistency: Without looking, distinguish rubber, wood, etc. = soft/hard.
Temperature: Cold (windowpane), warm (radiator).
Fetch some lukewarm water.

NAME: Peter   BORN _____

Date	13 Jan. 75			
BODY AWARENESS				
The child points, or names: head (nose, mouth, etc.)	+			
trunk (stomach, back, etc.)	+			
arms	+			
hands	+			
fingers	– 3			
legs	–			
feet	–			
toes	–			
Kinesthetic sense: Shut your eyes: is your arm straight or bent?	+			
Squeeze the ball hard, hold it loosely	+			
Arrange the boxes according to weight	+			
Sense of touch: Shut your eyes: Where am I touching you?	+			
Bag with familiar objects	+			
Surface & texture	+			
Consistency	+			
Temperature	– lukewarm			

Form 6: completed by teacher or psychologist

Form 7

Laterality and dominance
The side which is not to be moved moves slightly, i. e. Peter's motor ability is immature.

Peter does not know his own right and left, which is not surprising.

Direction and space
He has difficulty as to direction and the appropriate descriptive words; this is partly due to uncertain dominance and partly to unsure laterality. Memory plays a part here.

Hearing
Orientation good and hearing perfect. This can be tested roughly in various ways, e. g. the examiner rings a small bell in front, behind, at the side of the child and above and below, while the child points towards the sound. Repeat in a different order, with the child blindfolded.

Rhythm patterns. This is a question of listening to and distinguishing sounds. It is a help to be able to count. It was hard for Peter, partly because he only understands numbers 1, 2, 3 and 4 (see Form 10), but mostly because he has difficulty listening. The test can be performed by copying the beat (without looking) by tapping a pencil on a table. The test for normal children (Stambak) has been simplified here for subnormal children:

1) –   – = 2 slow beats.
2) – – = 2 quick beats.

Then a combination of quick and slow beats:

3) – –   – –
4) –   – –
5) – –   –
6) –   –   –
7) – –   –   –
8) – –   – –   – –
9) – –   –   – –
10) –   –   –   –
11) –   –   –   – –
12) – – –
13) –   – – –
14) – –   – – –
15) –   – – –   – –

The first time that educable subnormal children of school age try this, they usually do not get beyond nos. 3–5. With some practice they reach 8–9. Only a few subnormal children can get through the whole test without hesitation.

The quick beats are harder to catch. The speed should be the same in all tests.

NAME: Peter   BORN

Date	13 Jan. 75			
LATERALITY AND DOMINANCE: the dominant hand	right			
'Jumping Jack' auditive (page 101)	+ (–r./l.)			
'Jumping Jack' combined movements	–			
simultaneous movement on the opposite side	slight			
distinguish r/l on himself	–			
distinguish r/l on another	–			
DIRECTION AND SPACE: arm-stretching: up – down	+			
to the side	+			
backwards – forwards	+ –			
reaching out, slanting	–			
What is: in front of you	+			
behind you	+			
at the side	+			
describe pictures from left to right	+			
discriminate sizes	+			
crawl under a stick	+			
HEARING: What do you hear with?	+			
Orientation	+			
rhythmic patterns	+ 4			
auditory memory; number of orders carried out (out of 4)	3			

Form 7: filled in by teacher or psychologist

Form 8

Peter has normal sight; 6/6 in both eyes. There
is no squint or nystagmus and eye focus is
good. The eyes can follow a moving object
without jerking or flickering.

NAME: Peter   BORN

SIGHT: (visus = sight)
Diagnosis from case record:
Without glasses: visual acuity: r. 6/6 l. 6/6
                 field of vision: normal
                 binocular vision: normal
                 nystagmus (slight, quick, involuntary, rhythmic movements)
                 strabismus (squint)
With glasses: visual acuity: r.   l.

Date	13 Jan. 1975			
What do you see with?	+			
Eye focus: (both eyes together) following rolling ball	+			
(Holding your head still, follow an object ca. 80 cm from eyes): to the right	+			
to the left	+			
up – down	+			
slanting and	+			
clockwise, counter clockwise	+			
concentrated	+			
larger, jerky movements	–			

Form 8: filled in by doctor or physical therapist

Form 9

Shape. Peter can copy most of the common geometrical shapes after they have been shown for 1 second. That he does not know the rhombus (diamond) is natural at his stage of development.

Figure-ground. Peter should be able to differentiate between a circle, a square, a rectangle and a triangle which are drawn partly over each other.

Visual memory. In Kim's game Peter can remember four out of five objects which were shown for 4 seconds.

Colors. Peter confuses green and blue, which is rather usual in retarded boys of his age.

Montessori blocks with cylinders. The cylinders are mixed up and placed in front of Peter, who puts a cylinder in a wrong hole 18 times. He takes 53 seconds for this test. This shows very clearly that Peter is retarded, since he cannot estimate the overall situation. In this block all the cylinders had the same diameter. A normal child of the same age would begin with either the tallest or the shortest cylinder and then the next in size and so on.

Drawing and writing. Peter grasps writing tools using the low »cross-thumb« grasp, and the way he holds a knife and fork shows that his right hand is better than his left, which corresponds to his dominant side.

Ball play is poor. He takes 46 seconds to throw a large ball against the wall and catch it again 10 times at a distance of 1 to 2 meters. He can sometimes catch a small ball with both hands, but never with only one hand. This corresponds to the uncertain motor ability of his hands in general and shows that Peter certainly never tries to use his hands to play ball. (There may be additional reasons as well).

NAME: Peter   BORN

Date	13 Jan. 75			
SIGHT (continued): Shape: copy $+\bigcirc\ \square\square\triangle\diamondsuit$	+ −			
Figure – ground	+			
Visual memory, Kim's game: 5 known objects in 4 seconds	4 out of 5			
Colors: red, yellow, blue, green white, black	Confuses green/blue			
EYE-HAND coordination: Montessori cylinders: sec.	53			
Montessori cylinders: mistakes	18			
Drawing and writing: On the blackboard. Hand used	r.			
Grasp, chalk	nat.			
Grasp, pencil	low thumb cross-grasp			
Distance of eyes from paper	normal			
Placement of paper	normal			
Tension of muscles	+			
Eating: grasp, right	cross-grasp with straight index-finger			
left	ordinary cross-grasp			
Ball play: big ball: 10 times	46 sec.			
small ball (both) 10 times	now and then			
small ball (right) 10 times	–			
small ball (left) 10 times	–			
Tying a bow	–			
Zipping a zipper	–			

Form 9: filled in by teacher, psychologist and physical therapist

Form 10

Balance. Balance is best on the right leg, corresponding to the dominance, but is generally rather poor, because of the immature leg- pattern (see Forms 2 and 5, especially the extensors and abductors of the hip), and lacking free movement of the spinal column when walking. Sight and focus were satisfactory, so the cause cannot be found here.

NAME: Peter   BORN

Date	13 Jan. 75			
EYE-LEG COORDINATION: kicking a ball (r/l)?	r.			
BALANCE: hop 5 m on one leg, r:	+ flatfoot			
hop 5 m on one leg, l:	+ flatfoot			
stand 10 seconds on one leg, r:	+			
stand 10 seconds on one leg, l:	unsteady			
walk 5 m on a line	+			
Beam: 8 cm wide: (low) forward	+ insecure			
sideways	+ insecure			
backwards	−			
QUANTITY AND NUMBER: same – different	−			
many – one – none	+			
number concept; up to	4			

Form 10: filled in by teacher or psychologist

Form 11

Facial expressions. Peter's attainment here is rather satisfactory, but it is difficult for him to knit his brows and »look cross« and also to shut one eye. The last requires a really high degree of neuromuscular development, and could not be expected.

Movements of the tongue. The willed movements are quite good, but all quick movements are impossible.

Speech. Peter talks quite well in sentences, but slowly.

NAME: Peter   BORN

Date	13 Jan. 75			
ORGANS FOR EATING AND SPEAKING:				
Imitating: 　big smile	+			
pout lips	+			
whistle	+			
blow out cheeks	+			
wrinkle nose	+			
raise eyebrows	+			
frown	–			
shut one eye (difficult)	–			
blow your nose	+			
TONGUE: 　appearance	normal			
up – down	+			
to the sides (r.l.)	+			
sideways quickly (r.l.)	almost			
behind upper teeth	+			
behind lower teeth	+			
quick change: up – down	–			
wide – narrow	–			
Frenum:	normal			
what do you chew with?	+			
SPEECH: one-syllable words				
sentences	+ slowly			
lisp	–			
sniffle	–			

Form 11: filled in by speech therapist or physical therapist

Form 12

Lips. Peter's upper lip is a little tight, corresponding to a slight protrusion of the upper
jaw which pushes the lip up.

Speech organs in general. Natural. Peter
chews with a good rotating motion.

Form 12

NAME: Peter   BORN

Date	13 Jan. 75			
ORGANS FOR EATING AND SPEAKING: (continued)				
Palate: shape	normal			
soft palate movable	+			
Jaws' mobility: up	+			
to the sides (r.l.)	+			
Bite: molars	+			
incisors	slight protusion of upper jaw			
Teeth: regular or with spaces	regular			
Lips: tight	upper lip +			
can mouth shut	+			
is mouth usually shut	+			
Reflexes: sucking	–			
swallowing	+			
slobber	–			
coughing	+			
sneezing	+			
biting	–			
spitting	+			
chewing: up – down	–			
rotating	+			
Sensibility of oral cavity	+			
Obstructed air passages	–			

Form 12: filled in by speech therapist or physical therapist

Treatment of Peter

It would have been better if treatment and stimulation had begun at an earlier stage of Peter's life, so that some of the abilities he now lacks could possibly have developed naturally.

This is not to say that Peter could have developed like a normal child even just in terms of motor ability, but he could have learned many things more easily.

Peter apparently never had a chance to crawl at what would have been the right time for him, as can be seen in his immature, hand and foot patterns as well as his balance.

What should Peter practice now?

Everything which he cannot do now, but starting at a level which lies below his present attainments.

The idea is to start with the ability which comes first in the normal pattern of development, e. g. rolling before crawling, etc.

Most things can be done as play, but it will not do Peter any harm to learn that there are some things he cannot yet do, but which he can learn if he makes an effort.

Suggested exercises
  Rolling,
  crawl on the stomach,
  play, crawling on the floor (balance, hands, supple back),
  heel-raising and small springy jumps, one at a time (foot articulation),
  inward rotation of the legs: long-sitting (with legs stretched out),
  walking on a stripe, 8 cm wide,
  walking with feet pointing straight forward,
  running jump over a »ditch« (backward extension of the hip),
  run each day until he is out of breath (respiration and pulse),
  learn correct lifting technique,
  lying on the back: lifting legs one at a time with knees straight (hip-bending),
  get to know the back of the body better: lying prone and lifting the legs with knees straight (turn the leg slightly inwards),
  practice hand grasp (also practice getting to know the fingers),
  train the other weak muscle groups, especially those which extend the hips,
  arm signals, etc. (laterality, dominance),
  perception of direction and later right/left discrimination,
  auditive memory,
  distinguishing green from blue,
  play ball with the hands (eye-hand coordination).

This list seems formidable, but it can be quite easy, provided that many of the exercises are included in the school curriculum, some at playtime, and the rest are carried out by Peter himself (e. g. ball play) as soon as he knows what to do.

It would be best if a physical therapist trained Peter three times a week for a short period, after which the P. E. teacher and others could continue along the same lines.

Peter should be made to notice it each time he has learned to do something which he could not do before. This gives him the incentive to develop to the limit of his abilities, provided, of course, that mental development also progresses satisfactorily. All the different facets of a child are interrelated and it is the whole child that must be treated, taught and helped.

Last but not least, Peter must feel that those who train him and teach him are fond of him.

Evaluation form for severely subnormal children

In the case of normal infants in the first years of life or of older severely subnormal children, the evaluation must contain items which suit a lower level of development than described in the foregoing program.

Here is a short list of possible modifications to the evaluation form.

See also the Development Chart (folder) and the chapters on Reflexes and Motor development.

Forms 1 and 2. Additions:
Doctor's investigations of all the infantile re-
flexes.
How is the child fed: bottle or spoon?

Bowels:	Continent at night.
	Continent during day.
	Says when, but too late.
	Says when.
	Goes to the toilet by himself.
Bladder:	Repeat the same 5 points as for bowels.
Headbalance:	Lying on the stomach. Short lifting.
	Can hold head up.
	Lying on the back. Short lifting.
	Can hold head up.
Arm patterns:	Lying on stomach.
	Lying on back.
Leg patterns:	Lying on stomach.
	Position of hips.
	Position of ankles.
	Lying on back.
Sitting:	With/without support.
	Sits up by himself.
	Leg position.
	Back position.
Standing:	With/without support.
	Can get up by himself. With/without support.
	Hip position.
	Knee position.
	Ankles and feet.

Form 3
Leave out two tests: skipping,
                     lifting.

Form 4
No change.

Form 5
No change.

Form 6
Body awareness should be divided into two
parts: a) to point to the part of the body and to
b) name it. (This method must be used for many
of the items of severely subnormal children).

Add: taste and smell.
              salty – sweet – sour – bitter.
              »Smelling-bottles«.

Form 7
»Jumping Jack« must be performed by touch
and by sight (see page 101).
Leave out a few items:
              Discriminating right/left.
              Reaching arms out, slanting.
              Describe pictures from left to
              right.
With regard to discriminating sizes, they
should be clearly different in accordance with
the child's ability.
Regarding auditive memory, two words are
usually the limit.

Form 8
No change.

Form 9
Shape: Instead of copying shapes the child may
pair geometrical figures: a) three-dimensional,
b) two-dimensional.
Visual memory: For Kim's game use large,
well-known objects and no more than two or
three of them.
   Color: Divide into a) distinguishing and b)
naming.
   Ball play: Only with big balls. Roll, catch,
throw to an adult, bounce on the ground,
throw/catch up against a wall.

Add to this form:
   Build a tower of 2.5 cm cubes (record how
   many).
   Lay the blocks in a row to make a »train«.
   Make the train go.
   Undress himself.
   Dress himself.
   Large and small buttons, buckles, zippers.
   Can walk around the house alone.
   Can walk alone in the playground.
   Can walk alone in the street.

Form 10
No change.
   Notice that the beam should be an 8–10 cm

wide plank, which lies flat on the ground.

Form 11
Omit »shut one eye«. This coordination is attained late even in normal development.

Quick tongue movements will often be impossible.

Form 12
No change.

VI. Bibliography

Ajuriaguerre, J. de: Psychomotricité. Editions médecine et hygiene. Geneva, 1970.

Albitreccia, Stella: La preparation à la scolarité des enfants infirmes moteurs cerebraus. L'association nationale des infirmes moteurs cerebraus. Paris, 1961.

Andersen, Henning: Barnets første år. Gyldendal. Copenhagen, 1962.

Asmussen, E. & Heebøll-Nielsen, K.: Physical performance and growth in children. J. Appl. Physiol., vol. 8, no. 4, 371, 1956.

Ayres, Jean A.: Perceptual-motor-dysfunction-test. University of California. Los Angeles, 1964.

Barnes, K. H. J.: Language and the mentally handicapped. North Berks Society for the Mentally Handicapped. Abbey Press. Abinton, 1970.

Barsch, Ray H.: A movigenic curriculum, Bulletin 25. University of Wisconsin, 1965.

Beitema, David: A neurological study of new born infants. Heinemann. London, 1968.

Benton, A.: Right-left discrimination and finger localization. Development and Pathology. Harper & Brothers. New York, 1959.

Bergés, J. & Lëzine, I.: Test, d'imitation de gestes. Masson & Cie. Paris, 1963.

Bobath, Bertha: Abnormal postural reflex activity caused by brain lesion. Heinemann. London, 1965.

Brauner, A.: A la conquête du nombre avec les déficients menteaux. 8 mm film. Paris, 1964.

Brauner, A.: Pré-lecture. Paris, 1964.

Brinkworth, Rex & Collins, Joseph: Improving Mongol babies. National Society for Mentally Handicapped Children. Belfast, 1969.

Bucher, Huguette: Troubles psycho-moteurs chez l'enfant. Masson & Cie. Paris, 1970.

Chomsky, Noam: Language and mind. Harcourt, Brace and World. New York, 1968.

Christensen, Anne-Lise: Luria's neurological investigation. Text and Manual. Munksgaard. Copenhagen, 1975.

Clarke, A. & Clarke, A. D. B.: Mental retardation and behavioural research. Williams & Wilkins. Baltimore, 1975.

Comparetti-Milani, A. & Gidoni, E. A.: Routine development examination in normal and retarded children. Dev. Med. Child Neurol., vol. 9, no. 5, 1967.

Cowie, Valeria: Early development of mongols. Pergamon Press. London, 1966.

Cratty, Bryant J.: Perceptual and motor development in infants and children. Macmillan. London, 1970.

Crickmay, M.: Speech therapy and the Bobath approach to cerebral palsy. Charles C Thomas. Springfield, Illinois, 1967.

Cruickshank, W. M. & Bentzen, F.: A teaching method of brain-injured and hyperactive children. Syracuse University Press. Syracuse, 1961.

Dalcroze, Emile Jaques: Rhytmus, Musik und Erziehung. Schwabe & Co. Basel, 1921.

Daniels, Williams & Worthingham: Muscle testing. W. B. Saunders. London, 1965.

212

Dargassies, S. Saint-Anne: The development of the nervous system in the foetus. Nestlé. Paris, 1972.

Decroly, O.: La méthode globale. Maurice Lamertin. Brussels, 1929.

Descoeudres, Alice: L'éducation des enfants arriérés. Delachaux & Niestlé. Paris, 1932.

Doll, Edgar, A.: Vineland social maturity scale. America Guidance Service Inc. Vineland, N. J., 1947.

Dupont, A. & Heebøll-Nielsen & Holle, B.: Moron (debile) children: Physical treatment, training and education. The London Conference on the Scientific Study of Mental Deficiency, Proceedings, 1962.

Eklundh, Margit: Spare your back. Hawthorn Books. New York, 1966.

Erikson, Erik H.: Childhood and society. Norton, New York, 1963.

Fay, Temple: The origin of human movement. Am. J. Psychiat., p. 644, 1955.

Fiorentino, Mary: Reflex testing methods for evaluating CNS development. Charles C Thomas. Springfield, Illinois, 1963.

Frankel, Happ & Smith: Functional teaching of the mentally retarded. Charles C Thomas. Springfield, Illinois, 1967.

Frankenberg, W. K. & Dodds, J. B.: Denver developmental screening test. University of Colorado Medical Center, 1969.

Frostig, Marianne: The development program in visual perception. Follett. Chicago, 1966.

Frostig, Marianne: Move-grow-learn, Movement education. Follett. Chicago, 1974.

Gesell, A. & Amatruda, C. S.: Developmental diagnosis. Hoeber Medical Division. London, 1967.

Gesell, A.: The first five years of life. Harper & Brothers. London, 1954.

Getman, G. N.: How to develop your child's intelligence. G. N. Getman. Luverne, Minnesota, 1962.

Getman, G. N. & Harmon, D. B.: Proper chalkboards proper use. Optometric child vision care & guidance, Dec. 1964.

Gibson, J. James: The Senses considered as perceptual systems. Houghton Mifflin. Boston, 1966.

Goodenough, Florence: Measurement of intelligence by drawings. Harcourt, Brace & World. New York, 1926.

Goodnow, Jacqueline: Children's drawing. Fantane/Open Books. London, 1977.

Gotved, Helle: Musik og bevægelse. Rasmus Naver. Copenhagen, 1962.

Gray, William, S.: The teaching of reading and writing. An international survey. UNESCO. Paris, 1956.

Griffiths, Ruth: The abilities of babies. University of London Press. London, 1954.

Gunzburg, H. C.: Progress assessment chart. Birmingham, England, 1965.

Haeussermann, Elsa: Development potential of preschool children. Grune & Stratton. New York, 1958.

Harris, Albert: Harris test of lateral dominance. New York, 1955.

Herzka, Heinz Stefan: Die Sprache des Sauglings. Schwabe & Co. Basel, 1967.

de Hirsch, Katrina: A review of language development. Dev. Med. Child Neurol. vol. 12, no. 1, 1970.

Holle, Britta: Physical education. J. Ment. Subnormality. Birmingham, April 1966.

Holt, John: How children fail. Pitman, London & New York, 1968.

Holt, John: How children learn. Pitman. London & New York, 1968.

Holt, K. S. & Reynell, J. K.: Assessment of the cerebral palsy. Lloyd-Luke. London, 1967.

Houghton, W. F.: Educational gymnastics. London County Council. London, 1964.

Ilg, F. & Ames, L. B.: School readiness. Harper & Row. London, 1965.

Illingworth, R. S.: The development of the infant and the young child. Livingstone. London, 1980.

Jacobsen, Edmund: You must relax. Genuine Pocket Book. New York, 1945.

Jacobsen, Roman: Kindersprache, Aphasie und allgemeine Lautgesetze. Uppsala, 1941.

Kephart, Newell: The slow learner in the classroom. Charles Merrill. Columbus, Ohio, 1965.

Kephart & Roach; The Purdue perceptual-motor-survey. Charles Merrill. Columbus, Ohio, 1966.

Kinsbourne, M. & Warrington, E.: The

development of finger differentiation. Exp. Psychol. Q. Jl, 1962, 14, 223-234.

Kirk, S. A.: Educating exceptional children. Houghton Mifflin. Boston, 1962.

Kramer, Edith: Childhood and art therapy. Schocken Books. New York, 1979.

Laban, Rudolf: Modern educational dance. McDonald & Evans. London, 1948.

Luria, A. R.: The mentally retarded child. Pergamon Press. London, 1963.

Luria, A. R.: The man with a shattered world. Basic Books Inc. New York, 1972.

Luria, A. R. & Judovic, F. J.: Speech and the development of mental processes in the child. Stables Press. London 1959.

Lewis, M. M.: Infant speech. Routledge & Kegan Paul. London, 1951.

Lewis, M. M.: Language and the child. National Foundation and Education Research in England and Wales, 1971.

McCarthy, Dorothea: Language development in children. (ed.) L. Carmichael: Manual of child psychology. New York, 1954.

McCarthy, Dorothea: Organismic interpretations of infants vocalizations. Child Dev. vol. 23, no. 4, 1952.

McLean, James, Yoder, David E. & Schiefelbusch, R. L.: Language intervention with the retarded; Developing strategies. University Park Press. Baltimore, 1972.

Menyuk, P.: Speech pathology: Some principles underlying therapeutic practices. Paper presented at A.S.H.A. meeting, 1968.

Montagu, Ashley: Touching. Harper & Row. New York, 1978.

Montessori, M.: The Montessori method. Bentley. Cambridge, Mass., 1965.

Montessori, M.: The Montessori elementary material. Bentley. Cambridge, Mass., 1965.

Movement education for infants. London County Council. London, 1964.

Nuffield Mathematics Project. Chambers & Murray. London, 1967.

O'Connor, N. & Hermelin, Beate: Speech and thought in severe subnormality. An experimental study. Pergamon Press, London, 1963.

Ozeretsky, N.: Psychomotorik. Zeitschr. für angew. Psychol. 57, 1936, Leipzig.

Piaget, Jean: The origins of intelligence in the child. Routledge & Kegan Paul. London, 1953.

Piaget, Jean & Inherder, B.: La presentation de l'espace chez l'enfant. Press Universitaire de France. Paris, 1948.

Picq, Louis & Vayer, Pierre: Education psycho-motrice. Edition Dion, Deren & Cie. Paris, 1965.

Prechtl, Heinz & Beintema, D.: The neurological examination of the full term newborn infant. William Heinemann. London, 1965.

Renfrew, C. & Murphy, K.: The child who does not talk. Clinics Dev. Med. no. 13, London, 1964.

Robinson, F. & Robinson, J.: The mentally retarded child. McGraw-Hill. New York, 1965.

Schiefelbusch, R. L.: Language of the mentally retarded. University Park Press. Baltimore, 1972.

Schiultz, J. H.: Autogenic training. Grune & Stratton. New York, 1959.

Séguin, Edouard: Hygiène et education des idiots et des autres enfants arriérés. Paris, 1846.

Sheridan, Mary: The developmental progress of infants and young children. H.M.S.O. London, 1968.

Skinner, Charles E.: Child psychology. Macmillan. New York, 1941.

Soubiran, G. B.: La réadaptation scolaire des enfants intelligents par la rééducation psychomotrice. Edition Doin. Paris, 1965.

Stambak, Mira: Trois épreuves de rythme. Delachaux et Niestlé. Paris , 1964.

Stephens, Beth: Training the developmental young. John Day Co. New York, 1971.

Stevens, Harvey & Heber, Rich.: Mental retardation. University of Chicago Press. Chicago/London, 1964.

Stevens, M.: The educational needs of severely subnormal children. E. J. Arnold. London, 1971.

Strauss, A. & Kephart, N.: Psychopathology and education of the brain-injured child. Vol. II. Grune & Stratton. London, 1965.

Strauss, A. & Lethinen: Psychopathology and education of the brain-injured child. Vol. I. Grune & Stratton. London, 1965.

Transley, A. E. & Gulliford, R.: The education of slow learning children. Routledge & Kegan Paul. London, 1962.

André-Thomas, Chesni, Yves & Dargassies, Saint-Anne: The neurological examination of the infant. Heinemann. London, 1960.

Vygotsky, L. S.: Thought and language. M.I.T. Press. Cambridge, Mass., 1962.

Wing, Lorna: Autistic children. Constable. London, 1971.

Woodward, Mary: Developmental patterns of severely subnormal children. Brit. J. Educ. Psych. vol. 33, part 1, 1963.

Woodward, Mary: The behavior of idiots interpreted by Piaget's theory of sensori-motor development. Brit. J. Educ. Psychol. vol. 21, part 1, 1959, 29, 60–70.

Zachau-Christiansen, B. & Ross, E. M.: Babies. Wiley. London, 1975.

Zsanska-Brinken, M. & Wolanski, N.: A graphic method for the evaluation of motor development in infants. Dev. Med. Child Neurol. 11, 1969.

VII. Subject index